The Four Freedoms

The Four Freedoms

FRANKLIN D. ROOSEVELT

AND THE EVOLUTION

OF AN AMERICAN IDEA

Edited by Jeffrey A. Engel

SMU. | CENTER FOR
PRESIDENTIAL HISTORY

OXFORD
UNIVERSITY PRESS

OXFORD
UNIVERSITY PRESS

Oxford University Press is a department of the University of
Oxford. It furthers the University's objective of excellence in research,
scholarship, and education by publishing worldwide.

Oxford   New York
Auckland   Cape Town   Dar es Salaam   Hong Kong   Karachi
Kuala Lumpur   Madrid   Melbourne   Mexico City   Nairobi
New Delhi   Shanghai   Taipei   Toronto

With offices in
Argentina   Austria   Brazil   Chile   Czech Republic   France   Greece
Guatemala   Hungary   Italy   Japan   Poland   Portugal   Singapore
South Korea   Switzerland   Thailand   Turkey   Ukraine   Vietnam

Oxford is a registered trademark of Oxford University Press
in the UK and certain other countries.

Published in the United States of America by
Oxford University Press
198 Madison Avenue, New York, NY 10016

© Oxford University Press 2016

Library of Congress Cataloging-in-Publication Data
The four freedoms : Franklin D. Roosevelt and the evolution of an American idea /
[edited by] Jeffrey A. Engel.
pages cm
Includes bibliographical references and index.
ISBN 978-0-19-937621-6 (hardback : acid-free paper)   1. Roosevelt, Franklin D.
(Franklin Delano), 1882–1945—Political and social views.   2. Roosevelt, Franklin D.
(Franklin Delano), 1882–1945—Oratory.   3. Presidents—United States—Messages.
4. United States—Politics and government—1933–1945.   5. Liberty—United States.
6. Civil rights—United States.   7. National characteristics, American.   8. United
States—Politics and government—Philosophy.   9. United States—Foreign relations—
Philosophy.   I. Engel, Jeffrey A.
E807.F68 2016
973.917092—dc23
2015018909

Printed in the United States of America
on acid-free paper

CONTENTS

CONTENTS

ACKNOWLEDGMENTS

THIS VOLUME DERIVED FROM THE first conference produced by the Center for Presidential History, founded at Southern Methodist University in 2012. Special thanks must go to President Gerald Turner and Provost Paul Ludden for their vision in creating this center, and especially to Provost Ludden for overseeing its formation. Associate Provost Harold Stanley and the staff of SMU's Taos campus, especially Dr. Michael Adler, its executive director, graciously opened their doors for a workshop that made the ensuing volume infinitely better, especially when aided by the thoughtful contributions of Amanda Schnetzer of the George W. Bush Institute's Human Freedom project. Back on SMU's main campus in Dallas, thanks must go as well to two deans of Dedman College for their ongoing support, William Tsutsui and Thomas DiPiero, and in particular to the exemplary staff of the Center for Presidential History: Associate Director Brian Franklin and Assistant Director Ronna Spitz. Without them, the vital center cannot hold. Susan Ferber at Oxford University Press made the book possible, and better, with her suggestions and edits, and nothing would get written, or be worth writing, without Professor Katherine Carté Engel.

CONTRIBUTORS

FRANK COSTIGLIOLA is Professor of History at the University of Connecticut, and the author or editor of six books, including *Roosevelt's Lost Alliances: How Personal Politics Helped Start the Cold War*, for which he received the Robert H. Ferrell Book Prize from the Society for Historians of American Foreign Relations.

JEFFREY A. ENGEL is the Founding Director of Southern Methodist University's Center for Presidential History and a Senior Fellow of the John Goodwin Tower Center for Political Studies. He is the author or editor of nine books on American foreign policy, including *Into the Desert: Reflections on the Gulf War* and *The Fall of the Berlin Wall: The Revolutionary Legacy of 1989*.

LINDA EADS is Associate Provost for Faculty Affairs, Director of the Hunt Leadership Scholars Program, and Associate Professor of Law at Southern Methodist University. Formerly Deputy Attorney General for Litigation for the state of Texas, she is the recipient of the State Bar's President's Award, its highest honor.

WILLIAM HITCHCOCK is Professor of History at the University of Virginia and the Randolph P. Compton Professor at UVA's Miller Center of Public Affairs. He is the author or editor of five books on American and International History; his *The Bitter Road to Freedom: A New History of the Liberation of Europe* was a finalist for the Pulitzer Prize, winner of the George Louis Beer Prize of the American Historical Association, and a *Financial Times* bestseller.

MATTHEW JONES is Professor of International History at the London School of Economics and the Cabinet Office Official Historian of the UK Strategic Nuclear Deterrent. His works include *After Hiroshima: The United States, Race, and Nuclear Weapons in Asia, 1945–1965* and *Britain, the United States, and the Mediterranean War, 1942–1944*.

TISA WENGER is an Associate Professor of American Religious History at Yale University's School of Divinity. She is a specialist in religion in the American West and the former Bill and Rita Clements Research Fellow at Southern Methodist University's Clements Center for Southwest Studies; her publications include essays in *History of Religions, Journal of the Southwest, Journal of Feminist Studies in Religion,* and several edited volumes. She is also the author of *We Have a Religion: The 1920s Pueblo Indian Dance Controversy and American Religious Freedom.*

A part of the sacrifice means the payment of more money in taxes. In my budget message I recommend that a greater portion of this great defense program be paid for from taxation than we are paying today. No person should try, or be allowed, to get rich out of this program; and the principle of tax payments in accordance with ability to pay should be constantly before our eyes to guide our legislation.

If the Congress maintains these principles, the voters, putting patriotism ahead of pocketbooks, will give you their applause.

In the future days which we seek to make secure, we look forward to a world founded upon four essential human freedoms.

The first is freedom of speech and expression -- everywhere in the world.

The second is freedom of every person to worship God in his own way -- everywhere in the world.

Roosevelt's original reading copy of the Four Freedoms Address, delivered January 6, 1941. Franklin D. Roosevelt Presidential Library and Museum, Hyde Park, New York.

The third is freedom from want -- which, translated into world terms, means economic understandings which will secure to every nation a healthy peace time life for its inhabitants -- everywhere in the world.

The fourth is freedom from fear -- which, translated into world terms, means a world-wide reduction of armaments to such a point and in such a thorough fashion that no nation will be in a position to commit an act of physical aggression against any neighbor -- anywhere in the world.

That is no vision of a distant millennium. It is a definite basis for a kind of world attainable in our own time and generation. That kind of world is the very antithesis of the so-called new order of tyranny which the dictators seek to create with the crash of a bomb.

To that new order we oppose the greater conception -- the moral order. A good society is able to face schemes of world domination and foreign revolutions alike without fear.

(Continued)

PATRIOTS
CIRCLE
THE NATIONAL WWII MUSEUM

Dear Mr. McKeel,

I wanted to share with you Jeffrey A. Engel's edited collection of thought-provoking essays, *The Four Freedoms: Franklin D. Roosevelt and the Evolution of an American Idea*. Each essay written by a preeminent historian highlights how the Four Freedoms—freedom from fear, freedom from want, freedom of speech, and freedom of worship—shaped American policy during the postwar years. As Americans, and here at the Museum, we continue to explore how President Franklin D. Roosevelt's Four Freedoms created an enduring legacy of liberty.

I hope this book reminds you of your commitment to the Museum's mission of telling the story of the American experience in *the war that changed the world.*

Sincerely,

Michael Bell
Executive Director
Jenny Craig Institute for the Study of War and Democracy

Since the beginning of our American history we have
been engaged in a change -- in a perpetual peaceful
revolution -- a revolution which goes on steadily, quietly,
adjusting itself to changing conditions -- without the
concentration camp or the quick-lime in the ditch. The
world order which we seek is the cooperation of free
countries, working together in a friendly, civilized society.

This nation has placed its destiny in the hands and
heads and hearts of its millions of free men and women;
and its faith in freedom under the guidance of God. Freedom
means the supremacy of human rights everywhere. Our
support goes to those who struggle to gain those rights
or keep them. Our strength is in our unity of purpose.

To that high concept there can be no end save victory.

****

Franklin D Roosevelt

Orig. Reading Copy

The Four Freedoms

Franklin D. Roosevelt Presidential Library and Museum, Hyde Park, New York.

Introduction

The Four Freedoms: FDR's Legacy of Liberty
for the United States and the World

JEFFREY A. ENGEL

THIS IS A BOOK ABOUT freedom, the pursuit of which has shaped American and international history. It is also a book about the moment one man, Franklin D. Roosevelt, offered his own expansive vision of what freedom was and what it could yet mean, and the ways subsequent generations have sanctified, critiqued, misinterpreted, and otherwise manipulated his words to suit their needs.

Freedom has no universally accepted definition. Even those who praise Roosevelt's 1941 State of the Union address with his description of the four freedoms most essential to American life, the moment upon which this book both focuses and takes as a point of departure, cannot agree on the word's meaning. Freedom is nonetheless widely celebrated, even by leaders whose definitions not only contradict but also spur direct conflict. Simultaneously appealing and malleable, its invocation offers politicians of all stripes a powerful tool for advancing their own agendas, their credibility oftentimes enhanced by harkening back to this famous moment, and to this one man's particularly influential definition of what freedom could mean to his nation and the world, at that moment and for the future.

Franklin Roosevelt might well be thrilled or offended by the way his Four Freedoms address has been manipulated by later generations of politicians, but he surely would have understood. He was a famously flexible politician, and it was at heart a political speech, designed to rally popular support at a moment of crisis. The world was at war, Roosevelt told the Congress in January 1941, but the country's ocean moats no longer offered the same degree of protection as in the past. "At no previous time," he said, "has American security been as seriously threatened from without as it is today." In an age of aircraft and global trade, the country's only real protection from war's devastating reach thus lay in enhancing the country's defenses while simultaneously aiding those already fighting for the cause of democracy overseas. To remain at peace, the president argued, Americans needed to prepare to fight.[1]

Not everyone agreed, perceiving little danger from distant conflicts. Little danger, that is, unless Roosevelt intervened, whether foolishly or out of some more sinister design. "The destiny of this country does not call for our involvement in European wars," the famed aviator Charles Lindbergh had only recently intoned. Wildly popular more than a decade after piloting the first solo flight across the Atlantic, Lindbergh became controversial for his praise of the efficiency of German and Italian fascism. His résumé nonetheless lent particular gravitas to his pronouncements on airpower and geography. "One need only glance at a map to see where our true frontiers lie," he said. "What more could we ask than the Atlantic Ocean on the east and the Pacific on the west?" Congress was divided as well. Roosevelt's latest proposals were not only strategically unwise but also a danger to American democracy itself, Ohio senator Robert Taft railed, providing unconstitutional power "to carry on a kind of undeclared war all over the world." Tyranny, to their minds, could not be far behind.[2]

These were not isolated views, but rather along with Roosevelt's offered the basic parameters of what has subsequently been termed the "great debate," over whether, how much, and to what end the United States should engage the warring world in the last years of the 1930s and the beginning of the 1940s. They were thus passionate debates, with millions of lives hanging in the balance. "Historians have dealt with the policy issues," the noted historian Arthur Schlesinger recalled by the end of his career. But "justice has not been done to the searing personal impact of those angry days." In his view, the bitter argument over America's course during this era offered the "most savage political debate in [his] lifetime," outdistancing for its heat and vitriol subsequent bitter national debates over communism, McCarthyism, and even the Vietnam War. Given that American involvement in World War

II utterly transformed both the nation and its global position, centralizing the role of the federal government in citizen's lives while solidifying the United States as the epicenter of global affairs as never before, one might well argue that this was the most consequential public debate of the entire American century.[3]

Roosevelt thought Americans should be doing more to help defeat the fascist threat. He hoped above all else that January day to persuade a deeply divided Congress to support his proposals for greater military preparedness and aid to the nations aligned against Nazi Germany and its allies, in large part by appealing less to the legislators listening in person than to the millions of citizens well beyond the Capitol's chambers who hung on his every word. Every American had a stake in the war's outcome, he argued. The fighting would determine whether the freedoms Americans held dear would prevail or tyranny would conquer the world. Liberty would not long last in a world full of tyrants, he warned, no matter how wide the nation's ocean boundaries. "Armed defense of democratic existence is now being gallantly waged in four continents," Roosevelt ominously announced. "If that defense fails, all the population and all the resources of Europe, Asia, Africa and Australasia will be dominated by the conquerors. Let us remember that the total of those populations and their resources in those four continents greatly exceeds the sum total of the population and the resources of the whole of the Western Hemisphere—many times over." Despots were never satisfied, he warned. They would be next. "I have recently pointed out how quickly the tempo of modern warfare could bring into our very midst the physical attack which we must eventually expect if the dictator nations win this war."[4]

The dictators had to be defeated abroad, the president thus told the nation, if this generation of Americans were to safeguard for themselves, their descendants, and the world the freedom that was their due inheritance. Four freedoms in particular underlay the rest: freedom of speech, freedom for religion, freedom from want, and freedom from fear. At present the United States served as a beacon of hope and an arsenal of democracy to those equally dedicated to preserving these freedoms for their own people. But that was only a start. Someday, he told the American people, they and their children would ensure such freedoms would be found "everywhere in the world." Only then, in a world replete with freedom, could their own liberty truly be secured. "This is no vision of a distant millennium," Roosevelt said. "It is a definite basis for a kind of world attainable in our own time and generation."[5]

It would be nearly a full year before the United States entered the war, yet Roosevelt's words that afternoon helped define the entire Allied effort and visions of what a postwar world might hold. They provided the vocabulary for American desires to create an effective United Nations while rebuilding a shattered world immediately following the conflict; spurred efforts to eliminate global hunger and poverty during the 1960s and after;, catalyzed calls for universal human rights in the 1970s; and during the 1980s framed the surge of enthusiasm for democracy behind the Iron Curtain in European communism's final days. As the authors of this volume demonstrate, they were words that helped Americans consider the type of economy and government they wished to build at home, the ways in which they might debate and pray, and the means by which they pursued both national and personal security. Roosevelt's formulation even helped ease their collective sorrow after the terrorist attacks of September 2001, while providing a blueprint for Washington's response. "The survival of liberty in our land increasingly depends on the success of liberty in other lands," George W. Bush declared in 2005, employing one of the traditional synonyms for freedom. Thus "the best hope for peace in our world is the expansion of liberty in all the world." The two men occupied opposite ends of the country's political spectrum, with Bush wholly opposed to Roosevelt's expansive vision of government's role in society. Yet they mutually vowed that their generation of Americans would take the lead in fighting to advance the cause of freedom everywhere in the world to safeguard their own way of life.[6]

The distance between these two promises not only reveals how Roosevelt's legacy evolved over the intervening decades, but also in large measure tells the story of how far Americans journeyed from the anxious isolation of the early 1940s to the anxiety of a world globally integrated as never before by the twenty-first century. But what precisely did Roosevelt, Bush, and the generations of American citizens and leaders in-between truly mean when they spoke of safeguarding and expanding freedom against the forces of tyranny? For that matter, what does "freedom" itself even describe?

It is most certainly a malleable term, employed long before Roosevelt focused on his four. Pursuit of freedom energized the Greek polis, widely considered the progenitor of modern democracies, and inspired participants in the age of revolutions that swept the Atlantic World in the late eighteenth and early nineteenth centuries. It is an essential component of the liberal order that grew out of the enlightenment. Yet autocrats and dictators have employed the term as well, mingling it with related terms such as "liberty," "independence," and, in a national sense, "self-determination." The term and its synonyms are similarly deployed, reflexively and oftentimes without reflection, by religious zealots and atheists, conservatives and progressives, labor activists and capitalists, and with equal vigor by those who fight to remake society and by those who strive to keep radical change at bay.

It is not uncommon to see direct adversaries simultaneously adopting this language. Vietnamese revolutionary Ho Chi Minh, to cite but one of a myriad of possible examples, famously modeled his 1945 Declaration of Independence on Thomas Jefferson's 1776 proclamation declaring American independence from Great Britain. He hoped the homage might win him favor in Washington, yet "in a broader sense," the Vietnamese document continued, the declaration's real purpose was to situate Vietnam's quest for national sovereignty within a wider global discussion of humanity's universal birthright. "All the peoples on the Earth are equal from birth," Ho's declaration read, and "all the peoples have a right to live, to be happy and to be free."[7]

That statement is hard for American leaders to refute. One would think, therefore, if this document were the only thing one knew about Vietnam's struggle to throw off colonial rule, that leaders back in Washington, long critical of colonialism in their own right and heirs to a revolution purportedly conducted in pursuit of each individual's inalienable rights to "life, liberty, and the pursuit of happiness," would have supported Ho's cause as part of Roosevelt's pledge to ensure the spread of freedom "everywhere in the world." They chose instead to back French colonial rule, ultimately taking up the fight against Ho's communist regime once Paris faltered. Their reason: a communist's brand of freedom, in their book, was no freedom at all. Those whose perverted worldview denied individual liberties for the sake of a more efficient national state must be stopped, President Lyndon B. Johnson emblematically explained at the height of the American war in Vietnam, and not only for the sake of Southeast Asia. "Only in such a world," he said, "will our own freedom be finally secure."[8]

Johnson and Ho represent but two of many potential examples bolstering a key point of this book: people throughout the world frequently employ the language of freedom with radically different ideas in mind. It is therefore impossible to categorize an individual's sense of the word merely by noting its deployment. The yearning for freedom may well be universal, as American leaders routinely claim, yet the term has no universally accepted definition. Neither is logical consistency a prerequisite to its use. No greater irony exists in American history than the country's founding by men who simultaneously sought their own freedom and the preservation of slavery. Jefferson wrote "All men are created equal." He also owned hundreds.

The twentieth and twenty-first centuries are replete with similar disparities. Even Adolf Hitler, widely considered the modern age's singular evil and the principal "dictator" in Roosevelt's Four Freedoms address, believed himself a crusader for freedom. Under Nazi leadership, he routinely claimed, "the world will be set free" from the capitalists, communists, Jews, and colonialists who had for too long enslaved the globe. Germans would be set free most of all. It is no accident that he initially came to power on the basis of the political slogan "Freedom and Bread." Who doesn't want both? By the same token, men as different as George W. Bush and Osama bin Laden both considered themselves freedom's champion, to cite a more recent example. "Freedom itself was attacked this morning," Bush declared immediately following the terrorist attacks of September 11, 2001, "and freedom will be defended." Bin Laden, orchestrator of the attacks, responded with freedom-based language of his own. "It is both our responsibility and our privilege to fight freedom's fight," bin Laden retorted, in his mind safeguarding a way of life from outside intrusion. "How many acts of oppression, tyranny and injustice have you carried out, O callers to freedom?"[9]

Divergent understandings of this powerful and malleable term equally marked domestic American politics, where nearly every leader of note agrees that "freedom" is a value to be cherished and advanced. Few ever fully agree on a common sense of the word's meaning. The civil rights struggles of the 1950s and 1960s offer a case in point. "Free at last; free at last; thank God almighty we are free at last," Martin Luther King declared in what is widely considered his (and arguably the era's) most famous speech. Under his direction "freedom riders" fanned across the American South to challenge Jim Crow discrimination. Arch-segregationists such as Eugene "Bull" Connor, commissioner of public safety for Birmingham, Alabama, promised a particular brand of Southern hospitality: "100 new police dogs for use in the event of more freedom rides." His vision of freedom did not extend as far for African Americans as for whites, a point dramatically reinforced by Alabama governor George Wallace, who explicitly cast his own cause within the long march of freedom. "Today we sound the drum for freedom as have our generations of forebears before us done, time and time again through history," Wallace said in 1963. "Let us rise to the call of freedom-loving blood that is in us and send our answer to the tyranny that clanks its chains upon the South: . . . segregation today, segregation tomorrow, segregation forever."[10]

Although domestic actors cannot agree on a uniform vision of American freedom, Franklin Roosevelt was remarkably clear in his own definition of the term, or at least of the type of society he considered most likely to ensure freedom's maximum reach. "There is nothing mysterious about the foundations of a healthy and strong democracy," Roosevelt said in his 1941 State of the Union address. "The basic things expected by our people of their political and economic systems are simple":

> Equality of opportunity for youth and for others.
> Jobs for those who can work.
> Security for those who need it.
> The ending of special privilege for the few.
> The preservation of civil liberties for all.
> The enjoyment of the fruits of scientific progress in a wider and constantly rising standard of living.[11]

This agenda could be boiled down even further, to the four fundamental freedoms at the heart of this address: freedom of speech and religion, and freedom from want and fear.

This book argues that Roosevelt's Four Freedoms left a deep imprint on subsequent generations, yet also that American society largely failed to achieve FDR's particular vision of freedom. The details of his message have largely been lost in the haze of time, in particular his lofty aims of social equality and widespread economic opportunity. This is this volume's second major conclusion. Few remember his call for near universal health care; greater pensions and aid for the unemployed, infirm, and aged; and the promise of full employment. They were controversial even at the time. Even those who recall Roosevelt's message fondly have sought alternative approaches to solving society's problems. "In Franklin Roosevelt's view," President Bill Clinton proclaimed in October 1996, "government should be the perfect public system for fostering and protecting the 'four freedoms.'" Yet only months before, in his own State of the Union address, Clinton had uttered a phrase FDR would never have conceded: "The era of big government is over."[12] Nonetheless, a former U.S. Senator and Secretary of State, who also happened to be his wife, found no better place to kick off her own campaign for the White House than on New York's Roosevelt Island, at its Four Freedoms Park. "He [FDR] said there's no mystery about what it takes to build a strong and prosperous America," Hillary Clinton told supporters seventy-four years after Roosevelt's 1941 address: 'equality of opportunity ... jobs for those who can work ... security for those who need it ... the ending of special privilege for the few ... the preservation of civil liberties for all ... a kinder and constantly rising standard of living." Clinton paused before concluding: "that still sounds good to me."[13]

Moving beyond broad questions of government's role within a free society, Roosevelt's seemingly more easily digestible endorsements of particular freedoms ultimately proved problematic as well. As the chapters by Tisa Wenger and Linda Eads demonstrate, his calls for freedom of speech and for the free exercise of religion proved universally acceptable at first blush, but more controversial when put into daily practice by an increasingly diverse citizenry. Few could argue against these propositions, arguing in effect for widespread curtailment of speech or the imposition of acceptable forms of faith, though for each the devil remained in the details. As both Wenger and Eads reveal, consensus almost immediately broke down in these areas once individuals uttered words that inflamed passions or believed another person's religious expression hindered their own. A speaker's race, gender, and political views mattered as well when others judged their right to speak their mind or pray according to their conscience. It is easy to accept such freedoms for those who already speak like you, think like you, or look like you. Granting similar freedoms to others, especially those whose identities and desires are seemingly at odds with one's own, is a far more difficult proposition. The struggle to define those lines, Wenger and Eads both argue, has been neither simple nor uniform, being instead constantly recalibrated along axes well beyond mere speech or faith.

Roosevelt's vision of "freedom from want," conversely, as Matthew Jones argues in his contribution to this volume, garnered critics almost from the moment FDR uttered the phrase. He had, as noted above, a particularly broad vision of government's duty to ensure a basic living standard, having repeatedly been elected on a platform of expanding the social safety net while curbing corporate excess. He then made concessions to the exigencies of war once the United States entered the fray in late 1941, sacrificing further establishment of his New Deal program for the sake of political calm

and a speedier military victory. "Dr. New Deal" turned almost over-
night into the self-proclaimed "Dr. Win-the-War" after the Japanese
attack on Pearl Harbor. Jones shows that Roosevelt's sense of society's
responsibility to ensure both individual and collective security, a
term FDR used more to describe economic rather than physical comfort, was international in nature, with these words carrying greater
weight across the Atlantic than in his own country. Roosevelt's successors ultimately proved less able to see his vision to fruition than
America's wartime allies. Despite Roosevelt's powerful rhetoric and
domestic vision, "a rival conception of freedom," Jones concludes,
"one more in tune with the fundamental tenets of American political
culture—was to gain hold" in the United States, "where American
capitalism was allowed to operate in unconstrained form."

By the same token, "fear," as Frank Costigliola argues, not only
proved an elemental part of the human condition, but during the
Cold War in particular was often deemed by politicians too valuable to eliminate, even if it were in their power to do so. Freedom
from fear was a useful thing for Roosevelt to promise the American
people, Costigliola notes, though its invocation as a future goal
made Americans in 1941 feel less secure at that moment, and thus
more amenable to the president's proposals designed to guarantee the very security he claimed they lacked. The man who uttered
"We have nothing to fear but fear itself" in his first inaugural knew
how powerful fear could be as a political tool, though fear itself was
stoked and catalyzed by subsequent American politicians whenever
calmer rationales proved incapable of securing support for controversial policies. "Freedom from fear," Costigliola concludes, "was
more than merely one of Roosevelt's four aims outlined in January of
1941. Freedom from fear instead underlay his entire call to arms in
response to the growing Nazi threat, a tactic employed, repeatedly,
by American presidents ever since."

Taken as a whole, Will Hitchcock concludes in this book's final
chapter, the Four Freedoms offered a language of hope and political
change throughout the globe in the decades after Roosevelt spoke,
ultimately morphing in its most extreme version into a more dog-
matic freedom for the marketplace and for individual social choices
than Roosevelt ever would have endorsed. Freedom grew, in other
words, to include far less state influence over the kinds of individual
guarantees Roosevelt thought necessary for a truly free citizenry. The
Western world proved particularly good at securing "negative rights,"
Hitchcock demonstrates, constraining government imposition on
matters of conscience or belief. It simultaneously largely retreated

from FDR's vision of guaranteed "positive rights," those things citizens are guaranteed as part of the social contract, including universal education, housing, health care, and a minimum standard of living. By the twenty-first century most American politicians believed at least in a version of the proposition that political liberty cannot be divorced from unfettered economic opportunity, even if the combination also brought about unfettered individual risks. "I believe that free markets open the path to opportunity, that a successful society requires personal responsibility, that freedom is universal and transformative, and that every human life has dignity and value," George W. Bush said soon after leaving office. "History shows that the greater threat to prosperity is not too little government involvement, but too much."[14]

His successor largely agreed. "The free market is the greatest force for economic progress in human history," Barack Obama declared in 2011. "The free market only works when there are rules of the road that ensure competition is fair and open and honest," he continued, yet ultimately, "it's led to a prosperity and a standard of living unmatched by the rest of the world." Closer to Roosevelt than many of his more conservative White House predecessors, Obama outlined a sense of government's role in ensuring economic freedom that nonetheless bears only a faint resemblance to what Roosevelt envisioned seventy years earlier. Owing to the rise of conservatism in combination with the seeming failure of Lyndon Johnson's Great Society program to eliminate poverty, a program Johnson explicitly designed to complete his mentor Roosevelt's work, the entire American political spectrum shifted considerably to the right in the decades after World War II. Democrats occupying the White House since Johnson considered themselves more centrist than liberal and would likely have been out of place in a meeting of Roosevelt's brain trust.[15] They were further to the left than George W. Bush, but that is a relative position.

The overall trajectory of freedom as a commonly held American objective changed far less since Roosevelt's day when the topic of foreign policy arose. It remained in the twenty-first century as powerful a rhetorical tool as it was in the 1940s. There was no opposing position on the political stump whenever the goal of a freer society was invoked. Only someone seeking to derail a career would publicly disparage the notion of freedom. George W. Bush made it the central focus of his second term, announcing in his 2005 inaugural, much as Roosevelt had back in 1941, that American security at home demanded an expansive American engagement with the world. "We are led," Bush argued, "by events and common sense, to one conclusion: the survival of liberty in our land increasingly depends on the success of liberty in other lands. The best hope for peace in our world is the expansion of freedom in all the world." He called in turn for an end to tyranny the world over.[16]

Bush's profound faith in the power of freedom put him at odds with some of his closest advisers, who feared his conflation of "freedom" with American-style democracy might not sit well with many American allies, especially in the Middle East. Secretary of State Colin Powell, shown Bush's speech only days before it was to be delivered, worried that "it was over the top in terms of the democracy piece of it," though he deemed it too late to change the president's words. Even Condoleezza Rice, Bush's closest adviser and close friend, wondered how the president's goal of ending tyranny within a generation might be put into practice. "You know," she noted, "that is kind of a big goal there, end tyranny as we know it." Bush responded with characteristic bluntness. "Yeah, but what I really mean, of course, is we have to start toward getting everybody pulling toward this goal of a freedom agenda."[17]

Bush's profound faith in the power of his freedom agenda derived from two sources. First, he believed free peoples, identified by the democratic natures of their governments and the freedom of their markets, were most likely to be peaceful and productive global citizens. "The world has a clear interest in the spread of democratic values," Bush explained in 2003, "because stable and free countries do not breed the ideologies of murder." He also found divine inspiration for his expansive faith in freedom's power and in his nation's responsibility to expand its reach. Whereas other presidents avoided defining their sense of the term or its origins with specificity, Bush could be remarkably blunt on this point. "I come at it many different ways," he explained in 2007. "Really not primarily from a political science perspective, frankly, it's more of a theological perspective. I do believe there is an Almighty, and I believe a gift of that Almighty to all is freedom. And I will tell you that is a principle that no one can convince me doesn't exist."[18]

Continuing the comparison of the role of freedom in twenty-first-century American political rhetoric through the lens of the century's first two presidents, Barack Obama expounded the virtues of freedom with no less vigor, though with strikingly different characteristics. "I do have an unyielding belief that all people yearn for certain things," President Obama explained in 2009, all of which boiled down to a single idea: "the freedom to live as you choose." He too thought this desire was universally held, at least by those on the right side of history. "These are not just American ideals,"

Obama said. "They are human rights, and that is why we support them everywhere."[19]

Obama's thinking on the matter differed from Bush's in significant ways. So too did the list of freedoms, among Roosevelt's principal four, that he chose to emphasize. The political rights of free speech and religious expression mattered, but in his view conservatives defined Roosevelt's final two freedoms too narrowly. He preferred something closer, though not equivalent, to Roosevelt's own interpretation, with its greater emphasis on a guaranteed standard of living rather than the guarantee of unfettered opportunity. Fewer might accumulate wealth and power wildly in this formulation, but more would prosper and feel secure overall. "We must realize that the freedoms FDR once spoke of—especially freedom from want and freedom from fear—do not come from deposing a tyrant and handing out ballots," Obama explained. "They are only realized once the personal and material security of a people is ensured as well."[20]

Both Bush and Obama, not only successive presidents but representatives of the ideological and political divide over the American government's economic guarantees to its citizenry during the first years of the twenty-first century—the "great debate" of our own times—found reason to hark back to Roosevelt. Both took from him, however, different points of emphasis. It is worth noting the irony that it was the Republican Bush who offered the more engaged internationalist vision in line with Roosevelt's from the 1940s, whereas the Democrat Obama found greater common cause with those who thought the energy of FDR's internationalism better spent at home.

Each is thus an heir to Roosevelt's rhetoric of freedom, though to different parts. Obama claimed FDR's New Deal, Bush his global approach. Taking Bush's and Obama's formulations as points of comparison, this book ultimately concludes that three of FDR's four freedoms remain broadly if not universally appealing to Americans across the political spectrum. These are freedom of speech and religion, and freedom from fear if employed, as it typically is when the term "national security" is invoked by politicians during and after the Cold War, to mean security from foreign attack. Freedom from want, conversely, remains a pale shadow of what Roosevelt desired, not only for the United States but also for much of the world. Roosevelt's promise struck both contemporary supporters and critics alike for its scope and audacity. Even his closest advisers feared the reach of what he proposed. When Roosevelt was first dictating his speech to his staff, ending the enunciation of each of his four freedoms with the phrase "everywhere in the world," his longtime aide Harry Hopkins recoiled.

"That covers an awful lot of territory, Mr. President. I don't know how interested Americans are going to be in the people of Java." FDR was ready with a response. "I'm afraid they'll have to be some day, Harry," he replied. "The world is getting so small that even the people in Java are getting to be our neighbors now."[21]

How Roosevelt sold Americans on his vision of freedom, and how he made the four freedoms central not only to the nation's ensuing war effort but ultimately to the way ensuing generations defined freedom in their own lives and for their own times, is the story of this book. Even if ill-understood and improperly recalled, Roosevelt's speech proved one of the most influential presidential addresses ever delivered. It offers at once a snapshot of who Americans were in 1941, who they have become, and how the world has subsequently viewed American leadership and ideals. This book tells that tale through six essays. It begins by explaining Roosevelt's motivations for offering four freedoms to the world in 1941, traces the evolution of each particular freedom, and ends by detailing freedom's landing point in our own time. No book could possibly hope to detail the evolution and import of freedom as a concept and as an ideological tool in every land and at every time. We have instead striven in these pages to explain FDR's contribution, the story of which offers varied and frequently contradictory notions of this thing Roosevelt espoused and most everyone endorsed, this thing called "freedom."

Notes

1. The text of Roosevelt's Four Freedoms invocation, derived from his Annual Message to Congress on the State of the Union, January 6, 1941, is reprinted in the preface to this book (hereafter referred to as "FDR, Four Freedoms Address." For full text see the website Public Papers of the Presidents, the American Presidency Project, the University of California, Santa Barbara, http://www.presidency.ucsb.edu/ws/ (text of the speech itself is at http://www.presidency.ucsb.edu/ws/index.php?pid=16092). Hereafter references to the online UCSB project will be listed as PPP, with speech title, date, and URL.
2. For Lindbergh, see David Kennedy, *Freedom from Fear: The American People in Depression and War, 1929–1945* (New York: Oxford University Press, 1999), 433. For Taft, see Charles A. Beard's classic work, originally printed in 1948, *President Roosevelt and the Coming of the War, 1941* (New Brunswick, NJ: Transaction, 2003), 67–68.
3. Arthur M. Schlesinger, *A Life in the Twentieth Century: Innocent Beginnings* (New York: Houghton Mifflin, 2000), 241.
4. FDR, Four Freedoms Address.
5. FDR, Four Freedoms Address.
6. "Full Text of President Bush's Second Inaugural Address," *Washington Post*, January 21, 2005, A24.

7. Marvin E. Gettleman et al., *Vietnam and America: A Documented History* (New York: Grove, 1995), 26–27.

8. PPP, "Address at Johns Hopkins University: 'Peace without Conquest,'" April 7, 1965, http://www.presidency.ucsb.edu/ws/?pid=26877.

9. "Hitler Boasts Britain Will Be Broken," *Courier-Mail*, September 6, 1940, 1. For Bush, see PPP, "Remarks at Barksdale Air Force Base, Louisiana, on the Terrorist Attacks," September 11, 2001, http://www.presidency.ucsb.edu/ws/?pid=58056. For bin Laden, see "Full Text: Bin Laden's 'Letter to America,'" *Guardian*, November 24, 2002, http://www.theguardian.com/world/2002/nov/24/theobserver.

10. Martin Luther King, *I Have a Dream: Writings and Speeches that Changed the World* (New York: Harper Collins, 2003). For Connor, see the biography on the website of the PBS series *American Experience*, http://www.pbs.org/wgbh/american-experience/freedomriders/people/eugene-bull-connor. For Wallace, see Peter Applebome, *Dixie Rising: How the South Is Shaping American Values, Politics, and Culture* (New York: Mariner, 1997), 99.

11. FDR, Four Freedoms Address.

12. PPP, "Proclamation 6298—Roosevelt History Month," October 4, 1996, http://www.presidency.ucsb.edu/ws/?pid=52053, and "Address before a Joint Session of the Congress on the State of the Union," January 23, 1996, http://www.presidency.ucsb.edu/ws/?pid=53091.

13. "Transcript: Read the Full Text of Hillary Clinton's Campaign Launch Speech," *Time*, June 13, 2015, http://time.com/3920332/transcript-full-text-hillary-clinton-campaign-launch/.

14. "Bush Warns of Threats to Freedom, Economic Growth," *Washington Times*, November 12, 2009.

15. PPP, "Remarks by the President on the Economy in Osawatomie, Kansas," December 6, 2011, http://www.presidency.ucsb.edu/ws/?pid=97685.

16. PPP, "Inaugural Address," January 20, 2005, http://www.presidency.ucsb.edu/ws/index.php?pid=58745.

17. For Powell, see Wesley Widmaier, *Presidential Rhetoric from Wilson to Obama: Constructing Crises, Fast and Slow* (New York: Routledge, 110). For Rice, see Peter Baker, *Days of Fire: Bush and Cheney in the White House* (New York: Doubleday, 2013), 373.

18. PPP, "Remarks at the American Enterprise Institute Dinner," February 26, 2003, http://www.presidency.ucsb.edu/ws/?pid=62953. For "different ways," see Robert Wuthnow, *The God Problem* (Berkeley: University of California Press, 2012), 237.

19. PPP, "Remarks in Cairo," June 4, 2009, http://www.presidency.ucsb.edu/ws/?pid=86221.

20. Barack Obama, "Way Forward in Iraq: Remarks to the Chicago Council on Foreign Affairs," November 20, 2006, http://obamaspeeches.com/094-A-Way-Forward-in-Iraq-Obama-Speech.htm.

21. For the evolution of the term "national security," see Andrew Preston, "Monsters Everywhere: A Genealogy of National Security," *Diplomatic History*, 38, no. 3 (2014): 477–500. For Java, see Jon Meacham, *Franklin and Winston* (New York: Random House, 2004), 80.

CHAPTER 1

The Scene, the Phrase, and the Debate

JEFFREY A. ENGEL

I
T WAS A DRAMATIC SCENE. Legislators and a packed house assembled in the Capitol Building in the early afternoon of January 6, 1941, gathered to hear the president's annual State of the Union address. Millions more simultaneously huddled around radios, straining to hear some inkling of what their future might hold. All knew what he was there to discuss. Franklin Delano Roosevelt, the thirty-second president of the United States, only recently re-elected to an unprecedented third term, had been saying for weeks that nothing in the nation's history compared to the crisis now at hand. The world was at war, he repeatedly warned in press conferences and in his famous "fireside chats." War was creeping ever closer to American shores.[1]

The crowd settled into their seats amidst palpable tension. Speaker of the House Sam Rayburn of Texas shattered his brand-new gavel banging the sessions to order. Splinters showered the first rows. Following some good-natured applause for his vigor, the senators and representatives settled on command, then leapt as one to their feet as their president was introduced. Hailed by both parties in the traditional State of the Union fashion, Roosevelt slowly made his way into the hall, nodding and flashing his famous grin to political friends and foes alike. He then slowly ascended the podium, his pace contributing to the crowd's anxiety. He "walked," supported by aides, being paralyzed from the waist down following a bout with polio, a fact he constantly strove to make the world forget. Born to wealth and privilege, he'd become a tireless advocate for the poor and downtrodden, especially after polio taught him a degree of empathy his formal education at Groton and Harvard never could, earning him the ire of conservatives and elites and the epitaph "traitor to his class."[2]

He wore the curse as a badge of honor. "The old enemies of peace—business and financial monopoly, reckless banking, class antagonism, sectionalism, war profiteering," he had proclaimed in 1936, "they are unanimous in their hate for me—and I welcome their hatred." Little had changed to ease such feelings in the ensuing four years. Indeed, such passions had only come to the fore in the bitter election only recently concluded. No man had ever before won the presidency a third time. None had previously tried, leading critics to decry his campaign as an effort to enshrine for his own use dictatorial powers he deemed crucial to preserving democracy during the crisis of a global economic depression. Collectively known as the "New Deal," Roosevelt's agenda included banking and commercial reform and a new social safety net for the aged, infirmed, and impoverished termed "social security." No president had ever done more to reshape government's role in American society. In January of 1941 his supports hoped, and his detractors feared, he was not done yet.[3]

Clenching the podium with his left hand in order to stay upright, his legs locked into place by heavy steel braces, Roosevelt began to speak at a somber pace. His voice was flat. Gone was his normal joviality. Straining to hear, the audience in the room and those gathered around radios throughout the country instinctively leaned forward as he began. "I address you, the Members of the Seventy-seventh Congress, at a moment unprecedented in the history of our nation."[4]

The world, he said, was in flames. Germany controlled Western Europe, having accomplished in mere weeks what four years of brutal warfare had failed to achieve a generation before. France had fallen, and the Low Countries before that. Norway lay under the Nazi heel. So too Poland, Austria, and Czechoslovakia. Among democracy's champions in Europe only Britain remained, though for how long was anyone's guess. "We shall never surrender," Britain's prime minister, Winston Churchill, defiantly brayed, carrying on the fight "until, in God's time, the New World, with all its power and might, steps forth to the rescue and liberation of the old." Few international observers liked his odds.[5]

Events on the other side of the world looked little better in Roosevelt's estimation. Japan's army continued its brutal conquest of China, begun in 1937. It already ruled Korea. The well-trained and technologically advanced Japanese navy simultaneously sailed throughout the western Pacific, prowling, it seemed to wary onlookers in the Philippines, Hong Kong, Singapore, and Australia, like a tiger straining to be let out of its cage. Looking back once more toward the Atlantic, conduit for the bulk of American overseas trade, German ships and submarines seemingly multiplied every week, eager to ensure Britain's isolation, starvation, and ultimately, Nazi strategists hoped, submission. A new world would arise in place of the old imperial order Britain embodied, Germany's führer, Adolf Hitler, promised. "Come what may," he vowed, "Britain, the last island in Europe, will be broken," and the world finally "set free" from its colonial claws.[6]

Roosevelt painted a stark picture in response. Hitler's brand of freedom was empty and evil, he said. Fascism promised glory for the few, misery for most. "The democratic way of life is at this moment being directly assailed in every part of the world, assailed either by arms, or by secret spreading of poisonous propaganda." The crisis could no longer be confined to Asia or Europe. He feared the Germans even had designs on Latin America and the Caribbean, outposts for an inevitable Nazi struggle against the United States. Yet he also believed further fascist gains in the nearer term posed a more immediate threat, especially since Hitler's version of "freedom" ran so contrary to any definition of the word Americans might recognize or accept. "As your President, performing my constitutional duty to 'give to the congress information of the state of the union,'" Roosevelt solemnly explained, "I find it, unhappily, necessary to report that the future and the safety of our country and of our democracy are overwhelmingly involved in events far beyond our borders."[7]

Since 1812 the country's ocean moats had protected the American homeland from assault. Not anymore. He had long feared that modern aircraft might render Americans vulnerable to foreign attack, preaching restraint in aerial assaults on civilians even as his own military developed the means to strike foreign cities in time of war. "In times like these," he therefore explained, "it is immature—and incidentally, untrue—for anyone to brag that an unprepared America, single-handed, and with one hand tied behind its back, can hold off the whole world." On the contrary, if the country did not act, specifically if the Congress failed to endorse the measures he laid out that evening in support of Britain and the Allied cause and to increase overall military preparedness, all they could hope to secure was a "dictator's peace," and an end to "international generosity, or return of true independence, or world disarmament, or freedom of expression, or freedom of religion—or even good business." In short, nothing less than the American way of life depended on how Congress reacted to his pleas.[8]

He was therefore there to issue a call to arms, without resorting to a formal call for war, hoping that ramped-up military spending and foreign aid might yet keep his country out of the conflict. The United States was woefully unprepared for anything more. America at the start of 1941 boasted neither the military might nor extant industrial capacity, or for that matter the national will, to wage a global crusade. It had plenty of factories, though few were devoted to arms production. American industry overall continued to operate well below capacity more than a decade after the Wall Street crash of 1929 sparked the Great Depression. Growing European war orders stimulated an embryonic recovery by late 1940, but unemployment remained dangerously high. More than 15 percent of the nation's active workforce lacked steady wages or a job. This was better than the nearly 25 percent mark when Roosevelt took office in 1933, though no one knew for certain how many American workers had simply given up in the interim.[9]

With millions hungry and out of work, military spending of necessity lagged during the 1930s, following a decade of widespread international disillusionment and limited military budgets. Republicans and Democrats alike feared both the cost and the dangers of large standing military forces after World War One ended in 1918. Military spending was unproductive, Roosevelt's predecessor, Herbert Hoover, preached, contributing neither to industry or education while making the world more dangerous. As influential political journalist Walter Lippmann pithily summed up this pervasive line of thinking: "Big warships meant big wars. Smaller warships meant smaller wars. No warships might eventually mean no wars."[10]

Not surprisingly, given this political environment, the American navy's order of battle remained by 1941 far below the levels painstakingly negotiated at international conferences throughout the 1920s and 1930s. Japanese builders in particular routinely exceeded their negotiated limits while constructing a first-class navy; the United States, conversely, never approached its tonnage or vessel allotments. Its battleship fleet, imposing on paper and in the midst of a massive revitalization program, largely featured ships built for the Great

War, while the navy's newest battleship, the *North Carolina*, was by the start of 1941 still months from its maiden cruise after four years of construction. Naval planners had at least recently upgraded their main Pacific base at Pearl Harbor, reasoning that the security of this Hawaiian outpost—surely invulnerable to attack—would intimidate Tokyo into inaction.

Similar economic and political constraints limited spending on the army as well. Only eight ill-equipped and poorly trained divisions stood ready for combat throughout the whole of the American army when war first broke out in Europe in 1939. Germany, by contrast, fielded nearly two hundred divisions by January of 1941, with plans for nearly twice that number by 1943, many hardened by combat and sporting sophisticated weaponry. A year into the European war, American units meanwhile often trained with boards on wheels labeled "gun" and with aging trucks labeled "tank." Though spurred by European orders, American factories would require yet more time to retool for full-scale military production, while the armed forces would need time to learn how to use and deploy any new weapons that rolled off the production line. In mid-1940 Roosevelt called for a surge in aircraft construction capable of producing fifty thousand new planes a year. The number was supposed to both inspire and intimidate. Reality proved more daunting. American factories had provided only two thousand planes the entire previous twelve months, and in truth the amount of aluminum required to build fifty thousand aircraft exceeded the country's total annual production of that valuable metal. Americans could build the fleet FDR desired, in other words, provided they were unwilling to build anything else, and the president's audacious goal was less a realistic objective than an effort to shine a light on the woeful unpreparedness of both industry and the military for the conflagration they now faced.[11]

Each service wanted more as war erupted in Europe, hoping along with Roosevelt that a show of American strength might somehow keep Hitler at bay. "If we are strong enough," General George Marshall, the army's chief of staff explained, "peace, democracy, and our American way of life should be the reward." The country could only avoid a fight, he argued, if prepared to fight. By the time Roosevelt took to the podium in January 1941 Marshall commanded three times the combat troops his predecessor had in 1939, though expansion had not come easy. It was going to be a "dirty fight" to wring any money from Congress, FDR confided to a close aide, because pacifism, isolationism, and downright rejection of foreign affairs ran high throughout the American electorate as the 1940s began. "Do you realize that during the same length of time it has taken us to debate this bill," Vermont senator Ernest Gibson asked his colleagues in the midst of a bitter debate over national conscription in September of 1940, "Hitler was able to conquer France?" Both sides took the point as validation of their positions. The Nazis could not be ejected without immeasurable cost, isolationists argued. Those on Roosevelt's side thought any evil capable of such destruction had to be stopped before it became too late.[12]

"People have forgotten the great hostility of the time," Marshall later recalled, as Americans heatedly debated their role in a world rapidly descending into chaos. Some wanted to slowly rearm and wait. Many did not even want to do that much. The world's troubles seemed far away to their eyes, beyond America's traditional ocean moats. A vocal and steadily growing minority of Americans, conversely, clamored for immediate aid to the allies—though how much aid and in what form remained an open question—but with memories of the Great War fresh in their minds, most voters looked out on a world once more descending into bloody conflict and feared their nation was poised to repeat the mistakes of the past. It all seemed too familiar. Europe's war seemed to echo the last time—which was also the first time—Americans had sailed to Europe in defense of democracy. That crusade largely left bitter memories. Millions joined up to fight. Millions more bought war bonds and cheered their sons off to battle. More than one hundred thousand American soldiers, flyers, and sailors never returned home. More than twice that number would carry the scars of battle the remainder of their days.[13]

They won on the battlefield, but failed to secure a lasting peace. The postwar peace conference degenerated into bitter squabbles over reparations and national interest, and even the centerpiece of President Woodrow Wilson's strategic vision, a League of Nations designed to ensure disputes were resolved with words rather than arms, failed to gain the Senate's approval. World War I was never universally popular with the American people, making those who had supported the war, and especially those who went off to battle, that much more bitter over the outcome. By the late 1930s the ensuing conflict so many predicted, the war their crusade across the Atlantic had been designed to prevent, seemed tragically at hand, leaving few Americans eager to plunge once more into the bloody morass across the sea. "We were fools to be sucked in once in a European war,"

Ernest Hemingway complained, "and we should never be sucked in again."[14]

By 1937, nearly three-quarters of Americans polled believed it had been a mistake for their country to have entered the First World War. Similar numbers held steady through 1941, leaving Roosevelt little choice but to acknowledge the potential roadblock of the conflict's bitter legacy. "We need not overemphasize imperfections in the Peace of Versailles," he told the Congress as he delivered his 1941 State of the Union address, but "we should remember that the Peace of 1919 was far less unjust than the kind of 'pacification' which began even before Munich, and which is being carried on under the new order of tranny that seeks to spread over every continent today."[15]

American public opinion leaned increasingly toward the Allied cause at the end of 1940 as evidence of Nazi brutality spread, but many could not be convinced that Europe's woes were of any consequence to their nation, or that war itself could solve international strife. Roosevelt was squarely in the opposing camp. He saw no reason Hitler would cease his conquests unless stopped by force. Bullies never did. Only by being strong, and by being willing to fight, he believed, might Americans turn the tide against their fascist foes. The philosophical divide came down to this: Was peace secured through strength or seclusion?

From the comfortable distance of the twenty-first century, the passion of this debate has largely been forgotten. World War II is instead routinely recalled as America's last truly "good war," with clear-cut enemies defeated by national resolve. Hitler is widely considered the greatest evil of modern times, and his inconceivably brutal attempted extermination of whole peoples left one of modernity's deepest scars. Moreover, the Great Debate itself has faded in memory, because it was never fully resolved. Nothing Roosevelt or his opponents said or did decided the question of American entry into World War II. Japan instead decided for them. As the National Endowment for the Humanities rightly noted in a 2013 lesson plan for teaching the interwar-period debate over intervention, "After the Japanese attack on Pearl Harbor it suddenly ended, as both sides clearly recognized that, like it or not, the United States was at war." Indeed, the definitive work on the Pearl Harbor attack bears the apt title *At Dawn We Slept*. The attack occurred early on a Sunday morning, when much of the American force was still in bed. Yet this popular title simultaneously evoked a broader consensus reading of history that suggested Americans paid little attention to the conflict growing overseas until the war itself came crashing home. They snoozed, in other words, while Europe and Asia burned, waking only when their own homes caught fire.[16]

Reality was more complex than this easily digestible narrative. Rather than sleepwalk into war, Americans instead argued passionately over how best to proceed and respond to the international problems of their day. By the mid-1930s it had become commonplace to believe the Great War had not been waged for democracy or any other high ideal, but instead for crass capital. Senator Gerald Nye's investigative committee, to cite the best known example, concluded by 1936 that bankers and industrialists dubbed "merchants of death" had pushed the nation into the war in search of arms sales and to safeguard loans to the Allies. This widely held conclusion helped spur passage of a series of neutrality acts in the late 1930s designed to keep American shipping and business out of the line of fire in any future international conflict. In 1935 Congress forbade the export of "arms, ammunition, and implements of war" to any warring nation. Roosevelt opposed the legislation. Like most chief executives he believed in the power that came from diplomatic flexibility, though he ultimately relented under intense congressional pressure. Two years later a second neutrality act forbade Americans from extending loans to combatant nations, with the act further expanded following the outbreak of the Spanish Civil War to forbid American citizens from traveling on belligerent ships or from shipping arms directly to belligerents. Once more resisting congressional restraints, Roosevelt secured an important concession allowing export of materials not deemed "implements of war" so long as foreign buyers paid cash and transported the goods themselves.[17]

A fierce fight in 1939 over renewal of the law saw Roosevelt first lose a vote to include arms in the list of exportable goods, before winning his effort that November to allow weapons and other military goods to be exported, again so long as buyers paid in full and provided the transport. Taken as a whole, these legislative measures demonstrated the widespread view that if Americans were going to war it would be by conscious choice, not because they had been incrementally nudged closer and closer to the conflict, as had seemed to have occurred during the Great War.

Multiple reasons existed for resisting anything that even hinted of drawing closer to the war. Peace activists argued against conflict as a matter of faith. Leftist groups contended there was little reason to fight yet another foreign war for imperialism and wealth while problems remained at home. In this rare instance they made common cause with the far right, which feared that the kind of expansion of federal power required to meet the Nazi threat would invariably threaten American liberties at home. German- and Italian-Americans feared a reprisal of the Great War's antagonisms, while the electorally vital Irish American community typically objected to anything that even hinted of being good for Britain. Binding them all was the fear that Roosevelt in fact wanted war, or at the least believed war was unavoidable. Nothing in Europe was "worthy of the sacrifice of one American mule, much less one American son," Senator Nye declared.[18]

Roosevelt derisively lumped all these critics together as "isolationists," typically delivering the slight with a sneer in place of his usual twinkling eye. In private he described them as moral and intellectual shrimps, or "cheerful idiots," blissfully unaware of Hitler's pure evil. He saved the worst for those he considered not only foolish but sympathetic to Hitler's side. "I am absolutely convinced that [Charles] Lindbergh is a Nazi," FDR concluded about the famed aviator who beat one of the loudest drums against American intervention in the growing conflict. Lindbergh had "completely abandoned his belief in our form of government," Roosevelt told a close friend, "and has accepted Nazi methods because apparently they are efficient." Having recently returned from his self-imposed European exile, Lindbergh countered that it was Roosevelt who posed the greatest threat to American liberties, first by corrupting the free marketplace with his New Deal, and then by hawking war while simultaneously securing an unprecedented third term in office. "Democracy doesn't exist today," Lindbergh lamented, "even in our own country."[19]

While we should be wary of blithely adopting Roosevelt's collective dismissal of his critics as mere isolationists, or as he described them in his State of the Union address, "that small group of selfish men who would clip the wings of the American eagle in order to feather their own nests," he offered a singular condemnation in response. Those who refused to recognize the crisis of the day and its threat to American "national security"—a new term he used with increasing frequency as the great debate wore on—would, he argued, in time discover their dream of isolation and safety transformed into a "a nightmare of a people without freedom—the nightmare of a people lodged in prison, handcuffed, hungry, and fed through the bars from day to day by the contemptuous, unpitying masters of other countries."[20]

Words like these left little doubt over where the president stood on these issues. Wielding the bully pulpit as 1941 began, he determined to use it. With the contentious election of 1940 behind him, he could, in the words of one of his prime speechwriters, finally throw out the "namby-pamby euphemisms." He could "lash out against the apostles of appeasement" who failed to see the threat before them, or, worse yet, who quietly longed for a Nazi victory in Europe.[21]

Roosevelt thus called for many of the preparedness steps his critics most feared, including "a swift and driving increase in our armament production," and for the country to act as the vast "arsenal of democracy," a term he had first employed only weeks before. Having already secured revision of the constraining post–World War I neutrality laws, and the first peacetime draft in the nation's history, in late December 1940 he proposed further new avenues for arming Washington's allies without direct congressional oversight. Congress would appropriate the funds for this new program, dubbed "Lend-Lease," Roosevelt explained, and he would then, in the words of the ensuing legislation, transfer munitions and supplies "to the government of any country whose defense the president deems vital to the defense of the United States." Just put the money in my account, he effectively argued, and I'll take care of the rest.[22]

Critics howled in response. Such sweeping powers were never contemplated by the nation's founders and were nowhere to be found in the Constitution, Senator Robert Taft railed. They would allow Roosevelt, or any president, "to carry on a kind of undeclared war all over the world" and seemed to confirm their worst fears of Roosevelt's dictatorial aspirations. The *St. Louis Post-Dispatch* editorialized a blunt conclusion: "Mr. Roosevelt today committed an act of war. He also became America's first dictator."[23]

Roosevelt claimed other motives, telling the nation during one of his fireside chats that "the whole purpose of your president is to keep you now, and your children later, and your grandchildren much later, out of a last-ditch war for the perseveration of American independence and all of the things that American independence means to you and to me." It was better to arm Britain and the remaining forces of democracy now, he argued, than to wage a far harder fight later. "I deeply believe that the great majority of our people agree that the course that I advocate involves the least risk now," he said, "and the greatest hope for world peace in the future."[24]

Roosevelt was right in his assessment of public opinion, but only up to a point. As 1941 began 80 percent of Americans polled favored aiding the Allied cause, but the complexity of the issue was revealed in their unsteady support for particular measures their country might take on the Allies' behalf. Only 60 percent approved of granting aid even at the risk of war. A mere 20 percent of those polled stated that they would vote for war in a national referendum. Only 10 percent believed Congress should declare war immediately. This was the situation Roosevelt faced as he stared down at the Congress in early 1941: a crisis and a nation largely unprepared in his view to meet the challenge ahead, but also a powerful chorus of opponents. "It is a terrible thing," he had earlier complained, "to look over your shoulder when you are trying to lead, and to find no one there." In one form or another he had been on this crusade for rearmament and for the American people to recognize the sinister nature of the Nazi threat since at least September of 1938. "The president was sure then," his close aide Harry Hopkins subsequently wrote, "that we were then going to get into war." Roosevelt as a result ramped up his ongoing effort to help the general public understand the severity of the threat. "I am in the midst of a long process of education," he wrote a friend, "and the process seems to be working slowly but surely."[25]

The most pressing point of his State of the Union address in January 1941 was therefore to clarify the muddled issue of aid by securing congressional approval for the controversial measures embodied in Lend-Lease. "We are committed to full support of all those resolute peoples everywhere who are resisting aggression and are thereby keeping war away from our hemisphere," FDR declared. "By this support, we express our determination that the democratic cause shall prevail; and we strengthen the defense and the security of our own nation." In the end he was there for votes, vowing, "I shall ask this Congress for greatly increased new appropriations and authorizations to carry out what we have begun."[26]

He then did something that transformed this speech from merely a short-term political plea into a memorable sermon. He defined what Americans had at stake in the growing conflict, as a nation, as a people, and ultimately as individuals. It was more than simply their basic security, Roosevelt contended. "As men do not live by bread alone, they do not fight by armaments alone." Therefore, "those who man our defenses, and those behind them who build our defenses, must have the stamina and the courage which come from unshakeable belief in the manner of life which they are defending." They had to be inspired. "The mighty action that we are calling for cannot be based on a disregard of all the things worth fighting for."[27]

Put simply, Roosevelt reminded the American people that his plan safeguarded freedom, on a global and also a personal scale. This was why they should arm the allies, he said. This was why they should view fascism as a threat. Ultimately, this was why they had to prepare for a war he still hoped to avoid. It was to protect their inheritance as Americans. In Roosevelt's view, the United States supported four fundamental freedoms from which all other liberties flowed. "In future days," he declared, "which we seek to make secure, we look forward to a world founded upon four essential human freedoms":

The first is freedom of speech and expression—everywhere in the world.
The second is freedom of every person to worship god in his own way—everywhere in the world.
The third is freedom from want—which, translated into world terms, means economic understandings which will secure to every nation a healthy peacetime life for its inhabitants—everywhere in the world.
The fourth is freedom from fear—which, translated into world terms, means a world-wide reduction of armaments to such a point and in such a fashion that no nation will be in a position to commit an act of physical aggression against any neighbor—anywhere in the world.[28]

Before Congress and by extension the whole of the American people, Roosevelt outlined the basic building blocks not only of a free society but also of a new world order, "the very antithesis of the so-called new order of tyranny which the dictators seek to create with the crash of a bomb." He proposed instead a "moral order," in which "society is able to face schemes of world domination and foreign revolutions alike without fear." Even though foreign policy was clearly the primary issue, he proposed fulfillment of his earlier New Deal promises of more widespread personal economic and social security. To win overseas, Americans had to achieve victory at home, Roosevelt explained, and the American people needed to know that their personal and individual needs would be met even as they turned to help the world. "These include equality of opportunity for youth and for others; jobs for those who can work; security for those who need; the ending of special privilege for the few; the preservation of civil liberties for all," and finally "the enjoyment of the fruits of scientific progress in a wider and constantly rising standard of living." By ensuring his four freedoms, Americans would not only protect liberty and ensure their own security but materially improve their lives as well.[29]

The rhetoric stuck. References to the Four Freedoms quickly became a rallying cry for the Allied cause and a shorthand means of expressing American wartime goals. Postage stamps were issued in their honor. Monuments were raised to their ideal. Artists found inspiration. Sculptors and mural designers during and after the war competed with orchestral composers to see who could best present their ideals. In Burbank, California, the new city hall, opened in 1943, boasted a wall-sized mural devoted to Roosevelt's Four Freedoms. "It was the intention of the painter to have the entire mural serve to illustrate the spirit of democracy," its artist wrote the city council. San Francisco's main downtown post office similarly boasted a Four Freedoms mural in homage to California's history. German-born sculptor Adolph Wolter carved a Four Freedoms monument atop a chapel in Troy, Michigan, while the graphic artist Arthur Szyk, newly arrived as a refugee from Europe, composed in 1949 a "Four Freedoms Prayer" as a tribute to his new country. During the war Szyk proved one of the most prolific and effective designers of propaganda posters and cartoons. His typical lampooning style previously used to ridicule Nazi and Japanese leaders was nowhere to be found, however, in his almost sacred rendition of the Four Freedoms. It depicts a Madonna and Child and iconography suggesting that Roosevelt's words had a far more divine original author. Several of the images produced in the first months and years following his pronouncement are reproduced in the photographic essay included in this volume.[30]

None of these works had a more lasting impact than Norman Rockwell's. His four illustrations, published in 1943 in issues of the widely circulated *Saturday Evening Post* (and discussed in detail in several of this book's chapters), each depicted a single freedom. They were immediately popular, and the Treasury Department ultimately published four million copies of the posters for widespread distribution. The originals toured the country during the war, reaching sixteen cities and nearly 1.25 million viewers, and helped raise $132 million in war bonds. The images were hung in "schools, post offices, Elks Clubs, ration-board offices, Sunday schools, and railroad stations," a journalist reported. Such commonplace venues no doubt pleased their artist. "I'll express the ideas in simple, everyday scenes," Rockwell explained in 1942 when first describing his vision for the series, and "take them out of the noble language of the proclamation and put them in terms everyone can understand." Taking the president's lead, Rockwell determined to show his fellow citizens what they had at stake in the conflict. Their freedoms were not merely lofty ideals; they were tangible and enjoyed by everyday Americans in their daily lives.[31]

Rockwell had a narrow conception of "everyone" by later standards. Though consciously constructed for widespread appeal, his illustrations nonetheless remain remarkably fixed in their particular time, place, and social milieu. His "Freedom of Speech" image, for example, first published in February 1943, featured distinct symbols of class and social mingling, designed to demonstrate the right all Americans possessed to speak their mind regardless of their station in life. The principle figure in the image, a man addressing a crowd, wears dungarees and the kind of shirt and jacket favored by farmers or blue-collar workers. Men with ties, one in a suit fully buttoned up (and sporting a wedding band as an additional marker of social stability) and another with ill-fitting shirt askew, attentively listen, representatives perhaps of business and the professional classes. They appear to be the man's social superiors, yet each listens with the same respect and intent shown by the rest of the audience. The speaker himself looks up while making his remarks, as though addressing an authority figure seated on a stage, and thus explicitly speaking truth to power. His hands clasp what appears to be a church pew, itself symbolic in Rockwell's mind of the equality all share before their maker.

Rockwell's images epitomize the term "iconic," ultimately appearing in everything from museum galleries to television programs. His image of a burnished turkey and fixings set the standard for how Thanksgiving should look, to the ongoing frustration of many a harried cook. Indeed, an internet search for the term "four freedoms," without the modifier of "Roosevelt's," produces not the text or context of the famous speech but instead this series of posters. Even iconic images have difficulty withstanding scrutiny, however, and as much as they inspired, Rockwell's drawings are also problematic. The setting for his "Freedom of Speech," a New England town-hall meeting, did not translate well in other parts of the country or the world. Only Caucasians are in attendance, for example. The Thanksgiving feast pictured in "Freedom from Want" is also a wholly white affair. Only the turkey boasts a non-white skin.

The parents tucking their children safely into bed in Rockwell's "Freedom from Fear" appear white and middle class as well. The artist sagely inserted in each of these images markers of the times, such as the writing on the father's newspaper that includes the words "bombing," "horror," and "Women and Children Slaughtered in Raids." Americans did not fear rampaging hordes or tanks pummeling their cities during World War II, his painting suggested, but instead their darkest fear involved aerial assault, the only real means the enemy had of striking at the American heartland (more a theoretical than a real threat during the 1940s). "Painted during the bombing of London," Rockwell later explained, "it was supposed to say 'Thank God we can put our children to bed with a feeling of security, knowing they will not be killed in the night." The only image Rockwell composed with a hint of racial diversity was "Freedom of Worship," though, as Tisa Wenger notes in her essay for this volume, even in this image his own cultural framework dominates. Of the seven clear faces shown, six appear with their hands clasped together in the kind of prayerful style most commonly associated with Christianity. Though of different hues, nearly all appear of European descent.[32]

Rockwell never intended his images to offer a universalistic view of what FDR's Four Freedoms meant to people throughout the world. His portrayal of American freedoms was consequently of the rights and privileges of predominantly white citizens of some means, fortunate enough to have clothes worthy of presenting in a town hall, warm beds to lay children upon, or, most dramatically, enough food to make the table sag. Most of the world neither looked nor lived like this, but that was not Rockwell's point. He was instead determined to show how freedom appeared to Americans like him, a state of being others might aspire to achieve, desiring to show "people of different faiths joined in the act of prayer," he later wrote of his "Freedom of Worship" image. In his Christocentric worldview, he did just that, believing he had created an image of diversity with universal appeal. Others agreed, including the United States Postal Service, whose stamps bearing his images appeared with an official press release explaining their goal to "impress upon the public the necessity of spreading the four freedoms throughout the world." Americans in this sense were encouraged not only to spread freedom and to share in the freedoms they actually enjoyed but also to spread the freedom they idealistically envisioned. In Rockwell's defense, his *Saturday Evening Post* publishers typically forbade him from showing social strife, poverty, or discrimination, themes Rockwell ultimately addressed in later years and in different forums. Yet insofar as his contribution to the war effort was concerned, as historian Liz Borgwardt has concluded, "Rockwell made the Four Freedoms so cultural specific that his rendition was almost incomprehensible even to America's closest allies."[33]

The artist himself conceded as much. Displaced war refugees in Europe "sort of resented" the image of abundance in the

"Freedom from Want" poster, Rockwell admitted. They could not even fathom such a bounty. He did not mention, or perhaps even consider, how Asian refugees might react. Contemporaries recognized these deficiencies in his work. "Rockwell would probably be incapable of portraying a really evil human being, or even a really complex one—perhaps even a really real one," one reviewer in *Time* magazine concluded. "Even the four freedoms posters fall short of artistic maturity through their very virtue as posters: they hit hardest at first sight." While recognizing that complexity was not what people wanted in iconography (or propaganda) designed to celebrate all that was worth fighting for, this reviewer ultimately concluded: "As a loving image of what a great people likes to imagine itself to be, Rockwell's work has dignity, warmth, value."[34]

It was neither the first nor the last time a president, or an artist, would try to articulate what it meant to be free, and Rockwell's iconography, like Roosevelt's formulation, touched contemporaries yet also served as permanent fixtures for nostalgia and memory of happier times. Put simply, they endured. Following the 9/11 terrorist attacks in 2001, for example, Rockwell's Four Freedoms drawings enjoyed a revival, appearing on mugs, posters, T-shirts, and even commemorative coffee cans. The *New York Times* published digitally altered versions of the posters, updated for the more recent trauma. Whereas the original "Freedom from Fear" poster featured the father's newspaper bearing the words "bombing" and "horror," the full-page version that appeared on November 2, 2001, displayed in their place "U.S. Attacked" and "Hijacked Jets Destroy Twin Towers and Hit Pentagon in Day of Terror." The *Times* ran seven full-page Rockwell images that month. Their point was clear: faced with a new national trauma described by many as a direct assault upon freedom, Americans instinctively turned to memories of an earlier unified moment of national clarity, whose clear lines of good and evil ultimately produced national triumph. Yearning to strum the mystic chords of memory that bound them as a people, they found Rockwell's halcyon images and Roosevelt's inspiring words.

We should not think Roosevelt's Four Freedoms rhetoric, or his simultaneous call for rearmament, met with universal approval. The speech, like, the man, produced its fair share of criticism as well. Detractors immediately assailed the audacious breadth of his vision in particular. "We have been asked to fight abroad for the four freedoms," Lindbergh responded, "but there are other freedoms that our president did not mention," and one of them was "the freedom to vote on important issues," such as the nation going to war. What FDR promised as a defense of democracy was nothing less than its elimination through a permanent war waged against any around the world—and at home as well—who might define freedom differently. "The bill is a blank check to permit him to make good the reckless assurances he gave the world when he overdrew on his authority," Wisconsin senator Robert La Follette, Jr., echoed, including his assurance that "the United States is committed to the establishment of the 'four freedoms' everywhere in the world." Robert Hutchins, president of the University of Chicago, argued the same. "We are stirred, but not enlightened, by the great phrase—the four freedoms—which the President has used as the general statement of our aims," Hutchins wrote in response. But, he continued, "if we are to be responsible for the four freedoms everywhere, we must have authority everywhere. We must force the four freedoms upon people who might prefer to do without them rather than accept them from the armed missionaries of the United States." Following Roosevelt's recipe for the defense of empire, he argued, would lead to nothing less than the very sort of imperial tyranny Americans despised and strove against.[35]

Within months of his 1941 State of the Union address, therefore, Roosevelt's Four Freedoms formulation offered a target for his critics, who saw in his vow to preserve certain basic values a greater threat from their own government's reach than from foreign foes. For conservatives who believed in limited government, already uncomfortable with the government expansion embodied in the New Deal of the 1930s, further government expansion of the kind required to wage a global war for liberty meant inevitable erosions of freedom at home. Americans must "stop this notion of ideological war to impose the four freedoms on other nations by military force and against their will," former president Herbert Hoover explained. "We have no fear of military defeat; our only defeat would be if we lost our own freedoms and our potency for good in the world." To wage war on the world, even in the name of freedom, would require such an expansion of state power and reach as to make real democracy and real liberty things of the past. Fortress America, in other words, even safe behind its ocean moats, was not the country they knew or desired.[36]

Roosevelt's Four Freedoms address hardly sealed America's fate as an ally in the war against fascism. Less than seven months after his speech Congress once more took up the question of selective service, otherwise known as the military draft, debating specifically in August of 1941 if draftees inducted the previous year might have their term of service extended another eighteen months. A no vote would have effectively liquidated the army Marshall had so meticulously built up over the preceding years. The fierce debate featured repetition of the same isolationist and interventionist arguments as before, ultimately resulting in passage by a single vote. Indeed, sensing his slim lead in the voting slipping away, Speaker Rayburn gaveled the proceedings to a close before wavering representatives could cast their lots. Roosevelt's plans survived, though barely, even with the backing of his popular Four Freedoms appeal. "The Americans are a curious people," a British observer commented. "I can't make them out. One day they're announcing they'll guarantee freedom and fair play for everyone in the world. The next day they're deciding by only one vote that they'll go on having an Army."[37]

In time the great debate ended with a bang, though not with a conclusion. By Roosevelt's next State of the Union address the United States, like most of the world, was at war. The steps FDR outlined in January of 1941 for greater preparedness and more active support of the Allied cause nudged the nation closer to the fray. Their more lasting impact, however, lay in his rhetoric, which marked a pivotal moment in the long story of American engagement with the world. Long isolationist, in tone and self-conception if not in fact, the majority of Americans believed they had sallied forth in 1917 on a crusade to make the world safe for democracy. In the nation's consensus view of history, streamlined for convenience like most widely accepted national narratives, their crusade represented an unprecedented level of engagement with the wider world. In 1941, Roosevelt went an important step further than Wilson, telling this later generation of Americans that they must now engage the world in order to safeguard their own freedoms, but also to ensure freedom's survival the world over. That clarion call became for most a central mission by year's end, when he once more stood before Congress to declare December 7 "a date which will live in infamy" after Japan's surprise attack on Pearl Harbor. They would be at war on two fronts across the globe within seventy-two hours.

They never went home. After 1945 American policymakers controlled more than three thousand distinct military bases around the world. The number approaches twenty thousand if a looser definition of military installation is employed. More than eight hundred major outposts on every continent (save Antarctica) and in every sea remained in American hands through the bulk of the Cold War. Millions served overseas, whether as soldiers, diplomats, of functionaries. Half a million were stationed in Germany alone by the mid-1980s. Add missionaries and businesspeople to the mix and one quickly sees that Americans were a global people set on defending democracy throughout the globe throughout the entire second half of the twentieth century and beyond. Theirs was the "one stabilizing influence," Washington insider John McCloy concluded in World War II's waning months, "capable of bringing this world into some semblance of balance again." It is a charge successive American administrations have taken up since. "If we have to use force," Secretary of State Madeline Albright explained in 1998, "it is because we are America; we are the indispensable nation. We stand tall and we see further than other countries into the future, and we see the danger here to all of us." As she further explained, "I know that the American men and women in uniform are always prepared to sacrifice for freedom, democracy and the American way of life."[38]

Franklin Roosevelt would not have put it any differently. The Four Freedoms marked an important step in that long journey from self-perceived isolation to global indispensability. His vision of freedom, while itself indispensable to the nation's ongoing debate on the term's meaning and import, did not endure unaltered. The ensuing chapters make plain that freedom's appeal might well be universal, certainly within American political circles, but its definition and practice is nearly always contentiously debated. In the final analysis, what Roosevelt provided in 1941 was a framework from which his successors and successive generations could strive for the more moral society he envisioned. His words helped Americans understand their fight in World War II, and helped provide a rationale for the nation's ensuing global mission. His words set the terms of debate. They were not the final word.

Notes

1. For general discussion of the era of Roosevelt's address, useful primers include Susan Dunn, *1940: FDR, Willkie, Lindbergh, Hitler; The Election amid the Storm* (New Haven, CT: Yale University Press, 2013); Michael Fullilove, *Rendezvous with Destiny: How Franklin D. Roosevelt and Five Extraordinary Men Took American Into the War and Into the World* (New York: Penguin, 2014); Alonzo Hamby, *For the Survival of Democracy: Franklin Roosevelt and the World Crisis of the 1930s* (New York: Free Press, 2004); Andrew Johnstone, *Against Immediate Evil: American Internationalists and the Four Freedoms on the Even of World War II* (Ithaca: Cornell University Press, 2014); David Kennedy, *Freedom from Fear: The American People in Depression and War, 1929–1945* (New York: Oxford University Press, 2001); Harvey Kaye, *The Fight for the Four Freedoms: What Made FDR and the Greatest Generation Truly Great* (New York: Simon & Schuster, 2014); and Lynne Olson, *Those Angry Days: Roosevelt, Lindbergh, and America's Fight over World War II,*

1939–1941 (New York: Random House, 2014). For discussion of American foreign policy and geopolitics, see Robert Dallek, *Franklin D. Roosevelt and American Foreign Policy, 1932–1945* (New York: Oxford University Press, 1995) and David Kaiser, *No End Save Victory: How FDR Led the Nation into War* (New York: Basic Books, 2014).

2. Biographies of Roosevelt abound. See, for example, H. W. Brands, *Traitor to His Class: The Privileged Life and Radical Presidency of Franklin Delano Roosevelt* (New York: Anchor, 2009); Alan Brinkley, *Franklin Delano Roosevelt* (New York: Oxford University Press, 2009); James MacGregor Burns, *Roosevelt: The Lion and the Fox* (New York: Harcourt, 1956); Doris Kearns Goodwin, *No Ordinary Time: Franklin and Eleanor Roosevelt; The Home Front in World War II* (New York: Simon & Schuster, 1994); and Jean Edward Smith, *FDR* (New York: Random House, 2008). For discussion of FDR and polio see James Tobin, *The Man He Became: How FDR Defied Polio to Win the Presidency* (New York: Simon & Schuster, 2013). For FDR as part of an incisive group biography, see Frank Costigliola, *Roosevelt's Lost Alliances: How Personal Politics Helped Start the Cold War* (Princeton, NJ: Princeton University Press, 2012).

3. PPP, "Address at Madison Square Garden," October 31, 1936, http://www.presidency.ucsb.edu/ws/?pid=15219.

4. FDR, Four Freedoms Address.

5. Winston Churchill, "We Shall Fight on the Beaches," June 4, 1940, the Churchill Centre, Selected Speeches of Winston Churchill, http://www.winstonchurchill.org/resources/speeches/1940-the-finest-hour/we-shall-fight-on-the-beaches.

6. "Hitler Boasts Britain Will Be Broken," *Courier-Mail*, September 6, 1940, 1.

7. FDR, Four Freedoms Address.

8. FDR, Four Freedoms Address.

9. Eric Arnesen, ed., *Encyclopedia of U.S. Labor and Working Class History* (New York: Routledge, 2007), 1399.

10. Walter Lippmann, *US Foreign Policy* (Boston: Little, Brown, 1943), 54. See also Ronald Steel, *Walter Lippmann and the American Century* (New York: Vintage, 1980), 252–55. For progressive disarmament theory, see Robert Van Meter, Jr., "The Washington Conference of 1921–1922: A New Look" *Pacific Historical Review* 46 (1977), 603–24.

11. Jeffrey A. Engel, *Cold War at 30,000 Feet* (Cambridge, MA: Harvard University Press, 2007), 19–21.

12. For Marshall, see Dunn, *1940*, 187. For "dirty fight," see Olson, *Those Angry Days*, xix. For Gibson, see Julian Zelizer, *Arsenal of Democracy: The Politics of National Security from World War II to the War on Terrorism* (New York: Basic, 2012), 48.

13. Olson, *Those Angry Days*, xviii.

14. Ernest Hemingway, *Hemingway on War*, ed. Sean Hemingway (New York: Simon & Schuster, 2003), 306.

15. FDR, Four Freedoms Address. For further discussion of public opinion, see Steven Casey, *Cautious Crusade: Franklin D. Roosevelt, American Public Opinion, and the War against Nazi Germany* (New York: Oxford University Press, 2001).

16. For the lesson plan, see "Lesson 4: The Great Debate: Internationalists vs. Isolationists," We the People Lesson Plans, http://edsitement.neh.gov/lesson-plan/great-debate-internationalists-vs-isolationists. For Pearl Harbor, see Gordon Prange, *At Dawn We Slept* (New York: Penguin, 1991). For further

discussion of Pearl Harbor's long-term meaning for American society, see Emily Rosenberg, *A Date Which Will Live: Pearl Harbor in American Memory* (Durham, NC: Duke University Press, 2003). For "those angry days," see Arthur M. Schlesinger, *A Life in the Twentieth Century: Innocent Beginnings* (New York: Houghton Mifflin, 2000), 241.

17. For discussion of the Nye Committee, see Justus Doenecke and John Wilz, *From Isolation to War, 1931–1941* (New York: Wiley-Blackwell, 2002), and David Reynolds, *The Long Shadow: The Legacies of the Great War in the Twentieth Century* (New York: W. W. Norton, 2014).

18. David M. Kennedy, *The Library of Congress World War II Companion* (New York: Simon & Schuster, 2007), 77.

19. For FDR's insults, see Dunn, *1940*, 43. For Lindbergh, see Richard Moe, *Roosevelt's Second Act: The Election of 1940 and the Politics of War* (New York: Oxford University Press, 2103), 75; Olson, *Those Angry Days*, xx; and Max Wallace, *The American Axis: Henry Ford, Charles Lindbergh, and the Rise of the Third Reich* (New York: St. Martin's, 2003).

20. FDR, Four Freedoms Address. Dunn, *1940*, 44. For national security, see Andrew Preston, "Monsters Everywhere: A Genealogy of National Security," *Diplomatic History* 38, no. 3 (2014): 477–500.

21. Dunn, *1940*, 273.

22. FDR, Four Freedoms Address. FDR first employed the term "arsenal of democracy" in his December 29, 1940, fireside chat. This legislation ultimately became the Lend-Lease Act (An Act to Promote the Defense of the United States), March 11, 1941. See "Text of Lease-Lend Bill," in Richard Overy, ed., *The New York Times Complete World War II, 1939–1945* (New York: Black Dog, 2013), 153.

23. For Taft, see Charles A. Beard, *President Roosevelt and the Coming of the War, 1941* (New Brunswick, NJ: Transaction, 2003), 67–68. For the *Post-Dispatch*, see Burns, *Roosevelt*, 441.

24. For "whole purpose," see David F. Schmitz, *The Triumph of Internationalism: Franklin D. Roosevelt and a World in Crisis, 1933–1941* (Washington, DC: Potomac, 2007), 115. For "deeply believe, see PPP, "Fireside Chat," December 29, 1940, http://www.presidency.ucsb.edu/ws/?pid=15917.

25. For "terrible thing," see Brands, *Traitor to His Class*, 484. For Hopkins, see Dunn, *1940*, 27. For "long process," see Casey, *Cautious Crusade*, 30.

26. FDR, Four Freedoms Address.

27. FDR, Four Freedoms Address.

28. FDR, Four Freedoms Address.

29. FDR, Four Freedoms Address.

30. Information about the Burbank murals is available on the city's website: http://www.burbankca.gov/about-us/burbank-history/burbank-city-hall/city-council-chamber-murals.

31. Elizabeth Borgwardt, *A New Deal for the World: America's Vision for Human Rights* (Cambridge, MA: Harvard University Press, 2005), 47.

32. Francis Frascina, "*The New York Times*, Norman Rockwell, and the New Patriotism," *Journal of Visual Culture* 2, no. 99 (2003): 105. See also Deborah Solomon, "Ideas and Trends: In Time of War; Once Again, Patriotic Themes Ring True as Art," *New York Times*, October 28, 2001.

33. Lester G. Olson, "Portraits in Praise of a People: A Rhetorical Analysis of Norman Rockwell's Icons in Franklin D. Roosevelt's 'Four Freedoms'

Campaign," *Quarterly Journal of Speech* 69, no. 1 (1983): 15–24. Borgwardt, *New Deal for the World*, 47.

34. For "resented," see Borgwardt, *New Deal for the World*, 47. For "loving image," see Frascina, "*New York Times*," 103.

35. "U.S. Democracy Totters, Warns Col. Lindbergh," *Chicago Daily Tribune*, May 1, 1941. For Taft, see Beard, *President Roosevelt*, 67–68. Robert M. Hutchins, "The Proposition Is Peace: The Path to War Is a False Path to Peace," *Vital Speeches of the Day*, March 30, 1941, 389–392.

36. George H. Nash, ed., *Freedom Betrayed: Herbert Hoover's Secret History of the Second World War and Its Aftermath* (Stanford, CA: Hoover Institution Press, 2011), 234.

37. Goodwin, *No Ordinary Time*, 269.

38. For American basing, see Jeffrey A. Engel, "Over There ... To Stay this Time: The Forward Deployment of American Basing Strategy in the Cold War and Beyond," in *Political and Social Impact of Military Bases: Historical Perspectives, Contemporary Challenges*, ed. Luis Rodrigues and Sergiy Glebov (Amsterdam: IOS, 2008), 17–28. For McCloy, see Walter Isaacson and Evan Thomas, *The Wise Men* (New York: Simon & Schuster, 2012), 335. For Albright, see "Secretary of State Madeleine K. Albright Interview on NBC-TV 'The Today Show' with Matt Lauer, February 19, 1998, as released by the Office of the Spokesman, U.S. Department of State," http://1997-2001.state.gov/www/statements/1998/980219a.html. Accessed July 21, 2015.

FDR speaking to a joint session of Congress, January 1943. Courtesy of the *New York Times*.

CHAPTER 2

Freedom of Speech

LINDA EADS

IT IS 1957, AND THE image is quintessentially American: the windows are a bit frosty from the late November air, and a family gathers in the tiny dining room of their small postwar house. The dinner fare is pure Thanksgiving—turkey, stuffing, mashed potatoes. Dinner is later than traditional; the father's overtime shift did not end until 5:30. The talk is lively and happy until the discussion turns to whether to join a union. The mother, seeking holiday cheer, insists that they change the subject, but the father laughingly protests: "Wait a minute, Roosevelt said I fought for freedom of speech everywhere, including here."

Their seven-year-old daughter wonders who Roosevelt is, and what is freedom of speech?

Fast forward to early May 1970. The dorm phones were always heavily used on Sunday nights. Parents expected their weekly call. This Sunday, a coed was particularly anxious to tell her parents of the week's events. She had been protesting the war in Vietnam. She was sure her mother would be upset but was confident her father would support her. He always told her to stand up for her beliefs. She was stunned when he angrily told her how disappointed he was in her behavior. But, she stammered, "I have the right to tell the government it is wrong." Her father replied, "Write a letter. But you should never be disloyal to your government in public." Walking away from the phone, she thought once more about Thanksgiving, Roosevelt, and what free speech really meant.

39

I am, or rather was, the seven-year-old and the coed, and the connection between these two scenes serves as a backdrop to the major themes of this essay. First, the United States offered much greater protection to its citizens' individual right to free speech after its World War II confrontation with fascism than before, and Roosevelt's Four Freedoms speech was an important part of this transformation. Second, Roosevelt's speech gave voice to the modern push for greater human rights throughout the world.

Roosevelt's speech opened the country to the expansion of free speech protection. It became part of the great American narrative of freedom's triumph over fascism. It was easy to embrace the call to liberty found in the speech. It popularized the idealized vision of what America symbolized to itself and to the world. In that way, his address helped create an atmosphere that fostered more robust free speech protection than existed prior to and even during World War II. It became part of the common man's understanding of freedom, as noted by my father in the Thanksgiving vignette.

Roosevelt was not particularly concerned when crafting his speech, however, with constitutional theory or the specific doctrines of how far free speech protection could reasonably be expanded.[1] He did not reflect on whether the United States actively protected the individual's right to criticize government and voice prejudice. He was unconcerned with the specific legal requirements necessary to indict a person for incitement to riot. His focus was instead the menace of fascism, and his goal that day was to gather votes in Congress for measures to halt Germany's Adolf Hitler and Italy's Benito Mussolini, by articulating democracy's superiority. He consequently painted in broad brushstrokes in order to motivate Americans and their elected leaders to embrace a concept of a world order that placed protecting human freedom foremost among the purposes for which government exists.[2] The fascists would never have placed freedom so high, he argued; thus they were enemy to anyone, such as Americans, who would.

The path toward greater freedom of speech was neither straight nor consistent in the wake of Roosevelt's address. Indeed, at times he did not follow his own ideals. Both Roosevelt and his country often acted based on the complex understanding by which they—and citizens of other nations—have traditionally balanced their nation's broad security needs against an individual's right to express his or her opinions and ideas. Terrible mistakes ensued in the pursuit of this balance. Just like the excessive tilting toward security after the United States' entry into World War I, World War II and the Cold War produced hysteria, xenophobia, restraint on political speech, and ultimately a Red Scare designed to root out domestic communists. The 1960s saw a turning point, however, with a significant shift toward more protection of an individual's right to speak freely. Ultimately, this essay asserts that Roosevelt's Four Freedoms speech sounded a clarion call for a new birth of free speech, yet it was not until decades later that the call was truly answered.

The United States quickly emerged during World War II as the world's most powerful and influential nation, and thus, by virtue of placing the protection of human freedom at the center of why governments exist, Roosevelt's Four Freedoms speech contributed to changing how the world looked at human rights. After World War II, following Washington's lead, many nations and international organizations became stronger advocates for and protectors of various liberties, particularly free speech. It is easy to dismiss the Four Freedoms speech as rhetorical manipulation used by Roosevelt to call his country to action. It most certainly was this, but it was also more, a significant step toward an increased awareness both at home and in the world that certain fundamentals of human freedom are worthy of maximum protection.

Protecting human freedom, and particularly free speech, is not as easy as the rhetoric supporting it would have us believe. What do we do with hate speech, or with pornography, or with terroristic propaganda? Disparate nations that claim an equal affinity for free speech nonetheless answer these questions differently, and these different approaches trigger intense debate. The United States might well be the nation that most strongly protects the most forms of speech, including hate speech and pornography. Many countries typically considered quite protective of human freedom, such as Germany and Canada, are much more willing to constrain free speech rights for the benefit of the community. The rhetoric of free speech might be widespread, in other words, but reality is more complex.

This essay traces the history of free speech protection in the United States, before and after Roosevelt included freedom of speech among his principle four. It also reflects upon whether this journey by the United States offers any insight into how best to protect a community from harmful speech without simultaneously damaging individual freedom. It begins by examining the legal history of free speech protection in the United States. Then it examines the limitations on free speech found today in Germany and Canada as comparable examples of how other similar states deal with these issues. Finally, it discusses how Roosevelt's speech contributes to the current debate on how best to protect this vital right.

A last point of explanation. This essay focuses on the law of free speech in the United States and in other countries rather than on the social customs or political argument surrounding free speech. Government is always at the center of any action limiting free speech. An employer can dismiss an employee for speech, but a person can only be imprisoned or have speech materials confiscated when the government acts and argues such restraint of free speech is legal. Necessarily, then, the limits on free speech are those imposed by the government and upheld by judges. Focusing on developments in free speech jurisprudence reveals how judges have responded to limiting free speech.

Judicial protection of free speech is built into the American structure of government. Protection of free speech is found in the First Amendment to the Constitution. The interpretation of this First Amendment protection is in the hands of the judiciary. Understanding freedom of speech in America demands looking at judicial interpretations of this freedom. As with any "sacred text," interpretation changes over time, the text is sparse, and its historical roots are not crystal clear. The courts consequently have the task of applying the general principle—free speech is not to be abridged—to specific facts, such as yelling fire in a crowded theater. Changes in interpretation, therefore, provide a window into the social backstory that helped to create the new judicial interpretation. Judicial opinions reflect the social forces at work in society at a particular time. To review these opinions is to review the American experience that helped forge them at that point in history.

American Free Speech Jurisprudence Prior to the Four Freedoms Speech

Freedom of speech as found in the American Constitution and, as explained by the United States Supreme Court, is, and always has been, a work in progress. Its promise is visionary and exuberant. The American people have always seen free speech as an integral part of a free society and important to their individual rights. Yet in application the jurisprudential history of free speech protection finds courts upholding serious regulation and punishment of political speech. Understanding the distance between the vision and the application increases understanding of Roosevelt's particular vision. Doing so reveals how Roosevelt's Four Freedoms speech contributed to changes in the concept of free speech both in the United States and in other nations.

American free speech doctrine can be divided into two branches; the first is concerned with protecting society, and the second with protecting the individual. The first branch traces its roots back to the common law of England.[3] Until 1694, no publication was allowed in England without a government license.[4] In 1704, English commentators endorsed punishment for seditious libel against the government, and rejected the defense of truth because the crime occurred when the speech caused mistrust of the government, not when the words spoken were lies.[5] The common law of England just prior to the American Revolution protected at most and only in some instances the prior restraint of speech or publication. Prior restraint was defined, and continues to be defined, as the government stopping publication or speech before it is made. However, forbidding prior restraint did not protect speakers from subsequent punishment.[6]

The second branch of the narrative is more recent, largely a late-twentieth century-story, although it too has important historical roots.[7] This branch is much more protective of speech; it accepts fewer justifications for limiting speech; it defines very few areas that are not protected from subsequent punishment. This branch has even extended First Amendment protection to pornography and political contributions. It supports very few government regulations that could result in chilling an individual's inclination to exercise their right to free expression. This expansion is arguably unique to the United States.

Indeed, the United States possessed little national free speech jurisprudence prior to the early twentieth century. The Supreme Court was seldom engaged in defining the parameters of the protection. Most free speech cases occurred at the state level, because the First Amendment to the Constitution was not binding on the states until 1927.[8] Most state constitutions did have provisions limiting state governments from abridging freedom of speech, but cases brought under state constitutions typically were not appealed to the United States Supreme Court and were decided instead by state courts. These jurisdictional limits on the reach of the First Amendment resulted in the US Supreme Court deciding very few free speech cases until after World War I.

The evolving American sense of national security as protection against threats from abroad and within to the nation's existence, as detailed in this book's introduction and in the discussion of freedom from fear (chapter 5) in particular, ultimately affected individual rights. During and immediately after World War I, the Supreme Court's decisions in a number of cases made it clear that the balance between national security and individual rights was weighted toward security. By the time Roosevelt made his Four Freedoms speech, the Supreme Court had already upheld serious restrictions on speech in order to protect the community and the social order. The press prominently covered this line of cases, and it seems safe to assume that an astute politician like Roosevelt would know how free speech principles had been construed by the nation's highest court. Thus, Roosevelt framed his Four Freedoms speech against this historical background. His speech was created in an America that would not recognize the almost absolute protection of free speech enjoyed today.

The story begins with the Supreme Court's 1919 decision *Schenck v. United States*,[9] a prosecution brought under the Espionage Act of 1917. This act was passed in reaction to the United States entering World War I. Sweeping in substance and scope, it made it a crime "to convey false reports or false statements with the intent to interfere with [the military success] of the United States or to promote the success of its enemies" and "to willfully obstruct the recruiting or enlistment service of the United States."

The defendant, Charles Schenck, was indicted for willfully conspiring to print and circulate to men drafted into military service a document arguing that conscription "was despotism in its worst form and a monstrous wrong against humanity in the interest of Wall Street's chosen few."[10] The leaflet did not call for any violent action and was confined to encouraging the reader to assert his rights against conscription. It is difficult to imagine that such behavior today would lead to an indictment, yet in 1919 the great Supreme Court jurist Oliver Wendell Holmes upheld the law and its application to Schenck. To Holmes, speech loses its protection depending on the circumstances surrounding its utterance. The test he articulated has been labeled the "clear and present danger" standard, and in his words from the opinion:

> The character of every act depends upon the circumstances in which it is done. The most stringent protection of free speech would not protect a man in falsely shouting fire in a theatre and causing a panic. [The] question in every case is whether the words used are used in such circumstances and are of such a nature as to create a clear and present danger that they will bring about the substantive evils that Congress has a right to prevent.[11]

Clearly, this standard is not particularly specific. Indeed, the doctrine was severely criticized.[12] Learned Hand, another important jurist of this era, described the problems with the Holmes test thusly:

> Once you admit that the matter is one of degree, [you] give to Tomdickandharry . . . so much latitude that the jig is at once up. [Even] the Nine Elder Statesmen have not shown themselves wholly immune from the 'herd instinct' and what seems 'immediate and direct' to-day may seem very remote next year even though the circumstances surrounding the utterance be unchanged. I own I should prefer a qualitative formula, hard, conventional, difficult to evade.[13]

Holmes himself wrote several dissents against how the majority of the court was applying the test.[14] Nevertheless, the "clear and present danger" test continued to be used periodically by the Supreme Court to support both state and federal government punishment of political speech.[15] This continued after World War I during the Red Scare period and into the 1940s and 1950s.

Fear of foreign political doctrines and foreign invasion were also used in earlier cases to justify repressive laws. For example, during the last decade of the nineteenth century and in the first two decades of the twentieth century, even prior to World War I, socialism, anarchism, and syndicalism were viewed as threats to the American way of life. This fear was magnified when an anarchist assassinated President William McKinley. In reaction to this political crime and to the broader threat, thirty-two states passed statutes against sedition, which prohibited advocating for a form of government like socialism, and which many judges interpreted as barring as well as the advocation of worker's cooperatives or unions.[16]

The restriction of free speech rights during this time was driven by the felt need for collective security from perceived threats to the nation and its people. These laws and actions, therefore, belong to the first branch of free speech jurisprudence—the branch protective of community. This is not to justify the brute excesses perpetrated in the name of security. Understanding this perceived need to protect the community leads to examining the merits of the "community protection" argument when it is used in the modern era.[17] Roosevelt, therefore, wrote the Four Freedoms speech in a country that permitted considerable control of political speech, and it seems entirely plausible that Roosevelt's overall concept of free speech would not have included the almost absolute protection of speech found in modern America. His, in short, was a world in which speech could be regulated to protect the state and the rights of the individuals were not as elevated.

American Free Speech Jurisprudence During and After World War II

From World War II until 1969, the permissible regulation of political speech in the United States was a moving target. Statutes passed by many states prior to World War I outlawing syndicalism and sedition remained on the books. In 1940, with war on the horizon, Congress enacted the Smith Act, essentially a federal sedition act. Sedition was defined as advocating, or belonging to an organization that advocated, the forceful overthrow of the United States government. In 1950, Congress passed the McCarran Act (over President Harry Truman's veto), which required Communist Party members to register with the US attorney general.

Both the Smith and McCarran Acts gave the United States government extensive power to investigate and prosecute American citizens based solely on their political beliefs and affiliations. Under the Smith Act, being a member of a local Communist Party was grounds for prosecution even if there was no evidence that the party member knowingly advocated the overthrow of the government. The Smith Act also allowed federal investigators to covertly investigate a citizen and obtain search warrants based only on the probable cause that this person was a member of the Communist Party. Under the McCarran Act, party members had to register with the attorney general even if they were charged with no crime.

Franklin Roosevelt signed the Smith Act into law on June 29, 1940, almost seven months before his Four Freedoms speech. Some commentators also claim that Roosevelt forced his attorney general, Francis Biddle, to bring a case under the Smith Act against individuals based on very weak evidence. This case, dubbed the Great Sedition Trial, began in 1944 and ended in a mistrial when the judge died. Eventually all charges were dropped.[18] The evidence of Roosevelt's role in pushing for this prosecution is not entirely persuasive, though several cases brought under the Smith Act note his involvement. Roosevelt's willingness to pursue various prosecutions under the Smith Act further reveals how his vision of freedom of speech should not be interpreted as akin to modern First Amendment jurisprudence in the United States, with its strong protection of almost all speech.

Despite widespread criticism of the Smith and McCarren acts, and expectation in some circles that the Supreme Court would rule them unconstitutional, the court did not. Rather, the Supreme Court in the 1950s followed the path created by earlier cases, deeming protection of the nation as sufficient cause to restrict an individual's free speech rights. The historical context helps explain these court decisions. Cold War tensions ran high in the early 1950s, particularly after the Soviet Union exploded its first atomic weapon in 1949, but more specifically after it became clear that communist spies and sympathizers within the American nuclear effort aided Moscow's path to the bomb. These few well-placed informants provoked widespread fears not only that communists were everywhere, but also specifically that they were in positions of power and capable of harming American national interests and state security.

Within a decade, however, free speech protection began following the approach of the second branch of First Amendment jurisprudence by increasingly protecting individual rights. Many factors turned the political mood of the country against restriction of free speech. Joseph McCarthy and his claims of communist infiltration of the nation and the government were eventually discredited.[19] The concurrent rise of the civil rights movement sparked awareness that affiliation with an organization that advocated change was not evil or dangerous. The Vietnam War led to protests by the sons and daughters of many average Americans, as in my opening vignette, and opened the nation to the idea that some protests honored American ideals. Ultimately, the social upheaval of the 1960s coincided with serious changes in the Supreme Court's precedent regarding political speech. The Supreme Court often reflects in its opinions the nation's political changes.[20] We see this currently with the heightened protection of homosexual rights. The question is what role Roosevelt's Four Freedoms speech had on the changed attitude of the public toward free speech protection. First, let's discuss the revisions made by the Supreme Court to free speech law.

In *Brandenburg v. Ohio*,[21] a 1969 case, the Supreme Court reached for the second branch of free speech jurisprudence—the branch that protected individual rights. Clarence Brandenburg was convicted under the Ohio syndicalism statute, a statute passed in 1919 at the height of that era's Red Scare. The Ohio statute made it a crime to "advocate the duty, necessity, or propriety of crime, sabotage, violence or unlawful method of terrorism as a means of accomplishing industrial or political reform." In *Whitney v. California* (1927), the Supreme Court held constitutional a similar California statute.[22] In 1969, however, the Supreme Court discarded the prior precedent and held the Ohio statute unconstitutional, reversing Brandenburg's conviction.

The remarkable nature of this jurisprudential change becomes much clearer when we compare the underlying facts of *Whitney* and *Brandenburg*. The defendant in *Brandenburg* was a member of the Ku Klux Klan, the infamous white supremacy group that has engaged in violent terrorist acts since its inception after the Civil War. Brandenburg spoke at a rally attended only by Klan members as well as a reporter invited by the defendant to cover the rally. The reporter filmed the affair and the defendant's speech. The film showed hooded figures, some carrying firearms. These hooded figures burned a cross and made anti-Semitic and racist remarks that indicated a desire to harm African Americans in particular.[23] It also showed Brandenburg telling the rally's participants:

> We're not a revengent [*sic*] organization, but if our President, our Congress, our Supreme Court, continues to suppress the white, Caucasian race, it's possible that there might be some revengeance [*sic*] taken.[24]

The prosecutor argued that Brandenburg was advocating the efficacy of violence to accomplish political reform—the very actions made criminal by the statute. In response to this legal argument, the Supreme Court distinguished between abstract teaching of "the moral propriety or even moral necessity for a resort to force and violence [as distinguished from] preparing a group for violent action and steeling it to such action."[25] The court rejected the application of the Ohio statute to Brandenburg because it failed to draw this distinction and thus "impermissibly intrude[d] upon the freedoms guaranteed by the First and 14th Amendments. It [swept] within its condemnation speech which our Constitution has immunized from governmental control."[26]

Now compare the defendant's actions in the *Whitney* decision, for which the defendant was convicted and whose conviction the Supreme Court upheld. Anita Whitney attended a national convention of the Socialist Party as a delegate from California. Those in attendance split, and one group formed the Communist Labor Party. Whitney joined this communist branch, which adopted a document called "The Left Wing Manifesto" pledging industrial strife and the debilitating of representative government. However, later Whitney attended another convention of the California Communist Labor Party, at which she supported a moderate resolution calling for achieving the party's goals through traditional political processes.[27]

Brandenburg's statements and actions—participating at a cross burning with hooded figures—were more likely to cause others to act immediately than Whitney's participation in political conventions were, particularly since she publicly supported change through traditional political processes. Timing explains the verdict. In 1927, the year of the *Whitney* decision, the Supreme Court and the country viewed the threat of communism as exceptionally dangerous—much more dangerous than the nation in 1969, the year of the *Brandenburg* decision, viewed the threat of violence from Ku Klux Klan. Regardless of whether these were accurate assessments of risk at the time, the level of the perceived threat no doubt contributed to the support of Whitney's prosecution and the reversal of Brandenburg's. And, clearly, something had changed between 1927 and 1969 in how much protection the Supreme Court was willing to afford a person free speech rights.

The *Brandenburg* holding was only one of many decisions beginning in the 1960s and continuing to the present that underscore this point. The Supreme Court had tilted in favor of protecting the individual and was less concerned with protecting the community from actions that did not appear to pose an imminent threat. We see, for example, in *Hess v. Indiana* (1973)[28] a reversal of a conviction against a Vietnam War protestor who the jury found had intended to incite to riot by stating during a demonstration, "We'll take the fucking street later" (or "again"). The Supreme Court found no likelihood that these words were likely to produce imminent disorder. And in *Texas v. Johnson* (1989)[29] the court reversed on free speech grounds a conviction for burning an American flag at a public rally. Contrast both *Hess* and *Johnson* with the decision in *Schenck* upholding a conviction for doing nothing more than passing out pamphlets encouraging draftees to demand their rights.

This leads us, then, to two important questions: First, did confrontation with fascism cause a reexamination within the United States of when government should be allowed to control speech, and, second, did Roosevelt's Four Freedoms speech contribute to this reexamination? The answer to both questions seems clear: yes.

America's fight in World War II was against more than enemies; it was against authoritarian and totalitarian governments that rejected liberal democracy and individual rights. These fascist regimes rejected the idea that government power came from the consent of the governed. These authoritarian regimes saw no limitations on a government's ability to achieve national glory even if individual liberty was compromised. When fascism was defeated,

Americans viewed this not just as a national triumph but also as a victory for the idea of democracy and the philosophy enshrined in the Declaration of Independence: "That to secure these rights, Governments are instituted among Men, deriving their just powers from the consent of the governed."

Eventually, the "consent of the governed" idea metamorphosed into a political creed that claimed individual rights are almost always more important than government and community needs. We can debate whether the pendulum has swung too far toward protecting the individual, but it is clear that in America today individual rights are more revered than community needs.[30] In the civil rights struggle, the arrests of Martin Luther King and Stokely Carmichael were considered illegitimate not only because the underlying cause was so important but also because the right to protest and to voice disagreement with the government was viewed as an essential part of the fabric of the nation. This concept of free speech rights also motivated protestors against the Vietnam War, and protestors against every American war since.

By placing free speech in the pantheon of sacred rights, Roosevelt's Four Freedoms speech anointed the right as special and treasured. Over time this came to mean that protecting controversial or dissenting political speech was an especially strong barometer of a nation's real freedom. The generations following World War II largely did not question their right to disagree with the government and to advocate for change by organized protest. It was part of the natural right of free people, secured by the war's victory. Eventually, the Supreme Court came to agree with this view, as seen in *Brandenburg* and in contrast to its holdings in earlier times. No direct line connects Roosevelt's Four Freedoms speech to the Supreme Court decisions that provided more robust protection to the individual's free speech rights. Yet, by casting the struggle against fascism as necessary to ensure the Four Freedoms, Roosevelt pushed the United States toward greater reverence for and protection of political speech.

Comparison of Free Speech Protection between the United States and Other Nations

Roosevelt intended the Four Freedoms speech to motivate the world to take up the cause of democracy and individual freedom, and he believed that American security was dependent on a world that fostered such liberal democratic principles.[31] As with any planting of seeds, however, his ideas grew at different speeds and with numerous variations in the world's varied soils and climates.

Many other nations have not extended free speech protection as far as the United States. For example, Canada and several nations in Western Europe have laws that restrict hate speech and pornography in ways considered to be unconstitutional in the United States. And the UK Terrorism Act, passed after the 2005 London bombings, makes it a crime to publish a statement that is likely to be understood as a direct or indirect encouragement of an act of terrorism.[32] The limitations these nations are placing on free speech often are more in accord with the first branch of the American free speech narrative, the branch that recognizes a community's interest in regulating harmful speech.

Hate Speech

What is hate speech? How is it defined? This modern concept gained currency in the mid-twentieth century. It is a product of the expanding definition of human rights that followed World War II. And it may not be too much to say the regulation of hate speech was helped along by Roosevelt's Four Freedoms speech. As discussed in other chapters of this book, Roosevelt's concept of essential human rights included more than those rights to be protected from undue government influence. It also included positive rights—rights due humans simply because they are human. The Four Freedoms are grounded in the idea of human dignity and the goal of creating governments that honor that dignity. His speech reached toward improving the human condition.

After World War II many national charters and international treaties were structured to also improve the human condition and advance human dignity. It is within the language of these governmental charters and international treaties that we find the regulation of hate speech. For example, in 1948 the United Nations issued the Universal Declaration of Human Rights (UDHR), proclaiming the importance of human dignity and the need for tolerance between peoples. The UDHR limits individual liberties, such as free speech, when necessary to secure "due recognition and respect for the rights and freedoms of others and of meeting the just requirements of morality, public order and the general welfare in a democratic society."[33] It also prohibits any incitement to discrimination.

In 1966, these general proclamations within the UDHR blossomed into explicit prohibition of hate speech in the International

Covenant on Civil and Political Rights (ICCPR). In its Article 20, the ICCPR limits free speech if it is hate speech, stating that any "advocacy of national, racial or religious hatred that constitutes incitement to discrimination, hostility or violence shall be prohibited by law." Further, the ICCPR encouraged nations to adopt legislation to prohibit hate speech. The majority of nations did so. Some of these statutes will be discussed below. As for the United States, the United States made a reservation that their ratification of this treaty did not require the United States to restrict the right of free speech. Further, the United States Supreme Court's decisions make it very unlikely that US federal or state governments can enact hate speech prohibitions without violating the First Amendment.

Much like "freedom" itself, defining hate speech is problematic, and definitions often reflect the historical experiences of the nation constructing the definition. For example, Germany's definition is focused extensively on forbidding glorification of the Nazis. Generally, hate speech is defined to include speech that is abusive, offensive, or insulting to an individual's race, religion, ethnicity, or national origin. The advocacy organization Human Rights Watch defines hate speech as "any form of expression regarded as offensive to racial, ethnic, and religious groups and other discrete minorities, and to women."[34]

The lack of specificity in these definitions of hate speech is troubling. Indeed, it has parallels with the "clear and present danger" test discussed above that led one critic to state: "I should prefer a qualitative formula, hard, conventional, difficult to evade." This same criticism could be applied to the definitions of hate speech used throughout the world. It has an elastic nature that could give too much power to government, as did the "clear and present danger" test.

The Regulation of Hate Speech in the United States

The United States has not followed the great majority of nations in prohibiting hate speech, no matter how defined. This was not always true, although the historical prosecutions for such speech were brought under criminal statutes that did not specifically refer to hate speech. For example, in 1942 the Supreme Court upheld the conviction of a person who denounced all religion as a "racket." At one point the defendant had singled out a member of the crowd and called him "a damned Fascist" and added that "the whole government of Rochester are Fascists or agents of Fascists." The court reasoned that free speech is not absolute and that individuals are subject to prosecution for "insulting or fighting words—those which by their very utterance inflict injury or tend to incite an immediate breach of the peace."[35]

Essentially, the Supreme Court decided that words that inflict injury by their mere utterance can be regulated, and a person can be prosecuted for their use. This decision has never been overturned, but it is doubtful it would be decided the same way today, as will be discussed below. Yet the concept of protecting citizens from injury inflicted by speech is exactly what animates hate speech prosecutions in other countries.

In 1952, the Supreme Court upheld the conviction of an individual, Joseph Beauharnais, who was president of the White Circle League in Illinois, for orchestrating the dissemination of pamphlets warning against allowing "the Negro" to reside in white neighborhoods because "the Negro" would bring "rapes, robberies, knives, guns and marijuana" into the white neighborhoods. The court agreed that the state had a right to punish group libel just as a person had a right to be protected from individual libel. The court did not see such law as contrary to free speech protection under the First Amendment.[36]

I place these cases in the first branch of free speech jurisprudence— the branch discussed above that tilts toward protecting the community from harmful individual behavior. The Supreme Court, however, reassessed this balance in the 1960s and 1970s, just as it reassessed its decisions limiting political speech protection. The court became much more protective of an individual's right to speak even when it could be viewed as hateful or provocative.

In a series of cases, the Supreme Court reversed convictions based on the use of abusive language such as "White son of a bitch, I'll kill you,"[37] or "Black mother-fucking pig."[38] However, the Supreme Court in these decisions did not directly address the issue of hate speech and its regulation. Rather, these decisions focused on "fighting words" or other forms of inflammatory speech that might incite a crowd to lawlessness.

Finally, in 1992, the Supreme Court specifically addressed the constitutionality of a statute designed specifically to punish hate speech. In *R. A. V. v. City of St. Paul*,[39] the Supreme Court declared unconstitutional a city ordinance that prohibited placing on property "a symbol, object ... or graffiti, including, but not limited to, a burning cross or Nazi swastika, which one knows or has reasonable grounds to know arouses anger, alarm, or resentment in others on the basis of race, color, creed, religion or gender."[40] (In American jurisprudence the use of such symbols and signs is considered speech.)

In this case several teens constructed a cross and burned it inside the fence of a black family who lived in the neighborhood. The teens were prosecuted under two ordinances, one of which is quoted above. The Supreme Court unanimously declared the ordinance to be unconstitutional. Five members of the court (the majority) rejected the constitutionality of the ordinance because it punished as hate speech only certain categories of statements—those that affect individuals on account of race, color, creed, religion, or gender. It did not punish invectives aimed at other groups based on, for example, their political affiliation or union membership or homosexuality. To the majority of the court, punishing hate speech as it applies only to certain individuals or groups amounted to the regulation of speech based on its content. The majority rejected this as giving government authority to force individuals to speak or not speak on certain subjects.[41]

Given this reasoning, it is difficult to see how the Supreme Court could find a hate speech statute constitutional as hate speech is defined under the ICCPR or Human Rights Watch. These definitions obviously do regulate based on content and do proscribe speech that targets racial, ethnic, or religious groups.

In the years following the *R. A. V.* decision, little has changed in the United States.[42] The United States Supreme Court did give a nod to the possibility of punishing harm from speech in *Virginia v. Black*.[43] This 2003 case involved a Virginia statute that made it a crime to burn a cross with the intent to intimidate. Virginia, the seat of government for the Confederacy during the Civil War, had a special sense of how cross burning had been used to intimidate newly freed slaves as well as other African Americans for decades. The statute required as proof of intimidation only the act of cross burning, and nothing more. The Supreme Court held this was not enough evidence of intimidation. Rather, there must be evidence of a "true threat." Under this concept of "true threat," the court found the cross burning at a Ku Klux Klan rally was not a true threat, since the burning occurred in a rural area, and those viewing it were only those participating in the rally. It therefore reversed the conviction for this particular cross burning. On the other hand, the court did not reverse the conviction of two men who were convicted for burning a cross on the lawn of an African

American family, holding that this action could constitute a true threat.[44]

These cases show the nuance inherent in First Amendment rulings. We see that even when cross burning is involved, an extraordinarily hateful action classified as speech, the Supreme Court would not agree that it could be banned outright. Rather, this hate speech had to come in a context that made it threatening in a direct and intense manner. This is not the same position toward hate speech taken by other countries, as discussed below.

The Regulation of Hate Speech in Other Countries

The approach of other democratic societies to hate speech is quite different from that followed in the United States. Countries that criminalize hate speech in some manner include Australia, Austria, Belgium, Brazil, Canada, Cyprus, Denmark, England, France, Germany, India, Ireland, Israel, Italy, Sweden, and Switzerland.[45] It is not the objective of this article to repeat the findings of literature addressing the particular cases. Some of this is found in Appendix A, along with a list of nations and various statutes that regulate hate speech. Instead, a brief investigation of two countries, Canada and Germany, provides a basis for a comparison with the United States.

In 1982, Canada enacted the Canadian Charter of Rights and Freedoms. The Canadian Charter has been interpreted by the Canadian Supreme Court as balancing the rights of the individuals with the protection of the community. Part 1 of the charter and its Section 2(b) guarantee freedom of expression, but explicitly state that freedom of expression may be subject to "reasonable limits prescribed by law as can be demonstratively justified in a free and democratic society."[46] This language, on its face, is not particularly different from how free speech has been interpreted in the United States, where, as we have seen, free speech is not an absolute right but subject to certain limitations such as those involving threats to the nation and to individuals.

The Canadian Charter, however, further qualifies individual freedom in Section 15 by stating that the prior sections do "not preclude any law, program or activity that has as its object the amelioration of conditions of disadvantaged individuals or groups including those that are disadvantaged because of race, national or ethnic origin, colour, religion, sex, age or mental or physical disability."[47] The Canadian Supreme Court has used Section 15 extensively in deciding whether speech can be punished when it is harmful to larger societal interests.

Regina v. Keegstra[48] is one of the most important decisions by the Canadian court on this subject. James Keegstra, a high school teacher, was convicted of promoting racial hatred. Keegstra explained to his students that one way to understand history was to analyze the "International Jewish conspiracy," which he blamed for many of the world's political problems. The Canadian Supreme Court upheld this conviction, and a concurring opinion explained that its decision departed from the prevailing attitude in the United States on punishment for hate speech. The concurring opinion states:

> The international commitment to eradicate hate propaganda and, most importantly, the special role given equality and multiculturalism in the Canadian Constitution necessitate a departure from the view, reasonably prevalent in America at present, that the suppression of hate propaganda is incompatible with the guarantee of free expression.[49]

The court went on to explain that while care must be taken to not suppress free expression, government has the power to curb expression when it is of the kind and magnitude to threaten civil society. The court noted that expression of hate propaganda toward a group might undermine a commitment to democracy by destroying respect for individuals and for human dignity. Hate propaganda, they ruled,

> can be used to the detriment of our search for truth: the state should not be the sole arbiter of truth, but neither should we overplay the view that rationality will overcome all falsehoods in the unregulated marketplace of ideas. There is very little chance that the statements intended to promote hatred against an identifiable group are true, or that their vision of society will lead to a better world. To portray such statements as crucial to truth and the betterment of the political and social milieu is therefore misguided.[50]

The Supreme Court of Canada has followed its *Keegstra* holding in virtually[51] every case challenging hate speech laws.[52] This is not to say that Canada permits a hate speech prosecution for every insult. Canada requires the government to establish that the reason for limiting such speech is so compelling as to justify the regulation. It also requires that the means chosen to limit free speech not be arbitrary or irrational and must impair the right as little as possible.[53] This is the government's burden, and a case against the speaker cannot go forward without the government meeting this standard. In Canada, the default position is that free speech is highly protected, but that some circumstances require control of hate speech in order to protect democratic society.

Clearly, attacks on disadvantaged groups listed in Section 15 of the Canadian Charter of Rights and Freedoms (groups disadvantaged because of race, national or ethnic origin, color, religion, sex, age, or mental or physical disability) will be more likely to provide a compelling reason for limitations on speech. Further, this list of disadvantaged groups in the charter is sufficiently broad to create concern that restrictions on speech will become so prevalent as to have a detrimental effect on free speech generally.

Interestingly, the Canadian Supreme Court expanded this list of disadvantaged groups to include sexual minorities, such as gays and lesbians. In the case of *Vriend v. Alberta*,[54] the Canadian Individual Rights Protection Act was attacked as unconstitutional because it did not protect homosexuals under its terms. This, it was argued, violated the Canadian Constitution and the Canadian Charter of Rights and Freedoms. The government contended, however, that the courts could not by judicial decision add to the list of protected groups under the act; adding to the list of protected groups was the prerogative of the legislature, not the courts. The Supreme Court of Canada disagreed, and in *Vriend* ruled the Individual Rights Protection Act in fact protects homosexuals, and the employment dismissal of a homosexual because of his sexual preference is forbidden. Therefore, in Canada judges may expand the list of disadvantaged groups in Section 15 without legislative action. This adds to the possibilities of further speech infringement in Canada.

Indeed, some Christians in Canada have complained that protection of sexual minorities will infringe on their religious liberty to preach antihomosexual sermons. In *Hellquist v. Owens*[55] one court upheld the decision of the Human Rights Board to fine Hugh Owens for a cartoon he placed in a paper. The cartoon "featured an icon of two stick figures holding hands. The figures [were] covered by a red circle and slash"[56] and were accompanied by four Biblical references that prohibited homosexuality, including one that called for the death of those who participate in such acts. The Human Rights Board found that the use of these Biblical references, in conjunction with the cartoon, exposed homosexuals to hatred or ridicule. Eventually, the highest court in Saskatchewan ruled that the cartoon did not violate the human rights code and that Owens had a constitutional right to express his sincerely held religious beliefs publicly.[57] In fact, Canadian free speech law protects statements made to establish an argument or opinion about religion if done so in good faith.

It is important to note that this case went to the highest court in Saskatchewan before the fine against Owens was reversed. Such a case would likely have been dismissed at a much lower judicial level in the United States. The "protect the individual" branch of the free speech narrative is so ingrained in American jurisprudence that a claim that the cartoon was unlawful hate speech almost certainly would have been rejected immediately. In contrast, Canada's current jurisprudence places greater limits on free speech in order to protect the community, which made the decision in *Owens* much more difficult than it would have been in the United States.

Germany also attempts to incorporate community interests into its free speech jurisprudence. Certainly, Germany's free speech jurisprudence comes from its understanding of how hate propaganda can push a people to actions that are lethal and grotesque. German history is scarred by such experience. In 1949, West Germany adopted a new constitution stating as its first principle that "all rights must be weighed against human dignity, which takes precedence over all other human values."[58] The Constitution also states that it is the duty of all state authorities to respect and protect human dignity. It goes on to list certain basic rights, including freedom of speech, but it makes clear that free speech rights "shall find their limits in the provisions of general law, in provisions for the protection of young persons and in the right to personal honour."[59]

We should note that the 1949 Constitution was written with assistance from the United States while it was occupying West Germany. As the earlier discussion underscored, Americans were familiar with restraints on free speech in order to protect community interests. Such restraints were at the heart of the *Schenck* decision and the Smith Act.

Germany's free speech law is complicated and multidimensional, and, as with Canada, this essay is not intended to fully explain every facet of this German law. But, because the power of government to limit free speech rights is written into the German Constitution, Germany allows free speech to be limited by acts of legislation. One such act is the German Criminal Code, which makes it a crime:

> 1) to incite hatred against segments of the population or assaulting the human dignity of others; 2) to deny or downplay the acts committed under the rule of National Socialism, including the Holocaust; or 3) to participate in a meeting that

disturbs the public peace in a manner that violates the dignity of the victims of National Socialism or glorifies National Socialism.[60]

In the Holocaust Denial Case, decided in 1994, [61] the German Constitutional Court examined a case brought by a far-right political party for permission to invite a British speaker who, in past speeches, denied the reality of the Holocaust. The German government would allow the invitation only if the speaker agreed not to deny the Holocaust. The far-right party sued, claiming this infringed on its free speech rights. The German government defended its power to impose this limitation based on Section 130(3) of the criminal code. This section prohibits historical revisionism and punishes a person who denies or downplays an act "committed under the rule of National Socialism."[62]

The German Constitutional Court rejected the party's claim and upheld the government's refusal to allow the speaker to deny the Holocaust. The court found that denying the Holocaust injured the human dignity of Jews in Germany because it continues the discrimination against Jews and robs them of an essential part of their identity. The court also noted that the denial of the Holocaust also threatens the German population as a whole, because it undermines an environment in which all people, and especially German Jews, are fully integrated into German society.

In another limitation on free speech, German law in Article 21 of the Grundgesetz[63] gives the German Constitutional Court the power to decide whether to ban a political party. Grounds for banning a political party are actions "that seek to undermine or abolish the free democratic basic order or to endanger the existence of the Federal Republic of Germany."[64]

The German Constitutional Court has twice banned political parties. In 1952, the Socialist Reich Party was banned because of its ties to Hitler's Nazi Party and because of its "revival of the mythical notions of an indestructible Reich and German racial superiority."[65] The Communist Party of Germany was banned in 1956 because "it directed all of its operations against the existing constitutional system."[66]

In deciding whether to ban a political party, the German Court examines whether a party's ideology is against democracy, as in the Communist Party case, and also will consider whether the party's ideology is based on falsehoods about racial superiority, the first step toward hate propaganda against others. It is interesting that many of the early United States free speech cases limiting political speech also punished those who advocated communism because it was antidemocratic.[67] Such laws are no longer considered viable in the United States, but they are in Germany.

In comparison to the United States, Germany and Canada allow for much more regulation of hate speech in order to protect other societal interests. The foundational organizational documents of each society explicitly provide for such regulation. The Canadian Charter of Rights and Freedoms states that free speech may be regulated in order to advance other social goals. The German Constitution also places limits on free speech, stating that "all rights must be weighed against human dignity, which takes precedence over all other human values." Both the Canadian Charter (1982) and the German Constitution (1949) came after World War II, and thus of course after the Four Freedoms speech. On its face, Roosevelt's statement that America stands for freedom of speech everywhere does not countenance such limits on this freedom. But as we have seen from our analysis of American jurisprudence, the practice in the United States in 1941 did impose limits on this freedom, and Roosevelt himself signed the Smith Act, a law that imposed extraordinary restrictions on speech.

In this sense, the position taken in Canada and Germany is in alignment with how the First Amendment's protection of free speech was interpreted by the US political establishment as well as by the Supreme Court before 1969. It therefore is not particularly surprising that many democratic governments have adopted free speech regimes that seriously regulate this freedom. This behavior is based on the concept that no freedom is absolute and that some societal goals cannot be compromised to protect individual rights.

What is most interesting here is the behavior of the United States and US courts. We see a significant transformation in American jurisprudence and rapid movement toward a position that forbids regulation of speech in almost every instance, even cross burning. In the United States, the courts have claimed that the most important role of government is to make sure that individual rights are always protected and that other social goals and community needs cannot be used to limit these rights even when the individual's speech promotes hatred against an identifiable group. The controlling legal position in the United States is that the best defense of human dignity comes with the protection of individual rights. We see this playing out again when American courts are faced with attempts to regulate exploitive sexual speech.

Exploitive Sexual Speech

It has been difficult for lawmakers to define the speech that falls within this category. Canada defines it as undue exploitation of sex, or the combination of the depiction of sex with one or more of the following subjects: crime, horror, cruelty, and violence. Several local ordinances in the United States forbid sexually exploitive speech because it creates gender discrimination by presenting women as sexual objects who enjoy pain or humiliation, or in scenarios of degradation or abasement. As with hate speech, the definition is not precise, and as with hate speech, critics worry that such an elastic definition is dangerous to individual expression.

As with political speech and hate speech, the United States has moved toward less regulation of sexually explicit speech after World War II and after Roosevelt's Four Freedoms speech. In 1942, the Supreme Court listed obscenity as speech unprotected by the First Amendment, thus allowing regulation and outright banning of such speech.[68] To the court, obscenity was "of such slight social value as a step to truth that any benefit that may be derived from [it was] outweighed by the social interest in order and morality." This attitude reflected judicial opinions from prior eras that allowed the banning of such books as D. H. Lawrence's *Lady Chatterley's Lover* and Henry Miller's *Tropic of Cancer.*

These judicial decisions created the problem of how to define obscenity, because only obscenity was unprotected speech, while other forms of sexually explicit speech were protected by the First Amendment. Prior to World War II, US courts were not particularly concerned with honing the definition of obscenity, often siding with the government and its regulators. After World War II, this attitude changed, and courts, particularly the United States Supreme Court, concentrated on defining obscenity so as to not unduly limit speech—even sexually exploitive speech.

In reading the important United States Supreme Court decisions from the immediate post–World War II era to the present, it is clear that the majority of the court's members are more concerned that obscenity not be defined too broadly in an effort to protect speech important to literature and art. In this spirit, the court invalidated total bans on viewing nude dancing[69] and affirmed a lower court's rejection of a ban on sexually exploitive material that degraded women.[70]

This lower court decision, *American Booksellers Ass'n v. Hudnut,*[71] is particularly instructive on the American legal reaction to regulating sexually exploitive speech. In 1985, *Hudnut* struck down as violating the First Amendment a local Indianapolis law that prohibited some sexual speech because it was a form of gender discrimination. The law stated that gender discrimination was created by some forms of sexually exploitive speech that presented women as sexual objects who enjoy pain or humiliation, or in scenarios of degradation or abasement. Indianapolis defended its ordinance by arguing that some sexual speech leads men to believe that women should be subordinates and should be dominated and degraded. This affects the workplace as well as women's lives generally.

The United States appellate court agreed with the Indianapolis argument. Indeed, it stated that "depictions of subordination tend to perpetuate subordination. The subordinate status of women in turn leads to affront and lower pay at work, insult and injury at home, battery and rape on the streets."[72] But the effect this type of sexually exploitive speech could have on a particular group did not persuade the court to uphold the law. Rather, the court saw this sort of speech as lying at the heart of what free speech protects—the power to affect the human mind. The court stated:

> This simply demonstrates the power of pornography as speech. All of these unhappy effects depend on mental intermediation. Pornography affects how people see the world, their fellows, and social relations. If pornography is what pornography does, so is other speech. Hitler's orations affected how some Germans saw Jews.... Racial bigotry, anti-semitism, violence on television, reporters' biases—these and many more influence the culture, and shape our socialization. None is directly answerable by more speech, unless that speech too finds its place in the popular culture. Yet all is protected as speech, however insidious. Any other answer leaves the government in control of all of the institutions of culture, the great censor, and director of which thoughts are good for us.[73]

We see once again the US judicial system demonstrating an ever-increasing receptivity to allowing all forms of speech and expression as part of protecting individual freedom and an ever-growing fear that regulating speech gives government too much power. Once again we see a diminishing concern for the effects of speech on the community or groups within the community. A comparison of the United States legal response to sexually exploitive speech with that of Canada provides a clearer understanding of how the paths of both countries diverged on the issue of regulation of speech.

Canada also permits the banning of obscenity, and as with the United States the difficulty comes in defining the term obscenity.[74] *R. v. Butler* is the leading Canadian Supreme Court case on this subject.[75] It allows obscenity to be defined broadly as any sexually exploitive speech, because

> the effect of this type of material is to reinforce male-female stereotypes to the detriment of both sexes. It attempts to make degradation, humiliation, victimization and violence in human relationships appear normal and acceptable. A society which holds that egalitarianism, non-violence, consensualism, and mutuality are basic to any human interaction, whether sexual or other, is clearly justified in controlling and prohibiting any medium of depiction, description or advocacy which violates these principles.[76]

Consequently, Canada permits the regulation and banning of sexually exploitive speech based on an analysis of the degradation or dehumanization displayed in the speech.

The *Butler* decision is in sharp contrast to the United States *Hudnut* decision, discussed above. The Indianapolis statute adjudicated in *Hudnut* was similar to section 163(8) of the Canadian Criminal Code, which defines as obscene "any publication a dominant characteristic of which is the undue exploitation of sex, or of sex and any one or more of the following subjects, namely crime, horror, cruelty and violence." Yet, despite the similarities, the outcomes were quite different. The United States court was not persuaded that perpetuation of subordination justified regulating such speech; the Canadian court was convinced that regulation was necessary to avoid such grim consequences. The United States court announced that speech, even insidious speech, is protected. The Canadian court held that the government has an obligation to regulate speech that threatens important communitarian principles.

Comparing *Regina* and *Hudnut* strikingly illustrates the two distinct paths taken by liberal democratic societies in searching for the balance between speech and community protection. The *Regina* court articulates the concern that sexually exploitive speech must be controlled to protect other values; the *Hudnut* court is more worried about giving the government power over individual will and thought. As in the area of hate speech, the seeds of free speech planted by Roosevelt and others as part of the rationale for World War II have flowered into exotic and distinct varieties.

Canada is not alone in focusing on the harm done to society and individuals by some sexually exploitive speech. For example, in 2009 a new law went into effect in England, Wales, and Northern Ireland that bans what is termed "extreme pornography."[77] This law was influenced by some of the same arguments that led to the adoption of the Canadian criminal law and the Indianapolis discrimination ordinance—a recognition that harm comes to many from such extreme sexually exploitive material. The English law, unlike the *Hudnut* decision, focuses on the injury to individuals and groups—including consumers of sexually explicit speech—rather than protecting individual freedom from government intrusion.

Conclusion

What, then, should be made of Roosevelt's Four Freedoms speech and its influence on freedom of speech at home and on a global platform? Perhaps the most relevant question is not whether a direct connection can be drawn between Roosevelt's words and the increase of freedom of speech in the world. The most relevant analysis is to examine all the variations on free speech that have developed since Roosevelt's invocation of the Four Freedoms. The most relevant analysis is not a linear one but rather one that acknowledges the power of an idea to transform the world and then to be transformed by the world. In giving this speech, Roosevelt held up a vision and handed it to the world to develop vigorously and with variation.

It can be argued that the particular variation that developed in the United States, with its almost absolute protection of speech, is a product of its own troubled history with free speech rights and attempts to limit these rights in order to protect certain community interests. Americans learned that attempting to protect the community may lead to unnecessary curtailing of speech; they learned that some speech may be radical and dangerous, but tolerating it is less dangerous than regulating it, even when it is hateful and evil. The unfair prosecutions of labor organizers and dissidents in the 1920s and 1930s and the power of Senator Joseph McCarthy in the 1950s provided ample evidence of the dangers of regulation.

The United States is also a product of the beliefs that flourished during and after World War II. Roosevelt's Four Freedoms speech may have had the limited purpose of motivating Americans to become involved in stopping fascism, but the idea of four essential freedoms became part of the fabric of the nation. Americans often do not know that freedom of association is contained within the First Amendment, to note one example, but if they know anything about the First Amendment, or the Bill of Rights more broadly, they know it protects freedom of speech.

Consequently, when faced with attempted regulation of speech even to protect disfavored groups such as African Americans or women, the American justice system almost always refuses to permit these regulations. The greater danger is seen to exist in the regulation of speech rather than the harm caused by speech. This fear of government and the desire to limit government power is very much a part of how the United States conceives of the right to freedom of expression. It is a negative right. It is intended to stop government action against the individual. In this paradigm, government does not protect an individual from the words of other citizens.

And this appears to be source of the split—government seen as the danger or government seen as offering protection. Both the Universal Declaration of Human Rights and the International Covenant on Civil and Political Rights focus on human dignity and tolerance. They emphasize the concept of "dignity" more than "freedom." They recognize that incitement to hatred on grounds of national identity, race, or religious beliefs is destructive of human dignity. They exhort governments to pass law prohibiting such behavior, and in so doing advocate for the use of government power rather than limiting government power.

Those who have faith in this approach have created a post–World War II variation of Roosevelt's free speech ideal. This variation is marked by concern for hate speech and for speech that has the power to subordinate one human being to another. It is the product of a world that has witnessed the damage and death caused by propaganda and hatred. Post–World War II humans have witnessed death camps and the modern power to decimate entire populations based on nothing other than hatred. Post–World War II social science research can document the power of propaganda and media on human behavior. In this context speech is not just at the core of human freedom; it also is a source of terror and evil acts. And this context has prompted the great majority of representative democracies to regulate certain kinds of speech as being destructive of human dignity.[78]

Some argue that hate speech is at its most dangerous when it is used by governments, and this is further proof of why government should never be permitted to regulate the content of speech even for supposedly "good" purposes. Others would note that the damage done by harmful speech, whether hate speech or sexually exploitive speech, is often done by individuals and not governments. A government's decision to ignore this type of speech causes the most harm. At every turn in this debate, strong arguments are made for the "American" approach—almost no regulation of speech—and other solid points are made for the "Canadian" approach—regulation of speech in order to build an egalitarian and multicultural society.

Wherever one comes out in the debate, it is clear that speech has the power to affect humankind's destiny. It can increase the power of authoritarian governments and cause their downfall. It can motivate people to struggle to improve the human condition, or it can motivate people to eliminate perceived enemies. It is at the heart of our struggle because it gives meaning—both good and bad—to our aspirations and our fears. What did Roosevelt's speech contribute to this debate? One may look at it as contributing very little. It was propaganda written to give the United States a reason to move closer to the Allied cause in World War II. No subsequent judicial decision states that the speech, or recollection of Roosevelt's words, caused the court to "see the light" and rule for less regulation of speech. Further, Roosevelt's view of free speech was formed at a time when courts were upholding repressive laws that often did not protect minority viewpoints.

Roosevelt's influence is thus at once more subtle and longer-lived. His endorsement of freedom of speech gave clear voice to one of the essential American beliefs—people are free to speak our minds and to disagree with government. It made Americans proud that they had this freedom and focused their desire that others have it too. When war finally came, the content of the speech was part of the purpose for fighting. In war's aftermath American society largely took it as a catechism of civic faith that the greatest opportunity for improving the human condition came from protection of each individual's essential rights, even when conversations prove distressing, such as when a daughter calls her father to say she had just protested against the government for whom he'd once fought. He'd fought, after all, for her right to do so.

Notes

1. The introduction to this book provides a detailed discussion of the drafting of the speech.
2. Indeed, parts of the Four Freedoms speech state clearly that US freedom is tied to the freedom of others. At one point, Roosevelt stated: "We are committed to full support of all those resolute peoples, everywhere, who are resisting aggression and are thereby keeping war away from our hemisphere. By this support, we express our determination that the democratic cause shall prevail; and we strengthen the defense and the security of our own nation."
3. David M. O'Brien, *Constitutional Law and Politics*, vol. 2 (New York: W. W. Norton, 2011), 430.
4. Erwin Chemerinsky, *Constitutional Law: Principles and Policies*, 3rd ed. (New York: Aspen, 2006), 922.
5. Ibid., 923.

6. William Blackstone, *Commentaries on the Laws of England*, vol. 4 (Oxford: Clarendon, 1766), 151–52; O'Brien, *Constitutional Law and Politics*, 430–31.
7. For example, James Madison argued that because the people in the United States are sovereign, the right of free speech, press, and conscience must be protected. He rejected punishment for exercising rights of free speech and free press.
8. *Fiske v. Kansas*, 274 U.S. 380 (1927). States, prior to 1927, were free to impose restraints on speech according to the dictates of state law. For example, southern states punished those expounding abolitionist sentiments as threatening the public order.
9. 249 U.S. 47 (1919).
10. The leaflet also asked those being conscripted to assert his or her rights and alleged that the Constitution was violated when anyone refused to recognize "your right to assert opposition to the draft." As described by the Supreme Court, the leaflet "denied the power to send our citizens away to foreign shores to shoot up the people of other lands, and added that words could not express the condemnation such cold-blooded ruthless deserves." Ibid. at 49.
11. Schenk at 52.
12. Ernst Freund, "The Debs Case and Freedom of Speech," *New Republic*, May 3, 1919.
13. Kathleen Sullivan and Noah Feldman, *Constitutional Law*, 18th ed. (Saint Paul, MN: Foundation, 2013), 913; Gerald Gunther, "Learned Hand and the Origins of Modern First Amendment Doctrine: Some Fragments of History," *Stanford Law Review* 27 (1975): 719–73.
14. Abrams v. United States, 250 U.S. 616 (1919) (prosecution of Russian immigrants who circulated pamphlets calling for a strike to stop the production of arms being using to fight Russia); Gitlow v. New York, 268 U.S. 652 (1925) (prosecution of Gitlow for his writings advocating the overthrow of the government).
15. O'Brien, *Constitutional Law and Politics*, 444–45.
16. Ibid., 438.
17. The reaction against the Soviet Union and communism that defined the McCarthy period came after Roosevelt's speech, and so does not neatly fit into this timeline. Yet the McCarthy period follows the same path—a fear of foreign political doctrines gaining adherents in the United States with the goal of overthrowing the American government.
18. Geoffrey Stone, *Perilous Times: Free Speech in Wartime from the Sedition Act of 1798 to the War on Terrorism* (New York: W. W. Norton, 2004); Maximilian St.-George and Lawrence Dennis, *A Trial on Trial: The Great Sedition Trial of 1944* (Chicago: National Civil Rights Committee, 1946).
19. Joseph McCarthy's behavior and coercive tactics were called in to question by the great journalist Edward R. Murrow. See Joseph E. Persico, *Edward R. Murrow: An American Original* (New York: McGraw-Hill, 1988); Bob Edwards, *Edward R. Murrow and the Birth of Broadcast Journalism* (Hoboken, NJ: Wiley, 2004).
20. For example, in 1948, the great progressive thinker Felix Frankfurter upheld the right of Wisconsin to prohibit women from serving alcohol in deference to the different spheres men and women occupy in society—one domestic and the other business. Goesaert v. Cleary, 335 U.S. 464 (1948). Yet, twenty-three

years later, the Supreme Court rejected the idea that women were so different from men that Idaho could exclude women from the role of estate administrator. *Reed v. Reed*, 404 U.S. 71 (1971). Between Goesaert and Reed, the United States had changed its view of women, and the Supreme Court changed the law. In another example, President Roosevelt threatened to alter how Supreme Court judges were appointed, because the court ruled against his New Deal legislation. Schechter Poultry Corp. V. United States, 295 U.S. 495 (1935). Eventually, a sufficient number of justices retired or had a change of heart so that the "court-packing" plan was not pursued, and the court changed its mind so as to allow New Deal legislation.

21. 395 U.S. 444 (1969).
22. 274 U.S. 357 (1927).
23. According to the court's decision, statements such as "Bury the niggers" and "Nigger will have to fight for every inch he gets from now on" were made at the rally.
24. Brandenburg, 274 U.S. at 359.
25. Ibid., 448.
26. Ibid.
27. Whitney v. California, 274 U.S. at 365–66.
28. 414 U.S 104, 107 (1973).
29. 491 U.S. 397 (1989).
30. Indeed, political commentators rebuking communism almost invariably note its failure to recognize individual political rights. President Ronald Reagan once stated: "Let us be aware that while they [the Soviet leadership] preach the supremacy of the state, declare its omnipotence over individual man, and predict its eventual domination of all peoples on the earth, they are the focus of evil in the modern world." PPP, "Remarks at the Annual Convention of the National Association of Evangelicals in Orlando, Florida," March 8, 1983, http://www.presidency.ucsb.edu/ws/index.php?pid=41023.
31. See note 3 above for statements made by Roosevelt in this vein.
32. Terrorism Act 2006, http://www.legislation.gov.uk/ukpga/2006/11/contents.
33. Universal Declaration of Human Rights, 1948, http://www.un.org/en/documents/udhr/.
34. The United Nations definition of hate speech does not include speech aimed at discrete minorities or women. It is more limited, defining hate speech as "any advocacy of national, racial or religious hatred that constitutes incitement to discrimination, hostility or violence" It is reasonable to assume that adopting a hate speech definition similar to the one used by Human Rights Watch would be difficult for the United Nations given its myriad of political influences involving discrete minorities. It almost goes without saying that including expression offensive to women within the definition of hate speech would threaten various misogynistic regimes.
35. Chaplinsky v. New Hampshire, 315 U.S. 568, 572 (1942).
36. Beauharnais v. Illinois, 343 U.S. 250 (1952).
37. Goading v. Wilson, 405 U.S. 518 (1972) at n.1.
38. Brown v. Oklahoma, 408 U.S. 914 (1972).
39. 505 U.S. 377 (1992).
40. Ibid. at 380.
41. Ibid. at 391–94.

42. In the late 1980s several universities responded to racially charged incidents on campus by promulgating university codes that prohibited speech expressing hatred or bias toward members of racial, religious or other groups. Federal and state courts uniformly rejected these university codes as an unconstitutional infringement on free speech. See *Doe v. University of Michigan*, 721 F. Supp. 852 (E.D. Mich. 1989). For a discussion of these university codes, see Thomas C. Grey, "Civil Rights vs. Civil Liberties: The Case of Discriminatory Verbal Harassment," *Social Philosophy and Policy* 8 (1991): 81–107, and Charles Fried, "A New First Amendment Jurisprudence: A Threat to Liberty," *University of Chicago Law Review* 59 (1992): 225–53.

43. 538 U.S. 343 (2003).

44. Ibid. at 364–67.

45. Alexander Tsesis, "Dignity and Speech: The Regulation of Hate Speech in A Democracy," *Wake Forest Law Review* 44 (2009): 521.

46. Canadian Charter of Rights and Freedoms, Part I of the Constitution Act, 1982, being Schedule B to the Canada Act 1982, c. 11, art 2(b) (U.K.).

47. Ibid.

48. 3 S.C.R. 697 (1990) (Can.).

49. Ibid. Dickson C.J.C. at para. 60.

50. Dickson C.J.C. at para. 92.

51. This decision was a change in Canadian law, which had been more in accord with the treatment of hate speech in the United States. One of the concurring decisions in *Keegstra* discussed earlier Canadian law at length, and noted that this prior law interpreted the criminal code under which Keegstra was prosecuted "narrowly, holding that the requirement of injury or the likelihood of injury to the public interest was not satisfied by simply a desire to fan hatred and ill-will between different groups, but rather needed something more in the nature of an intention to disobey openly or to act violently against the established authority." Ibid. at para. 20.

52. Kathleen Mahoney, "Hate Speech, Equality, and the State of Canadian Law," *Wake Forest Law Review* 44 (2009): 327.

53. R. v. Oakes, [1986] 1 S.C.R. 103, paras. 73–74 (Can.).

54. [1998] 1 S.C.R. 493, 498 (Can.).

55. [2002] 228 Sask. R. 148 (Sask. Q.B.), paras. 9, 21 (Can.)

56. Mahoney, "Hate Speech," 334.

57. Owens v. Sask. Human Rights Comm'n, [2006] 279 Sask. R. 161 (Sask. Ct. App.). paras. 86–88(Can.).

58. Claudia E. Haupt, "Regulating Hate Speech—Damned If You Do and Damned If You Don't: Lessons Learned from Comparing the German and U.S. Approaches," *Boston University International Law Journal* 23 (2005): 314.

59. Grundgesetz für die Bundesrepublik Deutschland [Grundgesetz] [GG] [Basic Law], May 23, 1949, art. 1, art. 5 (Ger.).

60. Haupt, "Regulating Hate Speech," 322–23.

61. Bundesverfassungsgericht [BVerfGE] [Federal Constitutional Court] Apr. 13, 1994, 90 Entscheidungen des Bundesverfassungsgericht [BVerfGE] 241 (F.R.G).

62. Ibid.

63. Grundgesetz für die Bundesrepublik Deutschland [Grundgesetz] [GG] [Basic Law], May 23, 1949, art. 21(Ger.).

64. Zachary Pall, "Light Shining Darkly: Comparing Post-Conflict Constitutional Structures Concerning Speech and Association in Germany and Rwanda," *Columbia Human Rights Law Review* 42 (2010): 31.

65. Ibid., 32.

66. Ibid., 32–33.

67. In 2003 in a case involving the far-right National Democratic Party of Germany, the German Constitutional Court dismissed the case without answering the question whether modern Germany would be less willing to ban political parties because it had less to fear from radical politics. Ibid., 33–34.

68. Chaplinsky v. New Hampshire, 315 U.S. 568 (1942).

69. Schad v. Mount Ephraim, 452 U.S. 61 (1981)

70. American Booksellers Ass'n v. Hudnut, 771 F.2d 323 (7th Cir. 1985), aff'd mem., 475 U.S. 1001 (1986).

71. Ibid.

72. Ibid., 329.

73. Id., 330.

74. Canadian Criminal Code section 163(8).

75. [1992] 1 S.C.R. 452.

76. Ibid. at para. 85.

77. The law defines extreme pornography to include "explicit serious violence in a sexual context and explicit serious sexual violence." Ministry of Justice, Circular No. 2009/01, Possession of Extreme Pornographic Images and Increase in the Maximum Sentence for Offences Under the Obscene Publications Act 1959: Implementation of Sections 63–67 and Section 71 of the Criminal Justice and Immigration Act 2008 (2009), available at http://www.cps.gov.uk/legal/d_to_g/extreme_pornography/

78. In addition to Canada and Germany, other countries that ban hate speech include France (banning racist speech and denial of the Holocaust), The United Kingdom (banning incitement to racial hatred), Israel (banning denial of the Holocaust and speech that offends human dignity), South Africa (banning speech that advocates hatred based on race, ethnicity, gender, or religion), and Australia (banning hate speech).

Franklin Roosevelt and Winston Churchill attend religious services at the Atlantic Charter Conference, August 10, 1941. Franklin D. Roosevelt Presidential Library and Museum, Hyde Park, New York.

CHAPTER 3

Freedom to Worship

TISA WENGER

THE MOST ICONIC VISUAL REPRESENTATION of Roosevelt's Four Freedoms is indisputably the set of illustrations by Norman Rockwell published in the *Saturday Evening Post* early in 1943. Rockwell's image for the "Freedom of Worship" features a group of individuals standing side by side, their eyes closed reverently and their hands clasped in prayer. In the context of the Second World War, this painting clearly communicated a shared American commitment to faith and freedom, placed in implicit contrast to the suppression of religious practice and belief under totalitarian rule. The artist attempted to convey a sense of religious inclusivity by subtly identifying several of his worshippers as Catholic or Jewish. The woman at center left holds a rosary; the man at bottom right wears what appears to be a yarmulke and holds an unspecified holy book in his hands. From a twenty-first-century perspective, however, this gesture toward diversity appears quite limited. Rockwell made no effort to move beyond the tri-faith framework of Protestant, Catholic, and Jewish, which had already become the standard way to map America's religious diversity. Even further, his illustration assumed specifically Protestant norms for religious practice and the meaning of religious freedom. The worshippers' shared pose—praying separately, although side by side—suggested primarily Protestant assumptions about prayer as a fundamentally individual communication with the divine. The phrase lettered across the top of the painting, "Each according to the dictates of his own conscience," similarly emphasized the primacy of individual faith. And finally, worshippers not otherwise identified are assumed to be Protestant, an unmarked presence that suggests the normative quality of Protestantism in American life.[1]

A far less famous representation of the Four Freedoms, a mural created by artist Hugo Ballin for the city hall of Burbank, California, provided a rather different twist on the meaning of religious freedom. Like Rockwell's illustration, Ballin's religious freedom panel portrayed Americans as united in their commitment to religious faith, whatever specific tradition they embraced. But his image gave far more weight than Rockwell's to religious authority and tradition. In a letter to the city, Ballin named the large symbolic figure that dominated this panel as "Moses, holding the tablets of the law." Below Moses, he portrayed the pope with the regalia of his office, a group of Jewish rabbis with a Torah and ram's horn, and a Protestant minister preaching from a pulpit to his congregants below. With its tri-faith cast of authority figures, this image was far more compatible with Catholic conceptions of the role of the church than it was with the individual path to salvation that Protestants espoused. This was in part a regional difference. California, with a long Catholic history dating to its eighteenth-century colonization by Spain, had never developed the kind of informal Protestant establishment that dominated the eastern states. Ballin himself, though not devoutly religious, had spent time in Rome, had close connections to Los Angeles's Jewish community, and quite clearly had no interest in privileging Protestantism.[2]

These two images provide a telling entrée into the contested meanings and the limits of religious freedom in wartime and postwar America. First, they exemplify the competing Protestant and Catholic ideologies that structured the vast majority of religious freedom debates at the time. Protestants generally emphasized the individual's direct accountability to God, and the consequent need for religious freedom as an individual right. The diverse array of Protestants did not consistently or uniformly advance this view, but it had emerged out of Protestant critiques of Roman Catholicism that dated to the time of the Reformation. Eighteenth-century Enlightenment thinkers, most of them Protestants or in dialogue with Protestant traditions, had given even greater weight to the conscience and reason of the individual. Yet despite the importance of Protestantism, the proponents of an individualist view of religious freedom had never been exclusively Protestant. Religious minorities of many kinds—including self-identified atheists and secularists, who considered themselves the heirs of the Enlightenment—rearticulated individualist ideas for their own purposes, often to defend themselves against the public authority of both Protestant and Catholic Christianity. But an image like Rockwell's, with its emphasis on a public religiosity in a Protestant register, left little space for their call for freedom *from* as well as *for* religion.

In contrast to these individualist conceptions of religious freedom, many Americans adopted far more communalist approaches to this ideal, stressing the rights and freedoms of the community rather than the individual. Although assumed over the course of US history by a wide variety of minority traditions, this communalist approach is most frequently associated with Roman Catholicism. The Catholic Church had long insisted on its right to define and advance what it considered a uniquely authoritative religious truth, and for the faithful to follow its teachings. Interpreting the American ideal of religious freedom through this lens, US Catholics insisted that the First Amendment protected the freedom of action and expression for the church as a corporate body. While the specifics of this vision were distinctive to Catholicism, it had much in common with other ideologies of religious freedom that stressed communal rather than individual rights. Conservative Protestants, some Jews, and American Indians were among those who also articulated communalist ideologies of religious freedom, claims grounded in each case by a complex and distinctive sense of peoplehood. These communalist ideologies existed in persistent tension, as we will see, with the individualist and generally Protestant assumptions of the dominant culture.

Secondly, these two images suggest that the barriers to religious freedom in American life were racial as well as religious. To their credit, both artists incorporated gestures of racial inclusivity. Rockwell's "Freedom of Worship" illustration includes one African American woman, the only person of color—or the only one identifiable as such—in any of his Four Freedoms illustrations. He later explained that he had wanted this painting to "make the statement that no man should be discriminated against regardless of his race or religion."[3] But by presenting religious freedom as an unequivocal success story, and referencing racial minorities only in that context, Rockwell offered a misleading impression of racial harmony that elided the lived realities of racial segregation and violence for African Americans and other racial minorities at the time. For them

the ongoing realities of racism created a persistent barrier to freedom of all kinds, including the freedom of religion.

Ballin's "Freedom of Worship" panel referenced a very different racial-religious minority, once again reflecting his regional location in the American West. Visible near the bottom of the panel is
an American Indian man, described by the artist as "protecting a
flame." Despite a rather stereotypical headdress—one that signified
a Plains rather than Pacific Coast tribal affiliation—Ballin apparently intended this Indian to honor the continued presence of native
peoples and traditions in California. But another Indian figure,
placed on the outside edge of the panel, revealed a far more hostile
reality. "A savage back of the Pope," Ballin later explained, "is learning how to pray."[4] If the first of these Indians granted a degree of
religious legitimacy to native people and traditions, the second honored the historic Spanish Catholic missions that had attempted to
eliminate them. Ballin's derogatory word "savage" assigned Indians
to an inferiority that was defined in simultaneously religious and
racial terms. And in fact Native Americans remained a subordinated
people, with little meaningful access to the promise of religious freedom.[5] In short, this essay contends that racism compounded religious bias so that African Americans, Native Americans, and other
racial minority groups found it far more difficult than their white
counterparts to claim the promise of religious freedom.

The principle of religious freedom intersected with matters
of race in still another way. The First Amendment enshrined the
freedom of religion as an all-American ideal, one to which virtually
all Americans have paid homage ever since, however much they disagreed on precisely what it protected. By highlighting the "freedom
of worship" as one of the four key freedoms that all Americans were
bound to protect, Roosevelt's Four Freedoms address elevated the
importance of this cultural ideal even further, increasing the preva-
lence of appeals to religious freedom in American life. To articulate
a claim to religious freedom is also to assume, or to assert, a specifically *religious* identity. Yet this is only one of several possible ways to
categorize or define peoplehood—or, said differently, to frame the
terms of a community's identity—on the landscape of American culture. By pursuing claims to religious freedom, then, some minorities who might be defined in other contexts as primarily ethnic or
racial groups were instead able to forge a religious definition of
their communal identity. In other words, appeals to this freedom
enabled certain groups—particularly American Jews, and to some
extent Catholic immigrants as well—to reclassify their identities in

primarily religious rather than ethnic/racial terms. Once viewed as
only marginally white, and certainly not Anglo-Saxon, these groups
could in this way locate themselves as specifically *religious* minorities. This identification helped them escape some of the stigma of
racial-minority status, aiding their gradual absorption into the racial
status of whiteness in American life. In this sense, the prominence of
religious freedom in the Cold War era helped facilitate the expansion of whiteness in these same years to include Catholics and Jews.[6]

Perhaps inevitably, the cultural dynamics of religious freedom
exercised subtle pressures on minority practices and traditions. In
order to succeed in their religious freedom claims, minorities of all
kinds had to adapt or at least represent their traditions to fit existing norms for what counted as religion in American culture. As the
popularity of Rockwell's image suggests, these norms were to a large
extent set by the white Protestant majority. And those who appeared
most different from that majority, in racial as well as religious terms,
invariably had to work the hardest to gain such recognition. At
mid-century and beyond, predominantly African American movements that attempted to define themselves as religious were often
condemned instead as overly political, and to have their appeals to
religious freedom delegitimized on those grounds. Those who could
claim the privileges of whiteness were more likely to succeed in their
claims to religious freedom not only as a result of racial favoritism
as such but because public officials and the courts could most easily
recognize their practices and traditions as religious in the first place.
Religious freedom had facilitated the transition of some minority
groups into the racial status of whiteness. In turn, the privileges of
whiteness brought greater access to the promise of religious freedom.

This chapter provides a selective history of religious freedom
from the time of Roosevelt's Four Freedoms address through the
end of the twentieth century, highlighting the contested meanings
and the racially inflected limits of this ideal. In contrast to the other
chapters in this volume, it should already be clear that this essay
offers a primarily social/cultural rather than a political history of
religious freedom, and that it emphasizes events within the United
States over the impact of the religious freedom ideal abroad. These
choices are not a result of the freedom as such, but emerge out of
my own interests and methodological predilections as a scholar.
The range of emphases and approaches in this book is one of its
strengths, allowing each chapter to raise key questions that readers (and future scholars) are encouraged to apply across all four of
Roosevelt's freedoms, and to the ideal of "freedom" more generally.

I hope that this chapter will raise new questions about the range of meanings assigned to freedom in the United States and beyond, and about the complexities of race, religion, and freedom as intersecting concepts and categories in the historical development of American cultural and political life.

The chapter begins by examining Roosevelt's formulation of the freedom of worship, and why it became so popular in the Second World War and the early years of the Cold War that followed. Three case studies explore the promise and the limits of this freedom for Jews, African Americans, and Catholics as each group struggled to defend its interests (and redefine its identity) on the landscape of American culture. With these perspectives in place, the last section very briefly charts the cultural transformation of religious freedom in the courts and the larger society over the second half of the twentieth century. I argue that the lived realities of racial and religious bias continued to set the limits of this ideal, cutting across the familiar distinctions that remain at the center of public discourse around the freedom of religion today.

The Freedom of Worship in a World at War

When Roosevelt named the freedom of worship as the second of his Four Freedoms, he raised the profile of an already deeply resonant American ideal. Reaching for fresh and accessible language to convey something familiar, the president spoke of the essential freedom for each person "to worship God in his own way." Roosevelt's aim was to include all Americans within the embrace of all four of his fundamental freedoms. Indeed, he argued that these freedoms could only be maintained if they were extended universally to "every person," not only within the United States but also "everywhere in the world." Yet, like Rockwell's illustration, Roosevelt's formulation demonstrated an implicitly Protestant bias toward the freedom of the individual. From a Catholic perspective, for example, no single person had the right to worship or to interpret the Bible "in his own way." Rather, Catholics were expected to rely on the interpretive authority of the church. Moreover, by defining this freedom in terms of the right to worship God, the president assumed a normative status not only for Christianity and Judaism as monotheistic traditions, but for religious faith in general over and against the challenges of skepticism, atheism, and disbelief. Roosevelt's formulation, in other words, did not necessarily include the freedom *not* to worship, or to be irreligious, or even for nontheistic forms of religious practice (such as Buddhist meditation) that might not be construed as "worship." Instead this was a freedom *for* religious worship, articulated in an emphatically individualist mode.

The point here is not to attack Roosevelt, but to more clearly understand the development of the religious freedom ideal and its historical limits in American life. The president's views of this freedom built on a longstanding American political tradition that historians have named Christian republicanism. This was the idea that American democracy relied on religious faith and religious freedom as essential building blocks. A long line of American presidents and politicians had articulated similar claims about the vital importance of faith and freedom for an independent and virtuous citizenry. The experience of choosing one's own religion, they believed, would cultivate a citizenry accustomed to exercising the muscles of conscience. This was vital experience for participation in a democracy. But not just any religious faith would do. As they saw it, Christianity—and often Protestant Christianity in particular—was the only power capable of forming a citizenry with the moral strength and virtue that a democracy required. Throughout US history, the vast majority of political leaders had been Protestants who assumed the superiority of Protestantism as the basis for democracy, and took for granted a certain public role for the Protestant clergy. These leaders typically saw Catholicism as inherently incompatible with democracy because of its hierarchical structure, its doctrine of papal infallibility, and its claims to divinely appointed authority; and they regularly challenged any hint of Catholic public authority as a threat to American freedoms. Protestantism uniquely instilled the fundamentals of freedom, they believed, forming citizens capable of assuming the responsibilities of democratic citizenship. Roosevelt's "freedom of worship" reflected much of the bias of that tradition.[7]

Yet this president offered an updated and more inclusive version of Christian republicanism than had his predecessors in office. Roosevelt pushed the bounds of Protestant privilege, from the level of his political rhetoric to his cabinet appointments, to include both Catholics and Jews as equal partners in democracy's defense. This approach fit the political imperatives of the Democratic Party, the longtime political home for both Catholic and Jewish immigrants, and it built on the rising cultural momentum of the tri-faith ideal. His convictions on these matters had only grown stronger, moreover, with the rise of totalitarian governments in Europe. By denying the vital principles of faith and freedom, he believed, totalitarianism eliminated the nutrients most essential to a flourishing democracy.

Among the most dangerous features of fascism and communism, he told Congress in 1939, was that they "circumscribed or abrogated . . . the right to worship God in one's own way."[8] The war taking shape in Europe had added urgency to the president's desire to unify all Americans under the banner of religious freedom. Writing to Michael Williams, the founding editor of the liberal Catholic journal *Commonweal*, Roosevelt praised Catholic contributions to the cause of American religious freedom. "The lesson of religious toleration," he explained, "is one which . . . must be inculcated in the hearts and minds of all Americans if the institutions of our democracy are to be maintained and perpetuated." Roosevelt was thus firmly committed to an inclusive vision of religious freedom. Yet his vision assumed a tri-faith understanding of the American religious landscape, and maintained implicitly Protestant assumptions about the nature of religious conscience.[9]

Roosevelt was also a shrewd politician who hoped that emphasizing this ideal would build support for his policies from America's diverse religious constituencies. As it turned out, however, the address did not immediately or necessarily have that effect. In fact, many religious leaders seized on the president's ideas to argue *against* any sort of US engagement in the war. Some argued that getting involved would actually impede the progress of religious freedom. Civil libertarians pointed to a series of violent attacks against minority groups such as the Jehovah's Witnesses, for example, to show that the buildup to war already threatened the freedom of religion within the United States.[10] There could be no assurance, either, that American intervention would improve the situation abroad. Profoundly disillusioned by the aftermath of the First World War, many liberal Protestants had embraced pacifism and refused to be drawn in by pie-in-the-sky visions of what another global conflagration might accomplish. The previous war had not secured "liberty" or preserved "democracy or morality or Christianity," the prominent Methodist minister Ernest Fremont Tittle wrote. Instead it had simply created the conditions for the current war. However awful the Nazis might be, however horrific the situation for Jews and other European minorities, pacifists like Tittle were convinced that US intervention would only make the situation worse. Rather than vainly attempting to impose freedom abroad, Americans should instead focus on securing it at home. The only long-term hope for global peace and the spread of democratic principles rested on the United States staying out of the conflict, they argued, thus preserving its moral and material capital in order to advance these goals in the postwar world.[11]

The new US-Soviet alliance that developed that summer added fuel to the critics' fire. In June of 1941, breaking an earlier non-aggression pact between Hitler and Stalin, the Nazis suddenly invaded the Soviet Union. Roosevelt now proposed extending the Lend-Lease program—which he had created to help fund the British war effort—to the Soviets as well. Hoping to justify this program, the president began to portray Stalin as an ally in the struggle for freedom. Stretching the facts by any measure, he claimed at one press conference that the Soviet Union already provided complete freedom of religion to its people. But while the Soviet constitution did guarantee the "freedom of religious worship" along with the "freedom of anti-religious propaganda," Stalin's regime had advanced the latter with gusto and actively persecuted all sorts of religious groups. Some of Roosevelt's defenders believed (or hoped) that American influence could lead the Soviet Union to loosen its restrictions on religious life and ultimately toward a more robust conception of religious freedom. They pointed to the Soviet Union's more favorable policies toward the Russian Orthodox Church as evidence that this process had already begun. In fact Stalin was intentionally using the church, just as the Russian tsars had done before him, as a propaganda tool both for the benefit of the West and to help (re)gain the allegiance of Eastern European border populations who had been bombarded by Nazi propaganda portraying the Soviets as the enemies of all religion. Just as it was in the United States, the idea of religious freedom was becoming a propaganda tool for the Soviet Union.[12]

Few American Christians found this logic convincing, however. As one Methodist bishop angrily telegraphed the president, the "undisputed imprisonment and slaying of tens of thousands of priests, clergymen, and laymen, together with thousands of closed churches, speak louder than words."[13] Catholics joined Protestants in this groundswell of outrage. Monsignor Fulton J. Sheen, host of the popular radio show *The Catholic Hour* and an eloquent spokesman for his church, argued that the best outcome would be for Hitler and Stalin to exhaust one another's forces so thoroughly that neither could emerge victorious. No assistance should be given to the Soviet Union unless it established "complete freedom of religious worship," he insisted, while Russia should be required to entirely renounce communism as the condition for an actual alliance. Whatever their other differences, Catholics and Protestants alike considered the Soviet emphasis on freedom from religion a mockery of a principle that they defined above all as the freedom *for* Christian faith and practice.[14]

Yet as the Nazis steamrolled across Europe, more and more Americans came to support US entry into the war—and to view the freedom of religion as a primary rationale for that stand. The influential Protestant theologian Reinhold Niebuhr and his cohort of Christian realists argued that military engagement had become the lesser of two evils, necessary for the preservation of Christianity and democracy alike. Niebuhr's colleague Henry Pitney van Dusen wrote that the United States risked becoming "an island of democratic ideals and institutions," and would not be able to hold out for long as such. Under Nazi rule it would not be possible to "gather for worship without police surveillance," or to "declare belief in all mankind as of one blood under the fatherhood of God." Christians would be fools to oppose a war in which not only religious freedom but the very survival of religion was at stake.[15]

There can be no exaggerating how swiftly American public opinion shifted toward war after the Japanese bombing of Pearl Harbor that December. Even the antiwar stalwarts at the *Christian Century* now conceded the regretful "necessity" for the war. And while acknowledging the "perplexed conscience" of many of its constituents, the Federal Council of Churches (FCC) determined that the "momentous issues" at stake demanded a new clarity of purpose. FCC president and Yale theologian Luther Weigle now identified the defense of religious freedom as the cause that differentiated this war from its predecessor three decades earlier. This war, Weigle now believed, was truly being fought in the interests of Christianity and democracy. The churches had a responsibility, he concluded, to ensure that religious freedom remained a global priority after its conclusion.[16] Across the boundaries of religious difference, the vast majority of the nation's clergy agreed. A Gallup poll conducted in the summer of 1942 found that six out of ten Protestant ministers and Catholic priests nationwide had come to believe that "the church should support the war," even if they were opposed to war in general, because this war was being fought "to preserve religious freedom." Roosevelt's address in itself may not have moved them to this position, but he had articulated a rationale that Americans of virtually every religious persuasion found compelling as the nation entered the war.[17]

American Jews and the Ambivalent Promise of Religious Freedom

Roosevelt's heightened attention to religious freedom—and the growing cultural attention that it helped inspire—motivated a diverse array of Americans to articulate their own appeals in the terms of this ideal. Perhaps more than any other group, the experiences of American Jews embodied both the promise and the limits of this freedom. The Jewish festival of Hanukkah happened to fall less than two weeks after the bombing of Pearl Harbor. Virtually every sermon preached in New York's synagogues and temples that week—"The Maccabees and Religious Freedom," "Now It Is Our Battle," and "The Maccabees Defeated Hitler"—linked the current crisis to the struggles of the ancient Jews. The *New York Times* explained that the holiday commemorated "the triumphant struggles of the ancient Maccabees for freedom of worship against the oppressive forces of Antiochus Epiphanes, Syrian tyrant." Hitler was the new Antiochus, and now that the United States had entered the war, American Jews finally had the opportunity to take up their own triumphant struggle for his defeat. Through the annual round of Jewish holidays that year, American Jews from New York to Los Angeles reiterated this understanding of Jewish sacred history as a perennial struggle for religious freedom. The war against Hitler was simply the newest episode in this all-too-familiar saga. By framing the conflict in this way, the rabbis identified the Jewish tradition with the principles of American democracy, leveraging Roosevelt's "freedom of worship" for the cause of global Jewry.[18]

All this enthusiasm notwithstanding, Jews had a more ambivalent relationship to this ideal than their Gentile neighbors did. In most times and places around the world, religious freedom had not been a particularly important way of asserting Jewish rights. Being Jewish had been understood not as simply a religious identity, but as a far more complex form of peoplehood that blended what the modern West had come to see as distinct categories of race, religion, and nation. In Eastern Europe, the Jews had continued to live as a separate people with their own language and social institutions, and suffered from stark discriminatory restrictions on where they could live, travel, and work. Because they were not viewed primarily as a religious minority, the freedom of religion was simply not their primary concern. American Jewish leaders had recognized this reality in their lobbying for Eastern European Jews after the First World War, when they advocated not simply "religious freedom" but a variety of "minority group rights" for Jews along with the other ethnic or national minorities in the region.[19]

In contrast, in the United States and Western Europe, Jews had been granted equal citizenship rights by the mid-nineteenth century. Knowing that suspicions lingered against Jews as a "foreign" and disruptive element, the liberal Reform movement had attempted to demonstrate that Jews could be trusted as loyal citizens who merely had a different religion. Put simply, they wanted to be considered Americans whose religion happened to be Jewish, rather than "Jewish-Americans." Appeals to religious freedom went along with that cultural redefinition, and arguably helped to facilitate it. In 1893 the Central Conference of American Rabbis protested a recent trend toward restrictive Sunday laws as "antagonistic to the principles of our country's Constitution." "As a body of American ministers," they concluded, "[we] do emphatically protest against all religious legisla-tion as subversive of religious liberty." The rabbis' self-definition as a "body of ministers" laid claim to religious legitimacy by using a term most often associated with Protestantism. Similarly, their emphasis on religious liberty not only held America accountable to its prom-ise of religious equality but also helped position them as a religious group on the American cultural landscape in the first place.[20]

For many Jews, however, this redefinition of Jewishness never quite seemed to fit. Eastern European immigrants to the United States continued to maintain an ethnic or national sense of Jewish identity, expressed in Yiddish-language newspapers and an array of community organizations. Even within the Reform movement, the fact that Jews who were in no way religiously active still saw themselves as Jews—and were sometimes discriminated against as such—reinforced desires for a broader understanding of Jewish iden-tity.[21] These dilemmas only grew more intense with the emergence of a virulently racial anti-Semitism, a reality in the United States as well as in Europe. Discussions of a newly discovered "Jewish problem" paralleled the "Negro problem," and a variety of discriminatory bar-riers appeared against Jews in housing, higher education, and social life. Starting at the turn of the century, American Jewish leaders battled a decision by the US Immigration Bureau to classify Jewish immigrants according to "nationality" as "Hebrews," rather than by their country of origin, a classification that enabled a series of new restrictions on Jewish immigration. Rejecting Jewish protests that this practice violated the First Amendment, Senator Henry Cabot Lodge defended the classification of "Hebrews" as strictly racial, not religious, and therefore entirely justified. The Immigration Bureau maintained this practice until the mid-1930s. At a time of rising anti-Semitism around the world, then, American officials too were treating Jews more and more as an undesirable racial minority, a distinct (and distinctly foreign) people.[22]

The framework of religious freedom by itself could not address such forms of discrimination. It was even less relevant to the racially defined persecution directed more and more powerfully against Jews in Nazi Germany. Petitioning the US Secretary of State in 1935, the four leading American Jewish organizations detailed the "reign of terror" against the German Jews, calling for a formal United States protest against "racial and religious persecutions" that violated "the fundamental principles of human rights." This appeal referenced the "freedom of conscience," a gesture toward—and an effort to secure—the contested status of Jewishness as religious identity within the United States. But it was clear that the category of religion alone could capture neither the complexities of Jewish identity and experience, nor the terms of contemporary anti-Semitic persecution around the world.[23]

The language of race had become more problematic, yet harder to avoid. Morris Waldman, executive secretary of the Reform-dominated American Jewish Committee, wrote in 1942 that he could no longer consider Jewish identity simply a matter of religion. Like most other Reform Jews, Waldman had long opposed the Zionist movement's demands for a Jewish state in Palestine as a betrayal of the solely religious view of Jewish identity. He had feared as well that these demands would reinforce racially grounded attacks on the Jews in Germany and elsewhere. But the severity of Nazi persecution led Waldman to conclude that he could no longer oppose the creation of a predominantly Jewish state in Palestine. "You charge that a Jewish Palestine is in line with Nazi racist theory," he wrote to one colleague. "You say, in effect, we Jews are a faith and not a race. If so, what prompts us to collect Jewish money for a Jewish organization to be given to Polish or Roumanian Jews whose faith differs from ours as water from wine? ... Whether you admit it or not, there is a particular bond between you and me and every Jew in the world. The race and religion are indissolubly intertwined; one would be lost without the other." Such debates over whether Jews were a religious, a racial, or a national group—and which definition would provide the best defense against a genocidal anti-Semitism—reflected a lived complexity of peoplehood that could not be encompassed by any of the available categories of identity.[24]

Yet in the decades after the war, American Jews only intensified their appeals to religious freedom as their most prevalent strategy for communal self-defense. Increasingly this would mean allegiance to the complete separation of church and state as the only way to secure full religious equality in America. When the Synagogue Council of America and other Jewish leaders met in 1947 to formulate a common position on religious education in the public schools, for example,

they phrased their "Statement of Principles" with great care. They
began by articulating their commitment to the principles of faith and
freedom, emphasizing that they considered religious education absolutely essential to the nation's future. "Religion has always been and
continues to be the central core of Jewish life," they wrote. As Jews
they were "deeply concerned with [the] secularistic tendencies" that
threatened "the moral and spiritual basis of American democracy."
This statement suggested a felt need to prove the authenticity and
solidity of Jewish religiosity—assurances that the joint committee's
white Protestant counterparts rarely felt compelled to make. Only
then did the statement go on to denounce "all religious practices
or observances in the public elementary and high schools," including religious education classes on school premises or during school
hours, as a violation "of the traditional American principle of the
separation of church and state" and therefore of the freedom of religion. By framing their concerns in terms of religious freedom, these
leaders further reinforced the legitimacy of their Jewishness as a primarily religious rather than racial identity in America.[25]

The tri-faith model for American religion became even more
prominent during the early Cold War, serving as a way to assert faith
and freedom as the values of democracy in opposition to an atheistic and totalitarian Soviet Union. Articulated most influentially in
Will Herberg's *Protestant, Catholic, Jew* (1955), this formulation further
helped situate Jewishness in the American public imagination as a
primarily religious classification. Herberg argued that these three
religious groups had become the primary means of assimilation into
American life, and served as the backbone for American democracy.
Immigrants lost their ethnic distinctiveness, he claimed, and instead
embraced a *religious* identity as either Protestant, Catholic, or Jewish.
Presented as a descriptive analysis of American society—its subtitle
was *An Essay in American Religious Sociology*—the book served simultaneously as a moral critique of the ultimate emptiness its author
saw in the "American way of life" that all three traditions had come
to celebrate; and as another way of confirming the classification of
Jewishness as religious in the first place. Herberg himself had grown
up in a secular Jewish family, turned decisively against his early allegiance to communism, and embraced his Jewishness as a religious
identity. He offered a somewhat atypical critique of the American
Jewish emphasis on the separation of church and state, portraying
this as a defensive posture that was no longer necessary in a comfort-
ably Judeo-Christian America. Yet he could not overcome the basic
insecurity of American Jews as a demographically small minority in

an overwhelmingly Christian nation. And even as his work helped solidify the construct of a Judeo-Christian America, thus incorporating Jews into the American religious mainstream, it also imposed structural limits on that mainstream by claiming the mantle "religions of democracy" for Protestants, Catholics, and Jews alone.[26]

The all-American principle of religious freedom provided a powerful way to defend Jewish interests in an overwhelmingly Christian society. Its utility in defining Jewish identity as religious served as a key part of that defense. But this careful positioning of Jewishness as religion came with some very real costs. Jews had no choice but to conform at least some of the practices of their religious life after Protestant norms around worship, the role of the clergy, and much more. Herberg himself has often been criticized for modeling his theology and his views of Judaism on the ideas of his mentor, the influential Protestant Cold War theologian Reinhold Niebuhr. And his insistence on an underlying Judeo-Christian unity for America built on the Christian republicanism that had for so long supported Protestant public authority in American life. While asserting the place of Judaism as an all-American religion, Herberg implicitly (and sometimes explicitly) excluded other racial and religious others from that circle of inclusion.

In the process, the emphasis on Judaism as religion tended to undermine other ways of defining Jewish peoplehood. As the persistent figure of the "secular Jew" reveals, Jewishness had never become an exclusively religious identity. The invention of ethnicity—which was newly distinguished from race in the middle of the twentieth century—enabled a new way to ground Jewish peoplehood in shared ethnic origins and cultural traditions, while allowing American Jews to assume (for the most part) a white racial identity. Yet in the Cold War decades, when the cultural consensus identified Americans by definition as a religious people, such nonreligious conceptions of Jewish identity became harder to sustain. In a larger society committed to the tri-faith ideal, the most easily affirmed form of Jewish difference was the religious identity of Judaism—an identity that many Jews continued to find entirely inadequate as a way to encapsulate their experience of being Jewish.[27]

African Americans and the Racial Limits of Religious Freedom

Although African American leaders in the 1940s regularly invoked Roosevelt's model of the Four Freedoms to support their demands for racial equality, few of them devoted any real attention to the "freedom of worship" as such. In an essay titled "The Negro Has Always Wanted the Four Freedoms," Wilberforce University president and historian Charles H. Wesley surveyed the history of black freedom struggles from the abolitionist movement to more recent protests against lynching and Jim Crow. The setup of the Four Freedoms required him to address the freedom of worship, and as an ordained minister in the African Methodist Episcopal Church he certainly cared about religious life. Yet he devoted far less space to this freedom than to the other three, noting simply the restrictions that had been imposed on slave worship, the past "humiliation of the Negro pew," and the ongoing barriers to "Negro . . . membership in a 'white' church." This brief account gives ample evidence of the significant restrictions that had been imposed on African American religious life through the eras of slavery and segregation. But Wesley's historical narrative, and the list of seven "wants" that followed, made no further mention of the freedom of religion, stressing economic and social issues instead.[28]

Like Wesley, and in stark contrast to white Protestants, Catholics, and Jews, most African Americans demonstrated strikingly little interest in the specific principle of religious freedom. Although black Christians had long identified their own experiences with the Exodus account of the Jews' liberation from slavery in Egypt, for example, they had never renarrated this story in the language of religious freedom, as did their Jewish counterparts.[29] Forged in the racially defined experiences of slavery and segregation, black cultural and religious traditions in the United States generally foregrounded the ideal of freedom in general rather than the freedom of religion as such. For the most part, this particular freedom simply seemed less pertinent to the concerns of a people whose oppression had been so insistently defined in racial terms. Black Americans had of course met with very real restrictions on their religious lives, as Wesley noted. They had also faced demeaning religious stereotypes that continued to shape dominant cultural ideologies of race. Reinforcing images of black people as intellectually inferior, for example, white Americans had regularly depicted black religiosity as simplistic and overly emotional.[30] But because the larger society so insistently identified them as a despised racial minority—a categorization that American Jews were for the most part managing to escape—African Americans rarely found religious freedom a particularly useful way to frame their concerns.

It is instructive to attend to the contexts in which black Americans did use the language of religious freedom. At least some of those who did so were asserting their right to a primarily religious way of framing their identity, thus rejecting the insistent power of race to define their lives. This dynamic is evident in the new religious movements that flourished in black communities at midcentury, particularly in the urban North. In one way or another, many of these movements attempted to renegotiate their place in US society by rejecting an exclusively racial definition of African American identity, and to forge in its place an ethno-religious sense of peoplehood.[31] Noble Drew Ali, who founded the Moorish Science Temple in Chicago in the 1920s, taught that African Americans were "Asiatic" Moors, originally from Northwest Africa, whose rightful religion was Islam. W. D. Fard, founder of the Nation of Islam, likewise insisted that the people generally known as "Negroes" were in fact "members of the lost tribe of Shabazz, stolen by traders from the Holy City of Mecca 379 years ago."[32] And the various Black Hebrew or Black Israelite communities, most of them founded in the early twentieth century, staked out an African American claim to the Biblical status of God's chosen people.[33] All of these movements rejected the negatively racialized "Negro" or "colored" identity assigned to them by the dominant society. In its place they claimed a comprehensive ethno-religious identity, grounded in a powerful historical narrative that provided ultimate purpose and meaning for their adherents as a people.

In contrast to the black Protestant majority, these groups readily articulated their concerns in the language of religious freedom. And instead of defining religious freedom as an individual right, they articulated a far more communalist vision of the right to live and worship as a distinct people or nation. Noble Drew Ali's vision of peoplehood included the idea that each "nation" must have the right to practice its own religion. "Every nation shall and must worship under their own vine and fig tree," he taught, "and return to their own and be one with their Father God—Allah." These were separatist movements, more interested in withdrawing from the larger society and claiming the right to manage their own affairs than in any of the rights of individual citizenship under the US constitution. In certain respects their vision paralleled the "minority group rights" that Jews and other minorities were seeking in Eastern Europe at the time, a strategy that reflected the extremes of their marginalization within the larger society.

Forced to navigate within the framework of the US legal system, these movements necessarily formulated their legal appeals in a more individualistic register. But however they defined it, the freedom of religion served as a way for these movements to assert their religious identity—and thus their legitimacy—against the authority of the state. Black Muslims in prison, for example, used the language of religious freedom to protest prison rules that infringed on their standards of Islamic practice. Malcolm X, who later became famous as a spokesman for the Nation of Islam, joined the movement during his years in prison. In 1950 he led a group of his fellow prisoners in a protest against prison food and mandatory typhoid inoculations. By appealing for religious freedom he defined their identity and practice as religious—a defensive strategy and a claim to legitimacy that might seem to have a chance of succeeding under the First Amendment. Yet prison officials refused to accommodate their requests and, in hopes of silencing them, transferred Malcolm X to a different prison.[34]

Like these prison officials, the larger society proved unwilling to accept such redefinitions of African American identity or to accept their religious freedom claims. Before the war, most government agents, news reporters, and scholars had depicted black religious innovators simply as crackpots or frauds. W. D. Fard was stigmatized, for example, as the leader of a "Voodoo cult." The Nation of Islam increasingly came under suspicion as too political and a threat to national security. The FBI conducted a series of raids and imprisoned several Nation of Islam leaders in 1942, ostensibly because they refused to register for the draft. Their broader concern was the movement's anticolonial and anti-Western sympathies and connections. Fard's successor, Elijah Muhammad, had explicitly linked the African American struggle with the anticolonial movements of "darker races" in Asia and Africa. The Nation of Islam would become even more controversial at the height of the Black Power movement in the 1950s and 1960s, when Malcolm X rose to prominence and media coverage branded it as a black supremacist "hate group" rather than a real religion.[35]

Yet recent scholarship has challenged any dismissal of the movement's religious legitimacy on these grounds. Every religious commitment has political implications of one kind or another, and the divide between "religion" and "politics" has always been a definitional ideal rather than a clear distinction on the ground. These implications are simply less noticeable and less controversial when they support the status quo. As the story of the Nation of Islam reveals, religious freedom has been limited not only by overtly religious barriers, but by deeply racialized assumptions about what does and does not count as religious in the first place. For African

American Muslims the "freedom of worship," along with the rest of Roosevelt's Four Freedoms, was a hollow ideal that might as well have been marked "for whites and Christians only."[36]

Indeed, the celebratory discourses of religious freedom as employed by white Protestants, Catholics, and Jews could sometimes work to obscure, or even to reinforce, the ongoing realities of racial segregation and violence. The activities of the interdenominational Baptist Joint Committee on Public Affairs (BJC) demonstrate how an exclusive emphasis on religious freedom could help white Americans avoid the problem of race. Organized in the 1930s to lobby for persecuted Baptists abroad, the BJC immediately identified the historic Baptist ideal of religious freedom as its primary sphere of interest. During the war, when several historically black Baptist denominations were first invited to participate in the work of the committee, an African American delegate proposed that its scope of "public affairs" should include the issues of race and racial discrimination. The other delegates approved this proposal "in principle," but then closed off that possibility by resolving that "from now on" the BJC "should concern itself primarily with the question of making effective the Baptist position on religious liberty in the [postwar] peace settlement." Tackling the problem of racism would have alienated much of the BJC's white constituency, especially in the South. Maintaining its exclusive focus on religious freedom allowed the committee to maintain its tentative (and always fragile) collaboration between (white) northern and Southern Baptists. Yet in so doing the BJC avoided taking up the concerns most pressing to black Baptist churches. Perhaps for this reason, delegates from the black Baptist denominations rarely bothered to attend its meetings over the next two decades. In this way, the era's celebratory emphasis on religious freedom helped white Americans avoid the problem of racism, largely excluding African Americans themselves from the conversation.[37]

Some white Americans invoked religious freedom in ways that directly justified racial discrimination and the politics of Jim Crow. This rationale worked in concert with segregationists' emphasis on "freedom of choice" and "freedom of association" as a way to defend segregated schools, neighborhoods, and workplaces.[38] Donald R. Richberg, a former member of Roosevelt's New Deal administration, condemned the "civil rights hysteria" as a very real danger to individual liberties. Richberg argued in particular that by forbidding employers to discriminate on racial grounds, President Harry Truman's proposed Federal Fair Employment Practices Act would violate many

Americans' sincerely held religious convictions. In his eyes, any federal action against racial discrimination represented an unacceptable level of government control, veering dangerously close to communism and potentially infringing on every individual freedom. For anyone to freely "exercise . . . his religion, he must be free to restrict his associations with others in accordance with his feelings and his convictions as to what is necessary and desirable," Richberg wrote. "Yet the committee would have a man forced by law into associations which may be repulsive to him—not because of any narrow prejudice but because of his profound religious convictions." Richberg saw a religious foundation for racial distinctions and the "freedom of association," arguing that "race and color" were in no way arbitrary but had "divided mankind for centuries." In his eyes, any government programs aimed at forcing racial integration were "an intolerant violation of individual liberty," destroying the fundamental freedoms that Americans had so recently fought to defend.[39] And despite the ultimate successes of the civil rights movement, conservative articulations of religious freedom would remain as an impediment to racial integration across the suburban landscapes and neighborhoods of the United States.

Catholic Identity and the Contested Meanings of Religious Freedom

Catholics in the United States, like their white Protestant and Jewish counterparts, used the language of religious freedom quite successfully to help locate their place on the American cultural landscape. It served first of all as a way to position Catholics as loyal and patriotic citizens. Americans had been blessed with "true freedom . . . the right to live our lives under law and the right to worship God," said Boston's Archbishop William Cardinal O'Connell in his annual Easter address for 1942. They must now take up the "sacred obligation to preserve, defend, and perpetuate" that freedom.[40] At the time of O'Connell's address, soon after the United States entered the war, this was a potentially delicate task. In prior decades Catholics had worried far less about the Nazis than about leftists and communists in places like Spain, Mexico, and the Soviet Union—all countries ruled by openly atheistic regimes that severely restricted the rights of the church. The rise of fascists in Italy, Spain, and even Germany had at first appeared to the Vatican as a promising development, representing potential allies in the struggle against communism. The identity of so many American Catholics as second- and third-generation Italian and German immigrants also created potential suspicions around their loyalties in the war.[41] By stressing their commitment to religious faith and religious freedom, then, the archbishop identified Catholics as true Americans, dedicated to the principles of democracy and the fundamental freedoms that the president had named. Religious freedom thus provided Catholics too with a way to demonstrate their allegiance to American values, and the status of Catholicism as an all-American religion.

At the same time American Catholic leaders reframed religious freedom in distinctively Catholic ways, implicitly challenging the Protestant and individualist assumptions of mainstream political rhetoric. Nineteenth-century papal encyclicals had explicitly rejected individualist ideologies of religious freedom as heretical. For example, Pope Leo IX's 1864 Syllabus of Errors denounced the idea that "every man is free to embrace and profess that religion which, guided by the light of reason, he shall consider true" as a denial of the Catholic Church's claims to universal and exclusive truth. Responding to various efforts to control the church or to limit its authority, however, the Vatican had insistently defended the "liberty of the church."[42] According to official Catholic teachings, then, religious freedom rightly understood was the freedom of the church to advance its interests without interference from the state, and for the Catholic faithful to follow its teachings.

Archbishop O'Connell subtly redefined religious freedom in keeping with this view, pushing back against the individualist frameworks of the larger society. His address suggested a newly confident American church, one that assumed the right to speak for all Americans and advanced its own ideas about what religious freedom meant. And by omitting any mention of the individual conscience, his phrase "the right to worship God" silently rejected the president's emphasis on the individual. From a Catholic perspective, while the faithful must be free to fulfill the teachings of their church, they had no right to come up with their own religious beliefs or forms of worship. Instead, the freedom of religion primarily signified the rights of the church to instruct its members, to maintain its own forms of religious practice, and to determine for itself what aspects of life counted as "religion" and therefore fit within this freedom's scope. Grounded in their view of the church as the sole arbiter of ultimate truth, American Catholic leaders stressed the rights and freedoms of the church as a corporate body. This was an essentially communalist model of religious freedom, one that would assume growing importance in American political culture in decades to come.

A wartime controversy over Protestant missions in Latin America further illustrates the tensions between Protestant and Catholic ideologies of religious freedom. Protestants alleged that the Catholic hierarchy was pressuring Latin American governments to refuse visas to missionaries—and that church leaders had even colluded with fascist governments so as to preserve their "age-long status of privilege" in the region. Catholics were thereby violating the rightful separation of church and state, they claimed, as well as the religious freedom of the missionaries and of the Latin American people who were prevented from hearing the Protestant message or, if they so desired, joining a Protestant church.[43] But according to the US Catholic bishops the Protestants were the real culprits. The Jesuit weekly *America* explained that the only threat to the freedom of religion was from the attempted Protestant missions, which attacked the freely chosen Catholic faith of the Latin American people. *America* did not see how this freedom granted evangelical missionaries any right to disturb and harass committed Catholics. One of the aims of the war, *America* argued, was for "the oppressed nations" to "get from their own rulers a decent respect for the natural right to practice their own religion." Religious freedom in this sense already existed in the Catholic nations of Latin America, just as it did in the United States, and the offensive tactics of Protestant missions only undermined it. A nation that had legally established Catholicism—as long as its population was overwhelmingly Catholic and supported that establishment—posed no threat to the freedom of religion as these Catholics defined it.[44]

Catholics nonetheless found themselves adjusting to Protestant-inflected norms around religious pluralism and religious freedom. Even the need to assert Catholic commitments to these principles, as American bishops invariably did, reflected the pressures of the US context and shifted the terms of Catholic debate. The bishops formally opposed Catholic participation in the tri-faith movement, which in their view held the heretical implication that all religious commitments were equally valid. But a number of priests and Catholic laypeople joined in tri-faith events as a way to defend their church against anti-Catholic attacks. One pamphlet published in 1944 by the National Conference of Christians and Jews (NCCJ) profiled the Interfaith Clergy Council of Freeport, New York, as a model for other local committees in the tri-faith movement. They profiled Father John Mahon, a leading member of the council, as a Catholic spokesman for interfaith cooperation and religious freedom. "Our fathers came to America for religious liberty," Mahon said. "We in Freeport are trying to make their dreams come true." Tri-faith advocates insisted that their work did not trivialize religious commitment, but rather evidenced its depth. The Freeport council prohibited "discussions of theology," as well as any "attempt at common worship." Its objectives instead were to develop "community goodwill" and to prevent any resurgence of "hate movements" in their community.[45] Yet by taking part in these dialogues, Catholics like Mahan were tacitly accepting the location of their church as one among many American faiths. This was an attitude that sat somewhat uncomfortably with the Vatican's claims to exclusive religious authority.

Roosevelt's "freedom of worship" inspired a popular celebration of faith and freedom that had contradictory results for the nation's religious minorities. On the one hand, this ideology supported consensus-oriented models of public religiosity—especially in the early years of the Cold War—that effectively privileged the Christian majority. In venues ranging from media productions to military training manuals, cultural and political elites named religious faith, or the Judeo-Christian tradition, or even Christianity in particular, as the essential foundation for American democracy and freedom.[46] Both Protestant and Catholic educators and clergymen called especially for a new focus on religious values and religious education in the nation's public schools. If the schools could not impart "those religious values on which the whole democratic venture rests," wrote the Methodist Paul Hutchinson in 1946, they would become "our most prolific sources of cynicism . . . indifference as to morality in public affairs, and the worship of state power."[47] Many advocated for the "released-time" system, which provided denominationally specific religious education classes during school hours. In one community after another, local religious leaders organized committees to ensure that such programs operated smoothly and equitably. "[We are] satisfied that we are making a positive contribution to the lives of thousands of children in teaching them their duties to God and to neighbor," wrote Father Charles Walsh, who represented the Archdiocese of New York on one such committee. "We are satisfied too, that . . . though the religious education of these children we are strengthening the American Republic." Walsh saw such programs as a win-win proposition, enabling each church to direct the religious education of its own children and strengthening the nation's religious foundations in the process.[48]

At the same time, the ideology of faith and freedom empowered some religious minorities to challenge assumptions of consensus in the courts. The Jehovah's Witnesses became especially adept at using the courts to challenge the boundaries of legitimate religiosity. The Supreme Court had first ruled in their favor in *Cantwell v. Connecticut* (1940), finding that a system requiring the Witnesses to register with the state in order to canvas a local community had violated the First Amendment by empowering public officials to determine what counted as an acceptable religion. With this decision the court "incorporated" the free exercise clause, thus requiring states as well as the federal government to honor this constitutional guarantee. Significantly, the Witnesses had been proselytizing in the heavily Catholic neighborhoods of New Haven, where residents had protested against disruptive behavior that included the dissemination of virulently anti-Catholic tracts, and very loudly playing a phonograph record that portrayed the pope as the Antichrist. Local and state officials had sympathized with the interests of the Catholic community, which asserted a communal right to privacy and to freedom from harassment, and charged them with a breach of the peace and of evangelizing without the required license. Countering them, the Supreme Court ruling reflected an individualist view of religious freedom that was historically associated with anti-Catholicism. In this case, as in so many others that followed, the court came down in favor of individual rights and freedoms—and at the same time against a Catholic and communalist ideology of religious freedom.[49]

Another victory came for the Jehovah's Witnesses in *West Virginia State Board of Education v. Barnette* (1943). Here the court decided in favor of a child who had refused to salute the flag and recite the Pledge of Allegiance, patriotic exercises that Witnesses generally considered to be idolatrous. This ruling stressed the "fundamental freedoms" of the Constitution as America's best safeguard against totalitarianism. In a concurring opinion, Justice Murphy clearly echoed Roosevelt's phrasing from the Four Freedoms speech just two years earlier. However desirable Americans' loyalty to the flag might be, he argued, the compulsion to salute it against sincerely held religious beliefs violated the very "freedom of worship" that Americans were fighting to defend. "Reflection has convinced me that as a judge," he wrote, "I have no greater duty or responsibility than to uphold that spiritual freedom to its farthest reaches." Empowered by the wartime emphasis on religious freedom, the Witnesses were helping reshape First Amendment jurisprudence in ways that favored individual and minority rights over the claims of the religious majority.[50]

The Supreme Court soon moved to incorporate the establishment clause as well, bringing new challenges to the consensus model of public religiosity. The movement for the separation of church and state drew much of its energy from a growing anti-Catholic sentiment in the immediate postwar years. Especially where Catholic populations were high, some local governments had demonstrated their commitment to faith and freedom by approving various forms of indirect public support for (largely Catholic) parochial schools. In the landmark case *Everson v. Board of Education* (1947), a New Jersey taxpayer protested the use of that state's public education funds for transportation to parochial schools as a violation of the establishment clause. The state defended the busing plan by arguing that it did not benefit the parochial schools as such, but the children themselves who were simply using public transportation to get to their choice of schools. The Supreme Court accepted that theory and found the plan constitutionally acceptable, even as it declared that the constitution mandated an impregnable "wall of separation" between church and state. The decision sparked a firestorm of anti-Catholic agitation from critics who feared that a flood of public funding for Catholic institutions would follow.[51]

Anti-Catholicism was hardly the only motive for the separationist movement, however. Atheists, secularists, and members of religious groups with no significant local presence had compelling reasons to oppose any sort of school-based religious instruction, and separationist principles helped them make their case. Vashti McCollum, the mother of an elementary school student in Champaign, Illinois, and a self-identified atheist, filed suit in 1947 on the grounds that her son was being ostracized for not participating in the released-time classes there. The program stigmatized those children who did not participate, she argued, and structurally privileged the religious groups that were large enough to field such classes. In *McCollum v. Board of Education* (1948), the Supreme Court ruled in her favor, finding that Champaign's released-time plan privileged the religious majority and so violated the establishment clause. Most liberal Protestants, Jews, and a variety of religious minorities announced their support for *McCollum* as sound constitutional law. The separationist logic that had doomed parochial school benefits now posed a clear threat to religious education within the public schools, and potentially to other public expressions of Christianity as well.[52]

Conservative Protestants along with Catholics immediately attacked this decision as a dangerous misreading of the First Amendment and a direct assault on all religion (by which they mostly meant

Christianity) in America. Robert McQuilkin, a Southern Baptist
and the president of Columbia Bible College in South Carolina,
protested that religious liberty, properly understood, could not
mean that atheists had "equal standing with 'religion.'" To accept
the claim "that nothing should be tolerated in the public school
that would offend an atheist" was to destroy the Christian foundations of freedom and democracy, he believed, privileging a destructive secularism in its place.[53] The bishops of the National Catholic
Welfare Conference agreed. The court had abandoned "our original American tradition of free cooperation between government
and religious bodies," they protested, "cooperation involving no
special privilege to any group and no restriction on religious liberty
of any citizen."[54] On this issue the nation's mainline-to-conservative
Protestants had found a rare point of agreement with Catholics,
foreshadowing the evangelical-Catholic rapprochement that
would characterize the culture wars of the later twentieth century.
Religious freedom in their eyes meant the freedom *for* religion—or
more specifically for the Christianity that they saw as the necessary
grounding for all American freedoms—and the expectation that
the state would facilitate its practice.

Despite the separationist triumph in the courts, the faith- and-
freedom consensus met the political and ideological needs of the
Cold War so well that it remained powerful through the 1950s.
Even the Supreme Court backtracked on released time in *Zorach
v. Clauson* (1952), ruling that the specifics of a New York City program did not violate the separation of church and state. The court
in this case affirmed some amount of public accommodation to religion (which inevitably meant Christianity, or the "Judeo-Christian
tradition") because of its importance in American life. "We are a
religious people whose institutions presuppose a Supreme Being,"
wrote Justice William O. Douglas in the majority opinion.[55]
President Eisenhower similarly affirmed a tri-faith religiosity as the
foundation of American democracy over and against an atheistic
communism: "Without God there could be no American form of
government nor an American way of life," he said in 1955. A year
earlier Congress had added the phrase "under God" to the first sentence of the Pledge of Allegiance—an addition proposed by a DC
minister who complained that without it the same pledge could be
made to the "hammer-and-sickle flag in Moscow." When this word-
ing was accused of violating the establishment clause, supporters
insisted that the revised pledge was entirely constitutional because
it provided no support to "the church as an institution" and did not

compel any particular religious belief. The change would secure American freedoms, they insisted, not violate them. And in 1956 Congress declared "In God We Trust" an official national motto. For proponents these steps simply affirmed the grounding of American democracy in religious faith, maintaining the Christian republican principles that presidents like Roosevelt had endorsed for so long.[56]

Reconfigurations of Religious Freedom from the Cold War to the Culture Wars

In the decades after the Second World War, the familiar divide between Protestants and Catholics would gradually lose its place at the center of American debates over religious freedom. More and more often, the key points of contention lay instead between separationists on one side and accommodationists on the other, with each side insisting that it was defending the true principle of religious freedom. But there were many familiar dimensions to these reconfigured debates. The separationists—whose ranks included self-described secularists, liberal Protestants, Jews, and religious minorities of many kinds—continued to emphasize the primacy of the individual conscience and the need to protect minority groups against the overwhelming power of a religious majority. Arguing against them, the accommodationists called for a degree of government support and accommodation, at least in theory to be distributed even-handedly to all religious groups. Evangelical Protestants who had once supported the separation of church and state joined their Catholic counterparts to assert new rights and freedoms for religious communities and for the church as a corporate body. Catholic leaders whose predecessors had contested the privileges of Protestantism in the public sphere would gradually join forces with Protestant conservatives to insist on a public role for Christianity. And as we will see, through these transformations the racial limits of religious freedom would remain very much in place.

One factor in this shifting landscape was the growing acceptance of Catholics and Catholicism as a part of the American religious mainstream—an acceptance facilitated by shifts in Catholic ideas about religious freedom. Already during the war, Catholic intellectuals in Europe and North America had begun to rethink the theological foundations of this ideal. Painfully aware that the church had supported authoritarian regimes, especially in Spain and Italy, their goal was to realign Catholic social thought with democracy and human rights. They particularly emphasized the dignity of the human person as created in the image of God. In an influential series of essays, the American Jesuit theologian John Courtney Murray articulated a Catholic rationale for honoring the individual conscience, not so much within the church—where Catholics must of course continue to recognize the authority of the pope in matters of faith—but as a political principle for a pluralistic society. This was hardly mainstream Catholic doctrine at the time: Murray's Jesuit superiors ordered him in 1955 to stop writing on church-state issues. Yet the presence of Murray and others like him signaled important trends within the Catholic Church—trends affirmed less than a decade later by the Second Vatican Council (1962–65). Drafted by Murray himself, the Vatican II declaration Digitatis Humanae identified the separation of church and state and the freedom of religion for individuals as fully consistent with Catholic doctrine. In this and many other ways, Vatican II helped enable the dramatic movement of American Catholics into the cultural and religious mainstream.[57]

American Catholics experienced a variety of other changes at midcentury that brought them closer to the individualist norms of American religiosity. Upwardly mobile and moving to the suburbs as part of the midcentury "white flight" out of American cities, the new generation of Catholics was far less tied than their parents and grandparents to immigrant neighborhoods and ethnic Catholic identities.[58] This new social mobility reshaped Catholic interactions with the Protestants and Jews who were now their immediate neighbors, encouraging them to embrace mainstream models of religiosity and religious freedom. Consider John F. Kennedy's famous presidential campaign speech on religious freedom, delivered in September 1960 to rebut the anti-Catholic slanders that threatened his candidacy. By embracing a liberal idea of church-state separation, Kennedy helped shift American Catholic opinion—along with the broader public's perception of American Catholics—in this direction. "I believe in an America," Kennedy said, "where no public official either requests or accepts instructions on public policy from the Pope, the National Council of Churches, or any other ecclesiastical source; where no religious body seeks to impose its will directly or indirectly upon the general populace or the public acts of its officials; and where religious liberty is so indivisible that an act against one church is treated as an act against all." In Kennedy's formulation, religious freedom belonged above all to the individual and pushed against the public influence of any church or religious group in American life. Kennedy insisted on the primacy of his own conscience, and utterly rejected the right of any church body to influence public affairs. As he defined it, then, religion was an almost entirely private concern.[59]

Given just a few years before Digitatis Humanae, and received with some ambivalence by Catholic bishops at the time, Kennedy's speech symbolized a growing acceptance among American Catholics of a generally individualized and therefore privatized model of religious freedom. The descendants of Irish and Italian immigrants, once viewed as inferior in both racial and religious terms, were—like their Jewish counterparts—now gaining admittance into the white American mainstream. Part of the price of that acceptance was at least a temporary remolding of their Catholicism toward what might be called a Protestant-secular model of religious freedom as an individual prerogative. But the consequences of this shift went far beyond Catholicism. Kennedy's necessarily defensive posture contributed to a growing pressure to privatize all religious conviction in American public life in the 1960s. And this privatization threatened the traditional privileges accorded to Protestantism in American public life, along with the expanded vision of a Judeo-Christian America that Herberg and many other Cold War thinkers had articulated. Taken to its extremes in this way, the individualist model of religious freedom exercised a secularizing—or better, de-Christianizing—influence that moved well beyond the comfort level of most Protestants and most Catholics alike.[60]

The apparent consensus of faith and freedom finally unraveled with the cultural and political upheavals of the 1960s, when the liberal defense of individual and minority rights supplanted the previous generation's emphasis on shared religious values. Extending the logic of the *McCollum* decision, the Supreme Court now ruled school-sponsored prayer and Bible reading unconstitutional under the establishment clause. A series of free exercise cases further expanded the legal protections granted to religious minorities. In *Sherbert v. Verner* (1963), involving a Seventh-Day Adventist who had been denied unemployment benefits because she refused to work on Saturdays, the court ruled that states must grant accommodations for religiously motivated conduct unless they could demonstrate a "compelling interest" to do otherwise. Without such an interest even a law that appeared "neutral on its face," the court determined in *Wisconsin v. Yoder* (1972), would be unconstitutional if it "unduly burdens the practice of religion." Although the principle was unevenly applied, these cases complemented the court's establishment clause jurisprudence by emphasizing the rights of religious minorities over and against laws that favored majority cultural norms. All these rulings posited that religious freedom must include the right to be irreligious—anathema to the faith-and-freedom vision of American identity—and highlighted the rights of individual dissenters and minorities against the norms of the community.[61]

The pendulum began to swing back toward accommodation by the 1980s, however, as a newly vocal religious right protested the privatized and individualized forms of religion that separationist principles assumed. Conservative Catholics and Protestants ever since *McCollum* had pushed back against these standards as far too constraining, arguing that they imposed an ever-increasing array of limits on the public expression of religion. Now they sought to reassert the public presence and authority of Christianity in the name of religious freedom. They demanded at least some forms of prayer in the public schools, protested educational programs that they believed imposed an antireligious secularism on all Americans, and pushed for new legislation to outlaw abortion and later same-sex marriage as well. The Moral Majority, founded by Southern Baptist minister Jerry Falwell in 1979, publicized a host of evangelical crusades in the language of religious freedom. "Church schools and many preachers are being harassed by the liberal forces, and their religious liberties are being tampered with," complained Falwell's *Special Report* in 1983. "When decent citizens and religious leaders can be threatened and thrown into jail just for sending their children to a church school or preaching the Word of God, something is drastically wrong!" For the Moral Majority and likeminded evangelicals, religious freedom was becoming a key rallying cry, asserting first of all the right to practice and proclaim Christianity in the public sphere—a right that for many evangelicals seemed indistinguishable from the legal enforcement of Christian norms.[62]

Through all these reconfigurations of religious freedom, the racial limits to religious freedom remained very much in place. While the legal enforcement of segregation ended with the civil rights movement, de facto discrimination against African Americans and other racial minorities did not. As in earlier decades, white Christians all too often invoked the freedom of religion as a way to maintain racial segregation. According to historian Randall Balmer, at least some of the organizing impetus for the religious right was to defend white privilege against the successes of the civil rights movement. The new level of conservative evangelical mobilization in the late 1970s and early 1980s reacted not primarily against *Roe v. Wade*—as popular versions of its history have assumed—but against the IRS's move to revoke the tax-exempt status of Bob Jones University for its policies of racial segregation on campus. Falwell's rallying cry of religious freedom served as a way to defend de facto segregation, especially in the private Christian schools that were founded across the South as a refuge from newly desegregated public schools.[63] Given these racial politics, it is not surprising that black Christians rarely found the vision of the new religious right, or its rallying cry of religious freedom, to be particularly compelling.

Native Americans pursued a variety of legal claims to religious freedom in the 1980s and 1990s, but found that this ideal most often failed them. Native American articulations of religious freedom generally assumed a communalist frame, emphasizing the rights of the tribe or nation as a whole to maintain its traditions, but as with the Nation of Islam theirs was a communalism that never matched up with the dominant society's conception of religion. When public and private development projects threatened the landscapes that Indians named as sacred, for example, tribal leaders attempted to defend these places on First Amendment grounds. But in one case after another, the courts favored majority conceptions of land as merely property. "Whatever rights the Indians may have to the use of the area," wrote Justice Sandra Day O'Connor in one pivotal case, "those rights do not divest the Government of its right to use what is, after all, *its* land." The intertwined biases of race and religion meant that the dominant society, including the courts, were simply not willing to grant First Amendment rights to dimensions of Native tradition that did not fit the dominant society's model for religion—especially if those traditions conflicted with public or private interests in economic development. Separationist ideologies of religious freedom may have guarded against most forms of overt Christian authority in the public sphere, but they too imposed particular assumptions for what counted as religion—assumptions that were a far better fit for Christians than for Native Americans and other racial-religious minorities.[64]

Religious freedom also had significant limits for the array of new immigrants who arrived in the wake of the 1965 Immigration and Naturalization Act. Arriving from Africa, South Asia, the Caribbean, and many other parts of the globe, these immigrants certainly had legal access to religious freedom claims. Yet even their occasional successes in the courts could not resolve the intertwined racial and religious biases they faced. Especially those who were not Christians, including Hindus, Buddhists, Muslims, and practitioners of indigenous African traditions, found their religious identities and practices linked to negative racial stereotypes. Even before the terrorist attacks of 9/11, Americans linked Islam in particular to the racial image of the irrational, violent, and brown-skinned Arab. Most Muslims in the United States (and around the world) are not of Middle Eastern origin. Yet this image justified vitriolic and sometimes violent attacks on those who appeared to fit the racial stereotype, whether they were actually Muslim or not. The array of new immigrants also faced a myriad of legal regulations and cultural traditions that clearly favored Christianity. Town ordinances and zoning laws often seemed intent on blocking the construction of mosques or temples; and in fact they were sometimes intentionally redesigned for that purpose. Work schedules and school holidays were designed around the Christian calendar, so that practitioners of other religious traditions had to take off extra time for their own holy days, and often found themselves accommodating to the cultural norms of weekly worship on Sundays. Like other racial and religious minorities, then, the new immigrants found themselves adapting to a Christian model, shifting their own practices to conform to American expectations for what counted as religion.[65]

Conclusion

This essay has intentionally looked beyond more familiar subjects to explore the complex intersections of religious freedom with the politics of racial identity through World War II, the decades of the Cold War, and beyond. Throughout these years, religious freedom appeals proved most useful to those groups that most resembled the white Protestant majority in both racial and religious terms. Catholics and Jews alike drew on Roosevelt's formulation and the cultural politics of the tri-faith movement to claim a recognized place on the American religious landscape—and in the process helped solidify their racial status as white. Those groups whose racial-minority status proved more intractable, however, found it more difficult to claim the promise of religious freedom. At times, triumphalist narratives of the nation's apparent successes with this freedom actually reinforced the disparities of race by framing US diversity in primarily religious terms, thus diverting attention away from the more intractable American problems of racially defined discrimination and violence. Meanwhile, the most racially stigmatized groups found this freedom least relevant to their needs—and when they did make religious freedom appeals, were the least likely to succeed.

The rather sobering history charted in this essay unsettles more familiar triumphalist narratives of American religious freedom as an unequivocal success story. It is my hope that understanding the subtle and often taken-for-granted racial and religious norms that have limited this freedom may help inspire a more capacious and inclusive view of religious freedom—but also a greater humility on the part of its advocates. As we've seen, Americans rarely agree on what religious freedom means, or on how to achieve it. Some articulations of this freedom, moreover, have effectively functioned to reinforce the privileges of the white Protestant majority. In recent decades, the leaders of the Christian right have condemned separationist legal principles on the grounds that they impose secular norms that restrict everything marked as "religion" to the private sphere. Viewed from the perspective of non-Christian minorities, however, the accommodationist solutions they propose appear likely—and are sometimes intended—to restore the kind of cultural hegemony for Christianity, or for certain varieties of Christianity, that separationism unseated in the first place.

At the same time, my call for a more expansive vision of religious freedom recognizes the wide diversity of groups that have found individualist and separationist principles dissatisfying. This includes not only Catholic and Protestant conservatives but also racial-religious minorities—including Native Americans, African American Muslims, and in some respects Jews—who have not wanted to separate their religious traditions from a broader sense of identity as a people. Combatting religious discrimination cannot simply mean granting equal rights to individuals when such rights undermine the communities to which those individuals are most deeply committed, and when the shape of these rights are so deeply biased toward the religious traditions of the Christian majority. Perhaps, as Winifred Fallers Sullivan has argued, religious freedom is a philosophical and legal impossibility: the definition that must be reached in order to adjudicate this freedom, she argues, necessarily limits this freedom in one way or another.[66] But however impossible and imperfect it might be, religious freedom seems likely to remain in place for the foreseeable future as a foundational American ideal. Perhaps with a fuller understanding of its history, we can push toward new formulations of this freedom that will be less likely to privilege particular forms of religion, or to privilege the rights of "religion" over other forms of justice, or over that other American ideal of equality for all.

Notes

1. For Rockwell's reflections on this illustration, see Stuart Murray, *Norman Rockwell's Four Freedoms: Images That Inspire a Nation* (Stockbridge, MA: Berkshire House, 1993), 70.
2. Hugo Ballin, letter to the City of Burbank, (n.d. [1948]), available online at the City of Burbank, California, website, http://www.burbankca.gov/about-us/burbank-history/burbank-city-hall/city-council-chamber-murals.
3. Norman Rockwell, "The Four Freedoms," *Liberty: A Magazine of Religious Freedom*, August 1974, 7.
4. Hugo Ballin, letter to the City of Burbank.
5. Walter Echo-Hawk, "Native American Religious Liberty: Five Hundred Years after Columbus," *American Indian Culture and Research Journal* 17, no. 3 (1993): 33–52.
6. The growing body of scholarship on the history of whiteness in America has for the most part neglected religion as a contributing factor in American racial formations. See for example Matthew Frye Jacobson, *Whiteness of a Different Color: European Immigrants and the Alchemy of Race* (Cambridge, MA: Harvard University Press, 1998); David R. Roediger, *Working Toward Whiteness: How America's Immigrants Became White: The Strange Journey from Ellis Island to the Suburbs* (New York: Basic Books, 2005); Matthew Frye Jacobson, *Roots Too: White Ethnic Revival in Post-Civil Rights America* (Cambridge, MA: Harvard University Press, 2006).
7. Andrew Preston, *Sword of the Spirit, Shield of Faith: Religion in American War and Diplomacy* (New York: Alfred A. Knopf, 2012), 319, 321.
8. "President Flays World Tyrants: Governments Denying Religious Liberty Bitterly Attacked by Chief Executive in Congressional Anniversary Address," *Los Angeles Times*, March 5, 1939.
9. Franklin D. Roosevelt to Michael Williams, March 30, 1937, online at the American Presidency Project, http://www.presidency.ucsb.edu/ws/?pid=15382.
10. The Jehovah's Witnesses generally refused to join in patriotic exercises, which they considered idolatrous. For that reason—despite the fact that Jehovah's Witnesses in Germany were being placed in concentration camps—they were sometimes suspected of being Nazi sympathizers or even a "fifth column" for the Germans. For a contemporary statement on the issue see American Civil Liberties Union, *The Persecution of Jehovah's Witnesses: The Record of Violence against a Religious Organization Unparalleled in America since the Attacks on the Mormons* (New York: American Civil Liberties Union, 1941).
11. Ernest Fremont Tittle, "If America Enters the War, I Shall Not Support It," *Christian Century*, February 5, 1941; on the Christian peace movement in this era, see Joseph Kip Kosek, *Acts of Conscience: Christian Nonviolence and Modern American Democracy*, Columbia Studies in Contemporary American History (New York: Columbia University Press, 2009).
12. Steven Merritt Miner, *Stalin's Holy War: Religion, Nationalism, and Alliance Politics, 1941–1945* (Chapel Hill: University of North Carolina Press, 2003).
13. "Bishop Assails Statement," *New York Times*, October 2, 1941; "Are the Four Freedoms a Delusion?," *Christian Century*, October 15, 1941; see also Preston, *Sword of the Spirit*, 319–20.
14. "Mgr. Sheen Says Nazi Paganism Menaces World Christianity," *New York Times*, November 17, 1941.

15. Henry Pitney van Dusen, "If America Enters Into the War, I Shall Support It," *Christian Century*, January 29, 1941.

16. Federal Council of the Churches of Christ in America, *Biennial Report* (New York: The Council, 1942), 11, 29–30.

17. George Gallup, "Church Should Back War, Poll Discloses: Clergy Feel Justified in Opinion Because Conflict Waged to Preserve Religious Freedom," *Los Angeles Times*, July 11, 1942.

18. "Rabbis to Stress Hanukkah Theme," *New York Times*, December 20, 1941; "Spirit of Purim to Be Discussed," *Los Angeles Times*, February 27, 1942; "New Passover Meaning Told," *Los Angeles Times*, April 3, 1942.

19. For a detailed history of this effort see Oscar Isaiah Janowsky, *The Jews and Minority Rights (1898–1919)*, Studies in History, Economics, and Public Law 384 (New York: Columbia University Press, 1933).

20. Naomi Wiener Cohen, *Jews in Christian America: The Pursuit of Religious Equality*, Studies in Jewish History (New York: Oxford University Press, 1992), 91.

21. Eric L. Goldstein, *The Price of Whiteness: Jews, Race, and American Identity* (Princeton, NJ: Princeton University Press, 2006).

22. Cohen, *Jews in Christian America*, 97–98.

23. "U.S. Sympathizes with Reich Jews," *New York Times*, July 31, 1935. The secretary responded with a guarded letter expressing the administration's sympathy and commitment to "the concepts of religious freedom and liberty of conscience for all."

24. Morris D. Waldman to James N. Rosenberg, August 5, 1942, box 1, folder 33, MS 23, Morris D. Waldman Papers, American Jewish Archives, Cincinnati, Ohio.

25. Joint Conference of the Synagogue Council of America and the National Community Relations Advisory Council, "Statement of Principles on Religion and the Public Schools," June 10, 1947, Synagogue Council of America Records, box 10, folder 5, American Jewish Historical Society, New York.

26. Will Herberg, *Protestant, Catholic, Jew: An Essay in American Religious Sociology* (Garden City, NY: Doubleday, 1955); Laura Levitt, "Interrogating the Judeo-Christian Tradition: Will Herberg's Construction of American Religion, Religious Pluralism, and the Problem of Inclusion," in *The Cambridge History of Religions in America: 1945 to the Present*, ed. Stephen J. Stein, vol. 3 (New York: Cambridge University Press, 2012), 285–307.

27. Daniel Greene, *The Jewish Origins of Cultural Pluralism the Menorah Association and American Diversity* (Bloomington: Indiana University Press, 2011); Laura Levitt, "Impossible Assimilations, American Liberalism, and Jewish Difference: Revisiting Jewish Secularism," *American Quarterly* 59, no. 3 (September 2007): 807–32; Goldstein, *Price of Whiteness*.

28. Charles H. Wesley, "The Negro Wants the Four Freedoms," in *What the Negro Wants*, ed. Rayford Whittingham Logan (Chapel Hill: University of North Carolina Press, 1944), 90–112.

29. Eddie S. Glaude, *Exodus!: Religion, Race, and Nation in Early Nineteenth-Century Black America* (Chicago: University of Chicago Press, 2000).

30. Curtis J. Evans, *The Burden of Black Religion* (Oxford: Oxford University Press, 2008).

31. See also Sylvester A Johnson, "The Rise of Black Ethnics: The Ethnic Turn in African American Religions, 1916–1945," *Religion and American Culture* 20, no. 2 (Summer 2010): 125–63.

32. Edward E. Curtis, "Debating the Origins of the Moorish Science Temple," 70–90, and Sylvester Johnson, "Religion Proper and Proper Religion," 145–70, both in *The New Black Gods: Arthur Huff Fauset and the Study of African American Religions*, ed. Edward E. Curtis and Danielle Brune Sigler, Religion in North America (Bloomington: Indiana University Press, 2009).

33. Jacob S. Dorman, *Chosen People: The Rise of American Black Israelite Religions* (New York: Oxford University Press, 2013).

34. Richard Brent Turner, *Islam in the African-American Experience* (Bloomington: Indiana University Press, 1997), 197, 182–88.

35. Ibid., 148, 163, 151.

36. Ibid., 168, 170; Sylvester Johnson, "Religion Proper and Proper Religion," 145–70, in Curtis and Sigler, *New Black Gods*.

37. Joint Conference Committee on Public Relations Representing the Northern Baptist Convention and the Southern Baptist Convention, "Records of Meeting," April 27, 1943, Baptist Joint Committee on Public Affairs, Minutes, 1938–1979, AR 378, box 1:1, Southern Baptist Historical Library and Archives, Nashville, Tennessee.

38. Kevin Michael Kruse, *White Flight: Atlanta and the Making of Modern Conservatism*, Politics and Society in Twentieth-Century America (Princeton, NJ: Princeton University Press, 2005).

39. Donald R. Richberg, *Nor Can Government; Analysis and Criticism of S. 984—"A Bill to Prohibit Discrimination in Employment Because of Race, Religion, Color, National Origin, or Ancestry,"* American Affairs Pamphlets (New York: National Industrial Conference Board, 1948); for more on Richberg see his autobiography, Donald R. Richberg, *My Hero: The Indiscreet Memoirs of an Eventful but Unheroic Life* (New York: Putnam, 1954).

40. "Defense of Altars and Homes Duty of All, Says Archbishop," *Los Angeles Times*, April 5, 1942.

41. John T. McGreevy, *Catholicism and American Freedom: A History* (New York: W. W. Norton, 2003), 172–73; Peter R. D'Agostino, *Rome in America: Transnational Catholic Ideology from the Risorgimento to Fascism* (Chapel Hill: University of North Carolina Press, 2004), 197–257.

42. Pius IX, The Syllabus of Errors, December 8, 1864, Papal Encyclicals Online, http://www.papalencyclicals.net/Pius09/p9syll.htm; Leo XIII, Au Milieu Des Sollicitudes: On the Church and State in France, February 16, 1892, Papal Encyclicals Online, http://www.papalencyclicals.net/Leo13/l13cst.htm.

43. "Protestants Answer Catholic Latin-American Proclamation," *Los Angeles Times*, December 12, 1942; Committee on Cooperation in Latin America, *Religious Liberty in Latin America: Documents Relating to Recent Roman Catholic Campaign Opposing Protestant Missions in Latin America* (New York: Committee on cooperation in Latin America, 1943); George P. Howard, *Religious Liberty in Latin America?* (Philadelphia: Westminster, 1944).

44. "Protestants in Latin America," *America*, December 26, 1942.

45. Ralph W. Sockman, Edward J. Walsh, and Israel Goldstein, "A Call to the Clergy of America" (National Conference of Christians and Jews, 1944), National Conference of Christians and Jews, box 12, Records of Religious and Benevolent Societies and Organizations, record group 34, Special Collections, Yale University Divinity School Library.

46. Jonathan P. Herzog, *The Spiritual-Industrial Complex: America's Religious Battle against Communism in the Early Cold War* (New York: Oxford University Press, 2011).

47. Paul Hutchinson, *The New Leviathan* (Chicago: Willett, Clark, 1946), 193, 202–10.

48. Charles M. Walsh to Rabbi D. Bernard Stolper, May 16, 1947, Synagogue Council of America Records, box 31, folder 11, American Jewish Historical Society, New York.

49. James Jurinski, *Religion on Trial: A Handbook with Cases, Laws, and Documents*, On Trial Series (Santa Barbara, CA; Oxford: ABC-CLIO, 2004), 65–66.

50. West Virginia State Board of Education v. Barnette, 319 U.S. 624 (US Supreme Court 1943).

51. Jurinski, *Religion on Trial*, 55–56; David Sehat, *The Myth of American Religious Freedom* (Oxford: Oxford University Press, 2011); for a sampling of the era's anti-Catholic rhetoric see Paul Blanshard, *American Freedom and Catholic Power*, Beacon Press Studies in Freedom and Power (Boston: Beacon, 1949).

52. Jurinski, *Religion on Trial*, 113–14.

53. Robert C. McQuilkin to J. M. Dawson, September 30, 1948, Baptist Joint Committee on Public Affairs Records, 1946–1980, AR 709, microfilm edition, reel 9, Southern Baptist Historical Library and Archives, Nashville, Tennessee.

54. Cited in James M. O'Neill, *Catholicism and American Freedom* (New York: Harper, 1952), 36.

55. Sehat, *Myth of American Religious Freedom*, 239–40.

56. Kevin Michael Schultz, *Tri-Faith America: How Catholics and Jews Held Postwar America to Its Protestant Promise* (New York: Oxford University Press, 2011), 74–75; quotes on the Pledge of Allegiance debate are from Irving Goldaber, Memorandum to Joint Advisory Committee, May 27, 1954, American Jewish Congress Records, I-77, box 264, folder 9, American Jewish Historical Society, New York.

57. John Courtney Murray, "Current Theology: Freedom of Religion," *Theological Studies* 6 (March 1945): 85–113; McGreevy, *Catholicism and American Freedom*, 189–214.

58. John T. McGreevy, *Parish Boundaries: The Catholic Encounter with Race in the Twentieth-Century Urban North* (Chicago: University of Chicago Press, 1996).

59. John F. Kennedy, "On Church and State: Remarks of John F. Kennedy Addressed to the Greater Houston Ministerial Association," in John F. Kennedy, *The Kennedy Reader*, ed. Jay David (Indianapolis: Bobbs-Merrill, 1967), 364.

60. Mark Stephen Massa, *Catholics and American Culture: Fulton Sheen, Dorothy Day, and the Notre Dame Football Team* (New York: Crossroad, 1999), 128–47; David Hollinger, "The 'Secularization' Question and the United States in the Twentieth Century," *Church History* 70, no. 1 (March 2001): 132–43.

61. Sehat, *Myth of American Religious Freedom*, 246–51. *Brown v. Board of Education* (1954), the landmark case that overturned racial segregation in the public schools, reflected the same liberal emphasis on individual/minority rights and freedoms over and against the communal norms of the majority.

62. "Americans' Religious Freedoms in Jeopardy," *Moral Majority Special Report*, January 1983, MSS 2010/152, carton 73/26, People for the American Way Collection of Conservative Political Ephemera, 1980-2004, Bancroft library, University of California (hereafter PAW Collection); Jerry Falwell, "Special

Notice: Funds Desperately Needed for Religious Freedom TV Special," January 14, 1983, MSS 2010/152, carton 73/26, PAW Collection.
63. Randall Herbert Balmer, *Thy Kingdom Come: How the Religious Right Distorts the Faith and Threatens America* (New York: Basic Books, 2007).
64. Tisa Wenger, *We Have a Religion: The 1920s Pueblo Indian Dance Controversy and American Religious Freedom* (Chapel Hill: University of North Carolina Press, 2009).
65. Yvonne Yazbeck Haddad, Jane I. Smith, and John L. Esposito, eds., *Religion and Immigration: Christian, Jewish, and Muslim Experiences in the United States* (Walnut Creek, CA: AltaMira Press, 2003); Karen Isaksen Leonard et al., eds., *Immigrant Faiths: Transforming Religious Life in America* (Walnut Creek, CA: AltaMira Press, 2005); Stephen R. Prothero, ed., *A Nation of Religions: The Politics of Pluralism in Multireligious America* (Chapel Hill: University of North Carolina Press, 2006).
66. Winnifred Fallers Sullivan, *The Impossibility of Religious Freedom* (Princeton, NJ: Princeton University Press, 2005).

Photo Essay

The Great Depression caused mass suffering throughout the nation, including widespread need for soup kitchens and food relief, propelling FDR to electoral victory in 1932 on the promise of better times and codifying the New Deal ideals renewed in his January 1941 address. Franklin D. Roosevelt Presidential Library and Museum, Hyde Park, New York.

The Four Freedoms address was a call to arms, but it was not Roosevelt's first move toward rearmament. In 1940 he watched Secretary of War Henry Stimson draw the social security numbers of the first men to be called up for Selective Service. Franklin D. Roosevelt Presidential Library and Museum, Hyde Park, New York.

Inaugural parades typically include a show of military might, but Roosevelt's third, held January 1941, offered a particularly martial air. Franklin D. Roosevelt Presidential Library and Museum, Hyde Park.

Not everyone endorsed Roosevelt's rearmament plans, and of those opposing them none was more famous than Charles Lindbergh, admirer of Nazi efficiency, who became a frequent and influential Roosevelt critic. Courtesy of the *New York Times*.

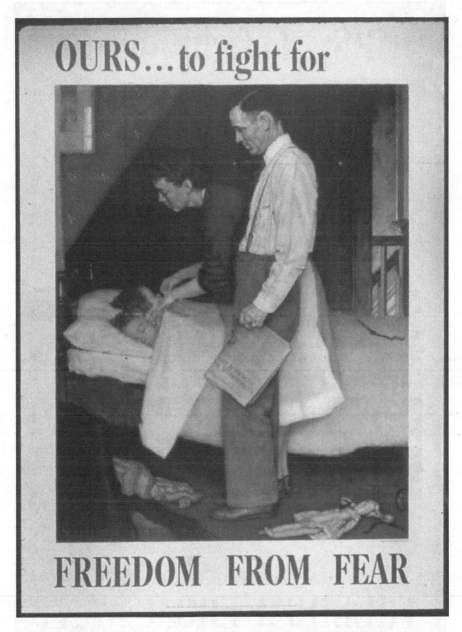

Roosevelt's Four Freedoms inspired a series of artistic impressions, none more famous than Norman Rockwell's images, shown here in their use as War Bond posters.

(Continued)

(Continued)

(Continued)

By Saul Steinberg

Even before Rockwell interpreted the Four Freedoms, other artists found inspiration in Roosevelt's words, including the political cartoonist Saul Steinberg, who depicted what the four freedoms might look like under Hitler in November 1941. The Saul Steinberg Foundation/Artists Rights Society (ARS), New York.

Four Freedoms imagery flourished in train stations, libraries, post offices, and other public buildings. Hugo Ballin painted this mural for the Burbank City Hall, dedicated February 12, 1943. Credit: Ben and Sarah Engel.

Located at the tip of Roosevelt Island, Four Freedoms Park in New York City is perhaps the largest memorial to the president's famed address, depicted here by Maira Kalman in 2012. Condé Nast Licensing.

Rockwell's iconography, and Roosevelt's message, enjoyed a resurgence of popularity after the terrorist attacks of September 11, 2001, adorning posters, T-shirts, and even commemorative coffee cans. Credit: Ronna Spitz

Franklin Roosevelt on the campaign trail, 1932. Franklin D. Roosevelt Presidential Library and Museum, Hyde Park, New York.

CHAPTER 4

Freedom from Want

MATTHEW JONES

OR MANY OF THE AMERICANS who crowded around their radio sets in January 1941 to hear President Roosevelt's State of the Union address, the third of the four "essential human freedoms" he proclaimed—freedom from want—probably had more immediate resonance than any other. With the United States having just endured the worst economic depression in its history, unemployment and acute social deprivation were not simply part of distant and unhappy memories, but had been intrinsic to recent everyday lived experience. As recently as 1937–38, to the despair of New Deal liberals who had believed steady recovery would follow FDR's resounding re-election in 1936, the economy had dipped again into a steep recession, and unemployment had returned to close to the levels last seen in 1932–33. Only with the surge in demand and industrial production that accompanied war orders from the beleaguered nations fighting in Europe and Asia, along with the effects of the domestic military preparedness program, did the economy start to move forward in 1940 and living standards begin to rise. Yet conditions remained hard: when liberal New York newspapers covered the State of the Union speech in January 1941, their editions also carried stories that featured the thousands of homeless and destitute people who still roamed the city by day and gathered in massed ranks at missions and flophouses at night. Huge numbers of men selected by the draft were graded

as unfit for military service, many of them afflicted by malnourish-
ment and poor nutrition.[1]

Over the next half century the contested meanings and understandings given to Roosevelt's idea of "freedom from want" would
touch on some of the central debates in American political discourse
and influence the course of public policy. Moreover, the activism
the phrase seemed to call for in the struggle against poverty, and
to meet the basic social needs of citizens, was also to infuse many of
the modernizing projects that became of fundamental importance
to the engagement of the United States with a developing world that
was emerging from colonial rule and exploitation. But just as in this
international sphere, a domestic political reaction against ambitious
plans for state intervention was soon to become evident. Instead, a
rival conception of freedom—and one more in tune with the fundamental tenets of American political culture—was to gain hold, where
American capitalism was allowed to operate in unconstrained form.
Taking Roosevelt's address as its starting point, this chapter explores
the tensions between such rival ideas about the essence of freedom
and the interplay between the foreign and the domestic spheres.

An expansive vision of the role of the state in providing for
essential human needs, through planning and enhanced social welfare provision, had been a developing component in liberal New
Deal thinking before 1941. Similarly, across other parts of the transatlantic community, there was discussion about the kind of world
and society that should take the place of the one that had failed
so conspicuously during the 1930s. Already in Britain, for example,
there was a vigorous debate developing from 1940 onward—spurred
by a searching examination of prewar failings and the requirement
to harness a national war effort—over the need to establish minimum standards of food, housing, and health care to accompany
any peace settlement, where the requirements of individual needs
were linked to larger issues of international security and stability. At
the first meeting of the War Cabinet's Committee on War Aims in
October 1940, held five months after the formation of a coalition government in London, the Labour Party's Ernest Bevin, and the new
minister of labour, proposed that one of the principles that should
inform the committee's work be "the direction of the economy to
achieve social security and the provision of a reasonable standard of
living and social welfare." By May 1941, Anthony Eden, the foreign
secretary and heir apparent to the leadership of the Conservative
Party, was giving speeches that made clear that social security at
home and abroad would be a priority for postwar government.[2]

One of the crucial points to recognize here is that, notwithstanding Prime Minister Winston Churchill's inability to engage with matters of postwar reconstruction, a consensus was beginning to form on cross-party lines that far-reaching changes were required that would place government provision and planning center stage in creating a better society after victory. There is evidence to suggest that developments in Britain had an influence on the ideas and terminology being employed by Roosevelt during this period. In September 1940 the president's attention had been drawn to passages in a book by Samuel Grafton that relayed British debates over the need for an "economic bill of rights," which combined the anti-Nazi struggle with "establishing 'minimum standards of housing, food, education, and medical care,' along with free speech, free press, and free worship." Roosevelt was also made aware of calls from both Protestant and Catholic Church leaders in Britain for protection for the family, universal educational provision, and removal of major inequalities of wealth.[3]

When he addressed Congress on January 6, 1941, Roosevelt's main task was to prepare his audience for the presentation of a bill that would offer lend-lease assistance to a beleaguered Britain, and so pull the United States even farther along the path toward confrontation with Nazi Germany. In order to give the necessary context to his request, however, the president also spoke of the sacrifices that would have to be made by all Americans in the "emergency" of the world crisis that they faced. Americans, the president proclaimed, were seeking to uphold a conception of economic democracy at home and abroad. This was no time, he said, to "stop thinking about the social and economic problems which are the root cause of the social revolution which is today a supreme factor in the world." In his estimation, there were several key foundations for a "healthy and strong democracy" that the people expected the political and economic system to produce:

Equality of opportunity for youth and others.
Jobs for those who can work.
Security for those who need it.
The ending of special privilege for the few.
The preservation of civil liberties for all.
The enjoyment of the fruits of scientific progress in a wider and constantly rising standard of living.

And he added, "The inner and abiding strength of our economic and political systems is dependent upon the degree to which they

fulfill these expectations." Pulling attention away from the immediate worries of the present, Roosevelt then mustered a rousing
peroration—the product of his own speech-writing work—that
featured the four freedoms that would underpin the world that
Americans might envisage for the future. The third he introduced
as "freedom from want—which, translated into world terms, means
economic understandings which will secure to every nation a healthy
peacetime life for its inhabitants—everywhere in the world."[4] Taken
together, the four freedoms represented a stark contrast with the values propagated by the Axis powers and, after Pearl Harbor, became
a favorite reference point for Roosevelt when he had to encapsulate
the war aims of the United States.[5]

Although the precise meaning of the phrase "freedom from
want" was far from clear, Roosevelt's listing of the components of a
strong and healthy democracy suggested to many that the war would
be an opportunity to advance a set of quite radical goals.

By the spring of 1941, some of Roosevelt's advisers hoped he
would give a clearer indication of future war aims by fleshing out
the ideas lying behind the Four Freedoms speech. An opportunity
seemed to present itself in August when Roosevelt and Churchill
came together at Placentia Bay for the first time as leaders of their
governments to agree to the Atlantic Charter as an official statement of their shared principles on which a better world might be
built. Included in the Charter, on the suggestion of the British War
Cabinet, was a reference to the "object of securing for all improved
labor standards, economic advancement and social security."[6] British
intervention had secured mention of an important component of
the evolving idea of freedom from want in the Charter—a document
that resonated around the world—and it became further elevated
in transatlantic discourse as a key objective for the postwar world.
By November 1941, Roosevelt was attempting to contrast the "progressive" notion of freedom with the freedom to dominate others
propagated by the German totalitarian regime. "There can be no
real freedom for the common man without enlightened social policies," he had said. "In the last analysis, they are the stakes for which
democracies are today fighting."[7] Roosevelt's use of the "common
man" archetype is striking at this juncture, for it had been a term
given currency during the 1930s in popular front and left-wing circles, and it was redolent of the idea that mass democratic politics
was refocusing attention on the ordinary citizen caught up in the
great maelstrom of events and with their individual needs, hopes,
and fears. Above all, then, for an American audience the evocative

but ambiguous phrase "freedom from want" represented ordinary aspirations for a brighter future, where painful memories of the Depression could be scourged and material abundance and prosperity enjoyed by all.

The domestic political standard-bearer for the idea of freedom from want was Vice President Henry A. Wallace. Speaking at a dinner of the Free World Association in New York City on May 8, 1942, in remarks that he had cleared in advance with the White House, Wallace assembled a barely concealed rebuttal to Henry Luce's earlier vision of an evolving "American Century" built on US omnipotence and the spread of free enterprise. There had, Wallace said, been talk of the coming American Century, but he saw emerging from the war instead the "century of the common man." He proclaimed that "men and women cannot really be free until they have plenty to eat, and time and ability to read and think and talk things over.... The march of freedom of the past 150 years has been a long-drawn-out people's revolution," and when Wallace came to think about the "significance of freedom from want for the average man, then we know that the revolution of the past 150 years has not been completed, either here in the United States or in any other nation in the world. We know that this revolution cannot stop until freedom from want has actually been attained." With peace would have to come "a better standard of living for the common man, not merely in the United States and England, but also in India, Russia, China, and Latin America—not merely in the United Nations, but also in Germany and Italy and Japan."[8] Wallace's promotion of economic development was expressly internationalist. He envisaged the United Nations, under multilateral direction, as performing the leading role in economic rehabilitation of the world's shattered societies, just as he anticipated the rapid dismantling of the European colonial empires after the war and the end of old-style power politics. His domestic program entailed support for proposals for extension of social security and inclusion of medical insurance coverage.[9]

Coming in the first six months of active US involvement in the war, Wallace's call seemed to catch a particular wave of public sentiment. Archibald MacLeish, poet, librarian of Congress, and New Deal advocate, reported to Roosevelt in May 1942 that latest polling showed the Four Freedoms had a "powerful and genuine appeal to seven persons in ten." From this he inferred that the American people were idealistically in favor of "helping to secure better working and living conditions all over the world," while four out of five believed the country "should and will help to feed the hungry peoples of the world after the war is ended." However, at the same time, seven out of ten expected to be worse off after the war, and three-quarters that there would be fewer jobs.[10] Wallace's challenge to the old order found its musical echo in Aaron Copland's stirring *Fanfare for the Common Man*, which premiered in March 1943. Copland's social-democratic sensibilities had been alert to the potential for radical change brought by the war; one of his early working titles for the piece was *Fanfare for the Four Freedoms*, and the composer had consciously figured his music—directly using the "common man" motif in its final title after hearing Wallace's speech in May 1942—as speaking to the aspirations of a previously unheard class of Americans.[11] No better symbolism for the hopes of many Americans was to be found than in Norman Rockwell's 1943 painting "Freedom from Want," one of a series of depictions of the four freedoms as they might be applied to small-town America (of which millions of reprints were sold), which showed an excited and joyful family gathered at a food-laden table for a Thanksgiving dinner. Rockwell's "Freedom from Want" was essentially apolitical, which helps explain its widespread appeal. Holding a job, providing for one's family, and aspiring to greater material well-being were all ideas that could unite Americans steeling themselves for the new challenge of global war, just as they resolved to never again experience the economic conditions that had blighted the 1930s.[12]

To New Deal liberals the war held the promise of creating opportunities for progressive change and for laying the basis for continuing federal intervention in order to preserve prosperity and growth once the stimulus of war orders had disappeared. During the early stages of US involvement in the war, their ideas were propounded through the Office of War Information (OWI).[13] Following its creation in June 1942 under the leadership of popular journalist and broadcaster Elmer Davis, OWI set about explaining to the American people the enlightened values for which the war was being fought. Davis himself had told Wallace that "the one thing he wanted to do" at the OWI was to promote the policies advocated in the "century of the common man" speech.[14] In the OWI's literature, freedom from want meant the federal government ensuring employment at fair rates of pay and providing basic levels of food, housing, and medical care. Rockwell's images were used by the OWI in its war bonds campaign and for posters in many schools and government buildings.

Transatlantic influences regarding schemes for postwar reconstruction and reform were again felt during 1942, with the culmination being the publication of the seminal Beveridge report in Britain in early December.[15] An experienced civil servant and trained economist who had helped coordinate the work of the Ministries of Munitions and then Food during the First World War, and then between 1919 and 1937 was director of the London School of Economics, William Beveridge had been selected in the summer of 1941 to lead an innocuous-sounding Ministry of Health interdepartmental committee that was "to undertake, with special reference to the inter-relation of the schemes, a survey of the existing national schemes of social insurance and allied services, including workmen's compensation, and to make recommendations." What some had first envisaged as a technical study of codification and methods of consolidation was soon transformed—under the prevailing zeitgeist of the overpowering need for postwar reconstruction—into a vehicle for a comprehensive approach to social security and the creation of a welfare state. By the time of Pearl Harbor, and even before his group had begun to take detailed evidence, Beveridge had given clear intent of what he envisaged when he told the fellow members of his committee that he saw the new system as based on the three props of a national health service, the payment of family allowances, and the maintenance of employment.[16]

Widely trailed by the press in the months before its production, and assiduously promoted by Beveridge himself, the final report emerged at the end of 1942—just as fortunes in the war began to turn quite decisively in favor of the allies—and was greeted with almost universal public approval, selling over half a million copies. A comprehensive scheme of "cradle to grave" social insurance, underpinned by full employment, Beveridge had argued, would help to establish a national minimum level of living, and tackle the problem of "Want." But, as the report proclaimed, "Want is only one of the five giants on the road of reconstruction and in some ways the easiest to attack. The others are Disease, Ignorance, Squalor and Idleness."[17] Widely discussed among all British social classes as well as in the armed forces, and soon in Europe-wide circulation, the plan for social security spoke to the aspirations of millions for the kind of society that they were now fighting to create. To one letter from a soldier who had responded with enthusiasm to news of his scheme, Beveridge wrote that it was "heartening to know that the fighting men recognise that the social evil of Want must be overcome." Beveridge's wife, Janet, wrote later of how moved she was by one young married woman, who told her that the scheme "would lift an almost intolerable load of anxiety from their lives and would make them worth living. . . . Doctors' bills were the nightmare they dreaded most. The provision of allowances during pregnancy and childbirth was a kind of Utopian dream.' "[18] "Of all the social policy manifestos of the postwar era," Daniel T. Rodgers has written, "none matched Beveridge's in its transnational influence or its electrifying impact.... The first attempt to bring the piecemeal social politics of the prewar age into comprehensive design, the Beveridge Report set the model for welfare state developments across the world."[19]

After its production, American press reports described the Beveridge report as the first attempt to translate the four freedoms into practical action, building also on the mention of social security for all in the Atlantic Charter agreed to by Churchill and Roosevelt in August 1941. Even before the report's publication, in September 1942, the National Resources Planning Board (NRPB) was producing pamphlets called "After the War—Toward Security: Freedom from Want", which spoke of the "challenge to our national security caused by lack or inadequacy of jobs or income." It went on to assert that without "social or economic security there can be no true guarantee of freedom" and connected this to the needs of national defense.[20] At the end of December 1942, Wallace had given a radio address that looked forward to the peace that was to come after "this world wide people's war," and the need for "unity of purpose in promoting the general welfare of the world." Having read the speech beforehand, Roosevelt had stressed to Wallace that in the postwar world there would be "the necessity of young people who come out of the Army feeling that they have won a war in which there is more freedom from want and more freedom from fear." When "he talked about freedom from want," Wallace recorded, Roosevelt "brought up the question of the Beveridge report."[21] When Beveridge toured the United States and Canada between March and May 1943, he received a very positive reception, spending an hour with the president, while Janet Beveridge reported that Secretary of Labor Frances Perkins was "all for the Beveridge Plan," and that Wallace, with whom the Beveridges had dinner, was "a humanitarian who savoured the underlying philosophy of the Beveridge Plan and liked it."[22] In August 1943, marking the second anniversary of the Atlantic Charter, Roosevelt issued a statement that echoed exactly the Charter's call for improved labor standards and social security for all, and connected this with the passage in 1935 of one of the centerpieces of New Deal legislation, the Social Security Act.[23]

Yet the prospects for wholesale reform in the United States as a result of the war were, in fact, severely circumscribed by trends in congressional and party politics, the growing power of conservative business interests, and, even more fundamentally, a political culture that was singularly averse to radical social experimentation. For several years before the coming of the Second World War it had been apparent to many observers that the political appeal of the New Deal to a large number of Americans was waning, and strong sources of opposition—always present throughout the high tide of reform in the mid-1930s—were growing in confidence and effectiveness. Roosevelt's calamitous actions of 1937–38, including the poorly conceived court-packing plan and an ill-judged effort to intervene in the selection of Democratic Party candidates before the mid-term elections, had weakened his authority even before the sharp downswing in the economy in 1938 helped in some people's eyes to undermine the achievements of reform. As William Leuchtenburg noted, while during 1938 the New Deal's enemies were still on the defensive, by 1939 Congress was "moving aggressively to dismantle the New Deal. . . . The more successful the New Deal was [at alleviating social conditions], the more it undid itself. The more prosperous the country became, the more people returned to the only values they knew, those associated with an individualistic, success-oriented society." On their return visit to "Middletown" (Muncie, Indiana) in the mid-1930s, following their pioneering survey of 1929, the social scientists Helen and Robert Lynd, despite all the apparent upheaval of the depression, found that "essentially it had changed nothing at all: 'Middletown is overwhelmingly living by the values by which it lived in 1925.'" Again, in Leuchtenburg's succinct summary: "The New Dealers were never able to develop an adequate reform ideology to challenge the business rhetoricians. . . . As the nerve of the business opposition revived, the old conviction that business could run the economy with greater efficiency than bureaucracy reappeared."[24]

This evolving picture was reinforced by the economic and social changes brought by the Second World War. Unemployment was banished by the stimulus brought to industry by wartime orders, as well as the draft, with a consequent effect on income levels. Business leaders gained in power and confidence as they moved into strategic positions in the wartime federal agencies, and they took key roles in the patriotic cause of production for victory. Benefiting from generous contracts and tax concessions, the profits earned by large corporations, in particular, rose quite dramatically (from a total of $6.4 billion in 1940 to $10.8 billion by 1944).[25] Rejuvenated by their role in the national war effort, and no longer blasted as the "economic royalists" who had brought the country to the brink of collapse, business leaders and conservatives began to argue for the importance of freedom from government regulation and

control. One of the most vocal proponents of the American system of free enterprise was the increasingly influential Republican
figure of Senator Robert A. Taft from Ohio, who had won his seat
in the midterm elections of 1938. Embracing many of the important themes of isolationist opinion, Taft's greatest anxiety was that
burgeoning levels of government spending would destroy America's
financial institutions and threaten its basic freedoms. From soon
after Roosevelt's enunciation of the four freedoms, Taft was attacking the president's policy on Lend-Lease as leading inevitably to a
ruinous war. "War cannot impose on other peoples forms of government which they do not want," he had warned in February 1941. "It
cannot make other people happy. War will never spread freedom
of speech, or of religion, freedom from want or freedom from fear,
anywhere in the world. We can only spread democracy as we did in
the nineteenth century—by the example of our success."[26] By early
1943, irked by signs that the planning tendencies of the New Deal
were being revived, he complained, "Every economic panacea any
long-haired crank ever thought of is being dusted off and incorporated in a magnificent collection of glittering landscapes supposed
to lead to Utopia."[27] In May 1943, he made an explicit attack on
Wallace's idea of a worldwide effort to address freedom from want,
branding it as "too visionary," and professing, "I don't believe we are
engaged in any crusade for the four freedoms." When it came to
America's international policies, Taft preferred to conceive of the
limits to what could be accomplished: "[Even] with the utmost generosity we cannot improve materially the conditions of other countries or put them under any real obligation to us.... We can help
a people to help itself, and we ought to do so by reasonable trade
arrangements and by assisting countries which wish to improve their
industry, commerce and agriculture, but we certainly are not going
to do the world any good by setting up an international WPA [Works
Progress Administration]."[28]

A conservative voting bloc, composed of Republicans and southern Democrats alarmed by some of the more radical features of the
New Deal, had begun to emerge in Congress after the midterm elections of 1938.[29] Their hold over congressional business was consoli-
dated following the pivotal midterm elections of November 1942,
which had seen important Democratic losses outside the South; on
only a 46 percent share of the vote, the party lost forty-five seats in the
House, giving them a margin of 222–209, while in the Senate eight
seats were lost, giving the Democrats a lead of 57–37.[30] Determined
to defend their own sectional interests, a southern voting bloc in

Congress, in harness with the rump of the Republican Party, was henceforth able to stymie many initiatives at a national level, and work to rein back the gains made by organized labor during the war years. For Democratic Party legislators from the South, as Ira Katznelson has made clear, it was the potential for New Deal reform efforts, in league with labor, to challenge the region's white-dominated racial order—an order that ensured their own grip on power—that served as a powerful incentive for their resistance.

Successful southern opposition in 1943–44 to proposals from the Roosevelt administration that would have allowed the introduction of a standardized national ballot for voting in federal elections so that members of the armed services overseas would be able to cast their ballots was a clear example of the way federal intrusion into the traditional prerogatives of the states—in this case the sensitive issue of voting rights—had the capacity to mobilize powerful congressional forces able to block change.[31] The accelerated movement of African Americans to northern urban areas in the war years, where they were a potential source of electoral support for Democratic Party machines increasingly ready to profess support for civil rights, was already becoming a major source of division within the party.[32] To add to the alarm of southern Democrats, a "rights consciousness" was also influencing white liberal northern sensibilities during this period, where the contradictions of a war fought in the name of freedom and democracy against an enemy that preached racial supremacy, but by a country where basic freedoms were denied to millions of America's own citizens, were clear for all to see.[33] Tensions over race therefore underlay how the issue of "ballots for soldiers" was handled, but it also portended how the extension of state capacity and New Deal liberalism, with its implicit drift toward placing the issue of racial equality onto the national political agenda, would provoke fierce opposition from those committed to the status quo. "National" programs, which would have the effect of undermining local differences, were vulnerable to attack as forms of dangerous radicalism.[34]

Liberals found themselves fighting a succession of rearguard actions, as agencies and groups identified with the New Deal, or that might provide the impetus for further reform, were attacked by hostile voices within Congress, while antitrust measures were relaxed. The Depression-era emergency powers that had given the executive branch such license to intervene in the economy were subject to steady erosion during these final years of the war. By the end of 1943, Congress had wound up the Civilian Conservation Corps, the

Works Progress Administration, the National Youth Administration, and the Home Owners' Loan Corporation, and sought to curb the influence of organized labor. Having extolled the virtues of some of the more radical and egalitarian forms of the New Deal, and with a reputation as the home of liberal ideologues, the OWI had also drawn the attention of conservative critics. Divided within its own leadership over how far to translate the ambiguous language of freedom into concrete policy proposals, the OWI was dismembered by Congress in 1943, a fate described by its historian as "but one more example of the war's devastating impact on the whole liberal cause."[35]

Determined to make prosecution of the war his overriding priority, Roosevelt's own performance was the cause of discontent among New Deal liberals by this stage, as they found themselves sidelined from key policy roles, conservatives brought into government, and large corporations turning their domination of the war economy into political influence both on Capitol Hill and in the executive branch.[36] Roosevelt's soothing gloss on the demise of the WPA, for example, was that Congress had granted the New Deal agency an "honorable discharge."[37] Wallace's increasing marginalization was the clearest sign of what would befall the cause of radical reform. He had already incurred the wrath of Cordell Hull, Roosevelt's secretary of state, who complained that Wallace's supporters seemed intent on sparking a "world wide social revolution" and were ready to see revolutionary thinking spread to the United States itself.[38] When at the end of 1942 Wallace voiced his fears to Roosevelt that large corporations threatened to dominate the political economy after the war, the president had seemed indifferent. In July 1943, after months of inter-bureaucratic strife, Roosevelt made his political preferences clear by announcing the abolition of the Board of Economic Warfare, Wallace's power base and his vehicle for intervention in the war economy and for postwar international planning.[39] "Liberals meet in Washington these days," MacLeish lamented in 1944, "if they meet at all, to discuss the tragic outlook for all liberal proposals and the inevitable defeat of all liberal aims."[40]

Another sign of the times was the reception accorded to ambitious plans for new schemes for social insurance. To be sure, the Beveridge report was not accorded unqualified adulation in liberal circles, some finding its stress on minimum standards of living and its assumption of austere postwar conditions ill-suited to a dynamic American economy that was now showing a remarkable capacity for rejuvenation and growth.[41] Nevertheless, the notion of a new or second Bill of Rights that would underpin postwar planning and reconstruction had been put forward in the National Resources Planning Board's major 1943 report *Security, Work, and Relief Policies*, which advocated an expansion in social security and improvements to education, health care, and housing, along with work for all who were able to take up employment. When finally released by the president in March 1943—its initial publication having been held back by an uncertain White House—the report provoked mixed reactions. Some liberals and the labor unions hailed it as an American version of the Beveridge Plan. "It epitomizes, as no statement has done," *The Nation* maintained, "the contrast between the way of life of free men and the way of life in the dictatorships. It is a natural supplement to the Atlantic Charter, but it is ... far more inspiring to the average man." These plaudits were soon drowned out, however, by a wave of disapproval from conservative critics in the press, while congressional opponents of the New Deal swooped on its contents to excoriate the NRPB. Indeed, in June 1943, after a lukewarm attempt to keep it alive by the White House, the board's funding was peremptorily removed by Congress, while its wartime reports were seen by many as increasingly redundant.[42] Hopes that the power of the federal government could be mobilized to achieve progressive goals were stymied. The president, enmeshed in the diplomacy and strategy of the Grand Alliance, was clear about where his priorities lay: "Dr. New Deal," he memorably told reporters in December 1943, had been replaced by "Dr. Win-the-War."[43]

The arrival of a presidential election year in 1944 sparked a brief renaissance for the cause of reform. At the end of 1943 the NRPB's broad conception of economic freedom had been taken up and pushed forward by the energetic Chester Bowles, the liberal head of the Office of Price Administration (and a particular foil for Taft's strictures against government intervention in the economy).[44] Bowles had presented his own ideas for a second Bill of Rights to Sam Rosenman, the president's longtime speechwriter, who seemed interested in the proposals, while Roosevelt himself also proved receptive. Based on an initial draft prepared by Rosenman and Robert Sherwood, Roosevelt's State of the Union address message was sent up to Congress on January 11, 1944 (the president being too unwell with the flu to deliver in person, substituting a radio address instead).[45] In it, Roosevelt raised the point that essential to the peace would be "a decent standard of living for all individual men and women and children in all nations. Freedom from fear is eternally linked with freedom from want." He pronounced that, having grown under the protection of particular "inalienable political rights," including those of free speech and free worship, the republic had come to "a clear realization of the fact that true individual freedom cannot exist without economic security and independence. 'Necessitous men are not free men.' People who are hungry and out of a job are the stuff of which dictatorships are made." It was these "economic truths" that had become "accepted as self-evident," and the president had gone on to list the specific rights that he had in mind, including the right to "useful and remunerative jobs in the industries, or shops or farms or mines of the nation"; the "right to earn enough to provide adequate food and clothing and recreation"; a farmer's right to make him and his family "a decent living" from his produce; freedom from unfair competition from monopolistic practices; "the right of every family to a decent house"; "the right to adequate medical care and the opportunity to share and enjoy good health"; "the right to adequate protection from the economic fears of old age, sickness, accident, and unemployment"; and the "right to a good education." It was implementing this "Economic Bill of Rights" that Roosevelt commended to the nation as offering the road to "human happiness and well-being," and he exhorted Congress to consider the means by which they could be fulfilled.[46]

Liberals were for a time reassured and even exhilarated by this echo of the original Four Freedoms speech and message, where freedom from want might still find a place in the Democratic Party's postwar agenda. But little of substance was to follow from a president who was increasingly tired, overstrained, and suffering from a multitude of debilitating ailments. Many would soon come to doubt how much political capital Roosevelt was really prepared to expend in order to push reform into new fields, his rhetorical flourishes seen as designed purely to keep the heterogeneous forces within his party together. "The President certainly is a waterman," Wallace wrote with weary insight in his diary in March 1944. "He looks one direction and rows the other with the utmost skill."[47]

By this point, Wallace's own days as a member of the leading ranks of the Democratic Party were clearly numbered. In July 1944, after a masterly example of political chicanery from Roosevelt, Wallace was removed from the Democratic ticket for the upcoming presidential election. Instead, the party, with Roosevelt's approval, selected a compromise vice presidential candidate in the form of Harry S. Truman, a senator from a border state who was acceptable to Democratic political bosses from both the major cities and the South.[48] In his Chicago convention speech Wallace hid his

disappointment with a stirring evocation of his vision for what a rejuvenated postwar liberal state could achieve:

> The future belongs to those who go down the line unswervingly for the lib-
> eral principles of both political democracy and economic democracy regard-
> less of race, color, or religion. In a political, educational, and economic sense
> there must be no inferior races. The poll tax must go. Equal educational
> opportunities must come. The future must bring equal wages for equal work
> regardless of sex or race.[49]

Wallace's views, it is apparent, represented a threat not just to
the established economic order but to the racial order of the South.
In this way, the issues of radical reform and race were again intertwined in the politics of the late New Deal era. Optimists in the
liberal ranks of the Democratic Party nevertheless still found much
to remain positive about: New Deal reforms, they supposed, had
helped to save capitalism without the need to reshape state power so
that it would infringe individual liberties; social welfare schemes had
been extended to protect some of the more vulnerable or weaker
groups in society; and mechanisms to ensure full employment and
correct fluctuations in the economic cycle were now an intrinsic part
of a fiscal policy geared to generating future growth and prosperity
(and the economy itself excited expectations of the bounties that
could be achieved, with national income reaching the dizzy heights
of $180 billion in 1944).

The publication in 1944 of Friedrich A. Hayek's *The Road to
Serfdom*—a text that was a Book of the Month Club selection and
sold a remarkable three hundred thousand copies in the United
States—had meanwhile put respectable philosophical bones on
conservative opposition to attempts to enlarge the regulatory
functions of the state. Hayek's portrayal of state planning of the
economy as inevitably leading to the loss of individual freedom
and the imposition of tyranny had a deep resonance for an audience awakened to the dangers of totalitarianism during the 1930s
and wartime years. The fact that so many political refugees had
made their way to the United States to escape political oppression in Europe also contributed to an American self-image as a
country that was a repository of basic individual rights—with the
absence of coercion lying at their center—standing in opposition
to a world steeped in the political excesses and human costs associated with grandiose "state-making" projects. By connecting so
concretely the economic freedom of the market with the preservation of individual liberty, Hayek's insights endorsed the emerging

rhetoric, coming predominantly from the business community, of the importance of upholding a "fifth freedom" of free enterprise in the postwar world.[50]

As peace approached, liberals could not ignore the significance for their own outlook of being engaged in a war fought for freedom against totalitarian regimes and an ideology that lauded the supremacy of the state in all aspects of the life of an individual. The message of the 1930s and 1940s seemed clear to many observers: building state capacity when taken to extremes could represent a fundamental threat to human liberty and produce terror and violence of an almost unimaginable order. For many liberals, as Alan Brinkley has shown in his account of the late New Deal, ambitious efforts to reform the fundamentals of American capitalism were superseded by a switch in their agenda to a stress on the importance of consumption and growth to alleviate social problems, with full employment by 1944 having emerged as the cardinal goal of economic management. Writing in the wake of the publication of *The Road to Serfdom*, the liberal theologian Reinhold Niebuhr observed, "The rise of totalitarianism has prompted the democratic world to view all collectivist answers to our social problems with increasing apprehension." The limits to freedom and autonomy posed by a burgeoning federal bureaucracy were increasingly seen as a potentially bigger problem than the economic inequalities that state regulation of capitalism might help to mitigate.[51] Within the government bureaucracy itself, for example, this shift in emphasis was underlined by the contrasting fortunes of the Bureau of the Budget (BOB) and the National Resources Planning Board, both of which had been brought into the Executive Office of the President in 1939 as the principal instruments through which the president could provide strategic direction to the economy. Whereas the BOB went through a dramatic expansion in staffing and budget, which saw it emerge by 1945 as the most important arm of the Executive Office, the NRPB, as has been seen, was emasculated by Congress in 1943. Fiscal interventions, and attempts to manipulate the economy through budget measures, would henceforth characterize the federal government's approach to broad economic policy.[52]

It was almost inevitable that the liberals who had never lost faith in Roosevelt would see in Truman a poor and disappointing substitute after the former's death in April 1945 ("a small man of limited knowledge who wants to do the right thing," Wallace had contemptuously noted of Truman in his diary), who by bringing to Washington his Missouri political cronies was accused of sullying

the courtly tone and style of the White House.[53] Although Truman's
State of the Union in January 1946 invoked the familiar liturgies
of liberal reform, it was apparent that the new president was not
prepared to press forward such an ambitious program. In any case
Congress would have been very unlikely to have passed new measures. Nothing illustrated the political mood better than the fate
of the Full Employment Bill introduced with much liberal fanfare
in January 1945, which was intended to make it incumbent on the
federal government to provide work opportunities for all those who
were fit and able. In its final and much diluted form, the Employment
Act eventually passed in 1946 (with the word "Full" dropped from
its title) allowed for higher levels of "natural" unemployment than
its original authors had envisaged. The federal government was
relieved of an automatic obligation to intervene when levels of joblessness rose, while the onus of responsibility for providing remedies
was to be shared more widely among industry, labor, state, and local
governments. Moreover, the promotion of "free private enterprise"
was now stipulated as an essential part of federal economic policy. In
John Morton Blum's opinion, the act "acknowledged the concern of
the Congress and the American people with prosperity, their acceptance of the importance of the role of the federal government in
national economic life, and their recognition of the utility of expert
participation in the definition of economic policy. But the act guaranteed none of those conditions. It did not assert, and still less did it
assure, a right to work. It did not even address itself to the question of
'freedom from want.' It advanced none of the objectives on the long
agenda of liberal reform."[54] The congressional midterm elections in
November 1946, which saw Republican majorities returned in both
the Senate and the House, represented the culmination of wartime
political trends. The election result, in the opinion of the senior State
Department official Adolf Berle, "merely confirm[ed] what anybody
could see coming. The New Deal dissolved with Roosevelt, and the
country [was] voting for another shot at the laissez-faire economy."[55]

   While the prospects for liberal reform at home had clearly
faded in the immediate aftermath of war, many liberals found a new
venue overseas for their activism as the task of remaking the postwar
world assumed greater urgency after 1945. Wallace's Century of the
Common Man speech had echoed Roosevelt's Four Freedoms declaration by asserting that the ideas and values it enunciated had a
worldwide applicability; the war years inculcated among Americans a
greater sense that they were connected with the fate of a wider global
community. In contrast to the rejection of international political

engagement that had occurred after 1919—as they imagined it—they would not repeat the mistakes of the past and shirk the responsibilities that history and the logic of power now thrust in their direction. There was a clear connection made in Roosevelt's 1941 pronouncement, moreover, and the Atlantic Charter that followed it, between establishing economic security for the individual and creating the economic conditions for postwar international security and stability. Indeed, for some the concept of freedom from want implied that the United States would take the lead in the struggle against poverty in a world emerging from the ravages of war (a foretaste of this kind of global activism had, in fact, already been offered in the interwar year by the work of private American foundations on schemes of social improvement). It was American officials who proudly helped establish the United Nations Relief and Rehabilitation Agency (UNRRA) in 1943, which brought help to societies, such as those in Greece and China, decimated by the effects of occupation and civil conflict. UNRRA's first director, Herbert H. Lehman, the governor of New York, declared that "freedom from want is a basic component of an enduring peace. . . . The fate of attempts by all the United Nations to banish global wars may well be determined by the success of their first joint action in relief and rehabilitation."[56] With the inclusion of "rehabilitation" in the agency's title some reformers also saw the potential to promote a restructuring or "modernization" within countries that now had an opportunity to start afresh.[57]

An inspirational model for those seeking to export American ideas of development during this pioneering era of liberal internationalism was the New Deal's own Tennessee Valley Authority (TVA), which under the guidance of David E. Lilienthal had used planning techniques and public investment to regenerate a whole region that had once seemed irredeemably mired in backwardness. In his 1944 book *TVA: Democracy on the March*, Lilienthal emphasized that the TVA experience could be made universally applicable as the vehicle for postwar reconstruction. As David Ekbladh has made clear, the TVA was seen as offering the chance of genuine, grass-roots democratic participation in a public development corporation, with Wallace, for example, leading calls for an "international TVA."[58] There were others closely identified with liberal reform who saw it as incumbent on the United States to take the lead in overseas aid efforts. To optimistic Cold War liberals, the New Deal's state-making and reform efforts had helped to resolve the problems of American capitalism in the 1930s; American ingenuity might now be used to transform social and economic conditions abroad. Out of government following the abolition of wartime price controls, Chester Bowles, for example, began to turn his attention to the wider world stage, making a speech at Freedom House in New York City in January 1947 that proclaimed, "If the American people will support the investment of only 2 percent of our total income each year for the next twenty years in the development of less fortunate countries, we may change the tide of history."[59]

By this stage, of course, the imperatives of the Cold War and an expansive definition of national security were already beginning to mesh with the urge to do good in the world through overseas aid. Freedom from want in this new incarnation thus came to represent a key message in the ideological struggle of the Cold War, as the US system tried to demonstrate its superiority over communist alternatives. Fear of economic collapse and breakdown in the battered economies of Western Europe during 1947 and the possibility that as a consequence left-wing political parties might gain greater footholds in government was an important driver in the inauguration of a European Recovery Program by the Truman administration. But Marshall Plan aid was being channeled to economies that had largely gone through the process of industrialization and were recognizably "modern" in their organization and use of technology; American concerns by the late 1940s onward were increasingly focused on the newly independent and undeveloped states of the Third World that were emerging from colonial rule. Assuming that "backward" and "traditional" societies in Asia and Africa would be highly vulnerable to communist blandishments and be tempted to follow Soviet models of state-led rapid economic development, some US officials came to believe that American technical and scientific expertise would be the key to bringing such new states into the modern world and providing the economic growth that would ward off social revolution.

This desire found clear expression, at least in rhetorical form, in the Point Four Program of technical assistance announced by President Truman in January 1949. In his inaugural address following his surprise election victory of the previous November, Truman had referred to the enormous challenge of confronting the Soviet Union that now faced the American people. Alongside the political and religious freedoms that distinguished the United States from its adversary, Truman pointed to Americans' right to "material well-being," and ability of an individual to "achieve a decent and satisfying life." Having mentioned US support for the UN, the European Recovery Program, and the Rio and North Atlantic Treaties, the president added a fourth point, saying:

We must embark on a bold new program for making the benefits of our scientific advances and industrial progress available for the improvement and
growth of underdeveloped areas. More than half the people of the world are
living in conditions approaching misery. Their food is inadequate. They are
victims of disease. Their economic life is primitive and stagnant. Their poverty is a handicap and a threat both to them and to more prosperous areas.
For the first time in history, humanity possesses the knowledge and skill
to relieve the suffering of these people. The United States is pre-eminent
among nations in the development of industrial and scientific techniques. . . .
Our aim should be to help the free peoples of the world, through their own
efforts, to produce more food, more clothing, more materials for housing,
and more mechanical power to lighten their burdens. . . . It must be a world-
wide effort for the achievement of peace, plenty and freedom.[60]

Point Four had its immediate genesis in the Truman administration's desire to find a strong theme and foreign policy message for
the inaugural address. The idea of stressing technical assistance
had come from Benjamin Hardy, a public affairs officer in the State
Department who had served in Brazil during the war, where a small
scale program on these lines had been run under the auspices of
the Office of the Coordinator of Inter-American Affairs. Inspired by
the Marshall Plan, Hardy proposed expanding the Latin American
experience

into a dramatic, large-scale program that would capture the imagination of
the peoples of other countries and harness their enthusiasm for social and
economic improvement to the democratic campaign to repulse Communism
and create a decent life for the earth's millions.

With a commendable disregard for the usual bureaucratic niceties,
and at some risk to his career, Hardy bypassed the State Department
hierarchy, believing it would smother his scheme, and approached
the White House directly in December 1948. Hardy's paper found
its way to George Elsey and Clark Clifford, two of Truman's closest
aides, the latter finding it "the solution to our dilemma: while we
had a speech in search of an idea, Hardy had an idea in search of
a speech." Although the State Department tried to put up obstruc-
tions, feeling the proposal had not received sufficient preparation
and analysis, Hardy's idea was included as the fourth point in drafts
of the inaugural, with Hardy becoming "a clandestine member" of
the drafting team.

    In fact, Truman's speech had drawn together a great many
disparate ideas that had been fermenting for several years among
officials concerned with modernization and the receptivity of the

rest of the world to American models of economic development, including exporting the TVA example.[61] Truman himself, enthused by visions of creating new TVAs on the Danube and Yangtze rivers, would rhapsodize to Lilienthal that "when they happen, when millions of people are no longer hungry or pushed and harassed, then the causes of war will be less by that much."[62] Greeted with considerable enthusiasm by the press and public after it was promulgated by the president in January 1949, Point Four became, as Clifford put it with some degree of hyperbole, "the godfather to a host of American foreign assistance programs," and "a turning point in American foreign policy" that was the harbinger of changes to come. Believing that "economic progress and education were the strongest bulwark against the spread of communism and military dictatorship," Clifford later professed that he was "convinced" that the nation "should commit more resources to the worldwide struggle against such problems as illiteracy, malnutrition, poor irrigation and primitive farming techniques, and over-population."[63] Nevertheless, Point Four did not get off to a flying start. Much to the frustration of the White House, a disdainful and suspicious State Department, led by a Dean Acheson, whose Cold War gaze was invariably focused on Europe, dragged its feet in bringing forward proposals for an aid program. With the State Department according it little attention at first, an initial request from the White House to Congress for appropriations to support a program, made in June 1949, came so late in the session that it could not be considered until the following year (the total US foreign aid budget at this time was still less than $40 million).[64]

It was the emergence of a communist regime in China in October 1949, where Mao Zedong had managed to capture the power of the Chinese peasantry—hitherto considered mired in poverty and "backwardness"—that underlined the danger for the United States and its interests in Asia if it did not both understand the changes underway in mid-twentieth-century rural societies and devise approaches that could lead them along paths of Western-inspired economic development.[65] The victory of communism in China, Chester Bowles later wrote, "shocked" the American people into realizing "the extent of our new responsibilities"; after the help they had provided Europe through the Marshall Plan, they "discovered that not only Europe, but even more so all of poverty-stricken Asia and the vast underdeveloped world were in the midst of a 'revolution of rising expectations.'" In this context, Point Four was seen by Bowles as "potentially the most powerful constructive program against chaos

and communism which the free world has devised."[66] A vigorous new
program to export US technology and financial assistance was one
response to what was seen as the increasingly urgent need to halt
a looming communist drive in the underdeveloped world, and to
bring into being a stable, prosperous and liberal world order under
American tutelage.[67]

In the spring of 1950 the administration duly introduced an
International Development Bill to Congress, mandating the creation
of a new Technical Cooperation Administration within a still wary
State Department. After the bill became law in early June 1950, with
$25 million of initial expenditure authorized, a Point Four Advisory
Board was also created under Nelson Rockefeller, indicating that
the overseas aid program would try to tap into private foundations
and networks of assistance to promote American models of development abroad. Moreover, by this time the Truman administration
had a specific ulterior motive for its funding request: support for
the French war in Indochina had become a priority for US policy
in Southeast Asia, and the economic aid mission to the Associated
States of Vietnam that Point Four funding helped establish, became
a counterpoint to the military assistance given to French forces.
"Although it was billed as a new technical assistance program of
'shirtsleeves diplomacy' to help the less-developed nations improve
their living standards," one historian of American involvement in
Vietnam has written, "the real motivation for the program, especially
in South-east Asia, was the need to provide assistance to less developed countries threatened by the Communists, which, by improving economic conditions, could presumably provide greater political
strength and stability."[68]

The arrival in office of a Republican administration under
President Dwight D. Eisenhower in January 1953 signaled a change
in the tenor of overseas economic policy, with the invocation of
the mantra "Trade not aid" and a far greater skepticism toward
government-led schemes of economic development accompanied
by a new stress on private investment and military assistance.[69]
Nevertheless, the fundamentals of the credos of "modernization"
had been absorbed by whole groups of American officials, private
individuals, international organizations, charities, and foundations,
who spent the next decade spreading their ideas to expectant peoples in the developing world, while the Point Four label and ethos
survived bureaucratic struggles within the administration over control of foreign aid.[70] Ironically enough, however, US private investment in the Third World was very difficult to attract during the 1950s

and 1960s, which was one reason why it was government-sourced aid that was required to fill the perceived gap.[71] The urgency of the problem was underlined for US policymakers in the mid-1950s by the belief that the Soviet Union was itself now embarked upon an "economic offensive" in the Third World, where the Soviet premier Nikita Khrushchev was attempting to sell Soviet-style modernization to audiences in Asia who were looking to cultivate alternative sources of aid, free from association with dependence on the older Western colonial powers.[72] By the end of the 1950s, Washington had recognized the vital role that foreign aid played in the global Cold War that had by then developed, and was prepared to take a pragmatic approach to state-sponsored schemes of development.

Opening up during this period, moreover, there was also a new sense of national mission, as outward-looking Americans, many of them New Deal liberals disheartened by the turn to the right in US domestic politics, found a vindication for their beliefs among societies yearning for progress. Having completed his first stint as US ambassador to India, Bowles wrote in November 1953, "We Americans are a pioneer people, still respectful of the old Puritan concepts of common decency and hard work, still guided by moral principles, still stirred by the call of the frontier. Now a new frontier awaits us, working with peoples of all races and religions in the economic, social, and political development of every underdeveloped continent, which is this century's main adventure."[73] Amid the heterogeneous ideas that operated—sometimes in competition—under the rubric of modernization, the New Deal's methods of rural reconstruction played some role in the efforts of American officials to "uplift" the villages of the Third World, and most particularly in Asia. At the forefront here was the notion of "community development," conceived (in the words of Bowles again) as "an administrative framework through which modern scientific knowledge could be put to work for the benefit of the hundreds of millions of people who have long lived in poverty." Expert knowledge and "rational" management techniques would be brought to bear on the processes of village life—and adopted by villagers themselves on a "communal" and voluntary basis—in order to improve standards of health, education, crop production, and animal rearing. During the 1950s, community development programs, with the help of private philanthropy from the Ford Foundation, as well as official assistance from Point Four, were launched in India and spread to Indonesia and the Philippines, with the concept being given recognition by the UN in 1956. The links with domestic US experience were tangible: community development projects had brought new services, public housing, and ideas of self-help to deprived American urban areas in the late 1930s and 1940s. Urban planning ideas were applied to an Indian setting by such visionaries as Albert Mayer, who, after working on slum clearance and new designs for city living in New York, established a relationship with Nehru and went on to help plan the new Punjabi capital at Chandigarh and seek to reconfigure the organization of Indian village life. But the gap between expectation and performance was often immense in such grand schemes of rural regeneration. In India, for example, living standards in the villages touched by community development showed no great improvement over others (some of which appeared to adapt even more effectively to the challenge of increasing food supply for an expanding population), while, in Nick Cullather's words, "Rather than a supple, decentralized strategy, community development turned out to be a traditional, ineffective, and massively expensive public jobs program."[74]

Despite its setbacks, an American ideology of modernization had taken hold in US official and nongovernmental circles by the later 1950s, during the same period that the Cold War had assumed for many the character of a competition between differing economic systems. In 1960, in his *Stages of Economic Growth*, Walt W. Rostow predicted the takeoff of premodern societies toward American levels of prosperity, security, and political freedom if they followed the correct prescriptions.[75] When comparisons with Soviet models of development were made, American information policy had to convey the basic point that the United States had formed its own version of a "classless society" where the average workers could own their own homes, acquire all the material comforts of modern suburban living, enjoy health insurance, and still have the safety net of a social welfare system if they should fall on hard times. The message of the 1950s to overseas audiences was that capitalism was not only for the wealthy, and that social progress could be achieved without the need for social revolution.[76] During his famous Kitchen Debate with Khrushchev in July 1959, Vice President Richard Nixon had paraded the ability of US-style capitalism to offer not merely the necessities of existence but the luxury goods and items that could enhance the quality of life of the family living in a modernized society. It was almost as if amid such material abundance the notion of freedom from want was beginning to seem like a quaint anachronism. Khrushchev's taunt of "We will bury you" could be met with an army of washing machines, television sets, and automobiles.[77]

Yet the great irony of this period was that US economic and social problems remained readily apparent to those who cared to look, and were a standing rebuke to those who claimed that the American system could deliver for everyone. Using a minimum threshold of a $3,000 annual income for a family, and employing official data from the US Federal Reserve Board and the Commerce Department, Michael Harrington, a former member of the Catholic worker movement and then a socialist journalist, published an article in *Commentary* magazine in July 1959 that concluded that between forty and sixty million Americans, out of a total population of 180 million, were living in poverty. This disproved the "current myth," Harrington argued, that the numbers of poor were either small or declining significantly. Afflicted with their own subculture, poor communities required a broad program from the federal government—what Harrington called a "comprehensive assault on poverty"—involving action in the areas of housing, education, medical care, labor standards, and communal institutions if the problem was to be addressed. But Harrington was not optimistic, noting that an extension of the welfare provision had been blocked since before the war, and that without dramatic political change it was "likely that the poor will remain with us, through cycles of boom and bust and successive elections, and that their way of life will perpetuate itself, to their own hurt and the great damage of our own society."[78]

During the presidential election campaign of 1960 the debilitating effects of structural unemployment on communities were brought home to Senator John F. Kennedy when he toured West Virginia during the primaries; Theodore White later commented on the presidential candidate that "he could scarcely bring himself to believe that human beings were forced to eat and live on these cans of dry relief rations, which he fingered like artifacts of another civilization. 'Imagine,' he said to one of his assistants one night, 'just imagine kids who never drink milk.' "[79] As the November election approached, Kennedy used statistics on poor housing conditions and the meagre support available to the old when attacking the record of the incumbent Republican administration, declaiming that the "war against poverty is not yet over."[80] In February 1961, one month after Kennedy's inaugural address had exhorted his fellow Americans to bear the burden of defending liberty around the world, the number of unemployed still stood at 5.4 million, the highest figure in twenty years.

Yet the priorities of the Cold War, and the heavy defense spending that it entailed, remained paramount for the new president as he entered the White House, while conservative legislators still retained a strong lock on congressional business. A new Area Redevelopment Act did become law in May 1961, but the programs it was intended to inaugurate moved at a snail's pace, created very few jobs, and came under criticism for favoritism, and additional funding was denied them by Congress in 1963. Fleshing out the concerns of his previous articles, in March 1962 Harrington published a summation of his earlier findings in a slim volume entitled *The Other America*, where he reiterated the plight of the "invisible" poor who were trapped in a culture of poverty. One-third of the nation, Harrington wanted to impress upon his readers, was badly housed, ill-nourished and clothed, without proper access to health care and education, and scraping out a subsistence level of living.[81] The "visibility" of poverty was also becoming more pronounced at this time, as the numbers of poor (often old, or nonwhite, or families with only one female parent) living in cities or towns rose. Nevertheless, there remained a sense of optimism in some quarters that remedial action by the federal government could effectively address such problems. New government programs in education, health, welfare, and training for the unemployed, a major 1962 University of Michigan study financed by the Ford Foundation argued, were necessary to supplement economic growth if poverty was to be tackled. The cost was put at about $10 billion per annum, or about 2 percent of national income, but with such measures "poverty could be abolished easily and simply by a stroke of the pen."[82] Having heard of Harrington's work from his speechwriter Theodore Sorenson, in 1963 President Kennedy began to move on the poverty issue, charging his head of the Council of Economic Advisors, Walter Heller, with examining the possibility of a broader and less piecemeal approach to some of the problems that social commentators had identified.[83] If Kennedy had lived there seems a strong possibility he would have launched an antipoverty program during his second term, and there are indications he took the moral aspects of the issue seriously.

For Lyndon Johnson, however, the cause was much more personal. Brought up in the struggling towns in the Hill Country of Texas, Johnson had served his political apprenticeship under New Deal programs during the latter 1930s, when FDR was his hero. The Great Society program of reforms that Johnson sponsored so vociferously in the mid-1960s was intended to take up what he saw as the unfinished business of the New Deal, with echoes of the State of the Union messages delivered by Roosevelt in 1941 and 1944. "At the heart of it," Johnson later wrote, "I thought of the Great Society as an extension of the Bill of Rights. When our fundamental American rights were set forth by the Founding Fathers, they reflected the concerns of a people who sought freedom in their time. But in our time a broadened concept of freedom requires that every American have the right to a healthy body, a full education, a decent home, and the opportunity to make the best of his talents."[84] In his first state of union address on 8 January 1964 he declared an "unconditional war on poverty in America," and in August that year the Economic Opportunity Act was passed, which introduced a raft of different measures, including youth training to give people a better chance to move into the labor market, and the controversial Community Action Program, with its attempts to mobilize, organize, and empower the poor.[85] In ironic fashion, and again demonstrating the transnational flow of ideas between the international and domestic, the concept of community development that had formed an important part of the thinking of US modernization theorists as they addressed the problems of poverty in the Indian countryside during the 1950s returned home to influence the approach of Great Society reformers a decade later (with David Lilienthal, that *Zelig*-like figure, once again playing a role).[86]

Mirroring such ambitions in the field of domestic policy, Democratic administrations during the 1960s sought to promote economic development and uplift abroad. As President Kennedy told Congress in March 1961, Americans had "economic obligations as the wealthiest people in a world of largely poor people," while the consequences of failing to meet such obligations could be serious: "Widespread poverty and chaos lead to a collapse of existing political and social structures which would inevitably invite the advance of totalitarianism into every weak and unstable area."[87] A Cold War frame once again served to mediate how administrations in Washington approached the issue of development. During the tumultuous decade that was to follow, as communist insurgencies, either actual or potential, were held responsible for spreading instability and upheaval in Southeast Asia, it was earlier themes of community development that now found another outlet, as attempts were made to assert central government control and impose order on a countryside in ferment. Community development had become an instrument of the pacification program in Vietnam by the mid-1960s, just as it was taken up by the Peace Corps volunteers who fanned out across Asia, Latin America, the Middle East, and Africa. Intended to correct the "cultural deficiencies" in traditional patterns of village life that were holding back its participants from full participation in national economic development, or grasping opportunities for self-improvement, community development assignments were given to about 30 percent of all Peace Corps volunteers between 1961 and 1965.[88] As the Johnson administration made the fateful decisions in 1965 to expand the war in Vietnam, it delved once again into the idiom of the New Deal to provide a more uplifting vision of economic development to counterbalance its displays of conventional military power. Tapping into Lilienthal's expertise, in April 1965 President Johnson came forward to explain US involvement in Vietnam at his Johns Hopkins University address, and accompanied it with grandiose plans for a TVA on the Mekong river, underwritten by a billion dollars of multilateral foreign assistance. "The task is nothing less than to enrich the hopes and existence of more than a hundred million people," Johnson proclaimed. "The wonders of modern medicine can be spread through villages where thousands die every year from lack of care. Schools can be established to train people in the skills needed to manage the process of development.... For all existence most men have lived in poverty, threatened by hunger. But we dream of a world where we are all fed and charged with hope."[89]

By the end of his administration, President Johnson, with the assistance of private American foundations, was promoting the "green revolution" in Asia, where Western technologies and agricultural expertise were employed to boost crop yields, feed expanding populations, and generate export surpluses. Pacification efforts in South Vietnam, which had earlier drawn on the vocabulary of community development, by 1967 were leaning on the new "miracle" strain of rice, IR-8, developed by the US-funded and led (and Philippines-based) International Institute of Rice Research, to increase agricultural production through modern scientific techniques and give a graphic demonstration of the material benefits of following Western paths of modernity in the Asian rural economy.[90] As the United States pursued a form of freedom from want in the myriad villages of Asia, its armed forces tried to defend what was seen as the "freedom" of South Vietnam against the threat of communist insurgency and aggression. But just as the military and political struggle in Vietnam took a decisive turn for the worse from the US perspective after 1968, so too did the struggle to feed the expanding populations of Asia increasingly appear insurmountable as hopes for self-sufficiency in rice faded for many of the poorest states of the region. The continuing presence of widespread hunger and malnutrition in India during the 1970s, above all, highlighted the problems that still had to be overcome, as takeoff for traditional, rural societies into new levels of growth and development proved elusive. Attention shifted to population control and addressing such issues as civil conflict and unrest or gender equality as the most suitable targets for remedying the basic problem of access to adequate food supplies in the developing world.[91]

Although the 1960s were often labeled the "decade of development," they also witnessed growing US domestic political opposition to elaborate foreign aid programs. An early sign of this was the Clay Committee's withering criticism of the Kennedy administration's foreign aid proposals in 1963 and the cuts that Congress imposed in that same year, which reduced an initial request for $4.9 billion to $3.2 billion.[92] To many Americans by this time, aid seemed to be flowing to regimes that were led by unsavory characters, mistrusted neutralists, or leaders who were simply downright anti-American. From Sukarno's Indonesia, to Nehru's India, to Sihanouk's Cambodia, the developing world appeared to be filled with countries that were not only unfriendly but explicitly repudiated American influence. From the mid-1960s, the Vietnam War helped to underline the position even further, with a succession of Third World leaders falling over themselves to condemn US imperialism in Southeast Asia, and the way Washington seemed to assume that foreign assistance could buy influence in the developing world. In September 1965, the British ambassador in Washington was reporting what he described as a "distinct hardening from the President downwards in US policy towards the outside world, including the under-developed countries of Asia and Africa." Disputes over aid to India and Pakistan had been compounded by what the "Americans regard as an increased unwillingness by the recipients of American aid to pay any regard to American interests or feelings.... The Americans are ... getting very tired of seeing their money as they think squandered by ungrateful recipients of aid who do nothing to return American generosity."[93]

Beside these international factors had to be set the deteriorating position of the US economy, where balance-of-payments difficulties were becoming acute—fueled by the Vietnam War and the costs of overseas military expenditures—and federal budget deficits were starting to grow at a prodigious rate. In the opinion of many legislators, overseas development aid was a low priority when so much had to be done to alleviate the condition of America's declining urban centers and address the persistent issues of poor health care, education, environmental protection, and economic opportunity for those at the bottom end of society. Attacks on foreign aid were also increasingly launched from the left of the political spectrum, as it was depicted as simply another form of Western imperialism designed to keep the Third World in a condition of subjugation and dependence. The Nixon shocks of 1971—where the free convertibility of dollars to gold at a fixed exchange rate was ended—marked a point of new economic nationalism in the United States, where the needs of the domestic financial system would trump those of acting as the guardian of global financial stability.

The stress in US foreign economic policy shifted quite decisively in the 1970s toward reductions to international barriers to trade and promotion of direct private overseas investment. Between 1969 and 1980, as Congress chipped away at its budget, the total spending of the Agency for International Development increased from $1.4 to only $1.8 billion, representing a real-terms cut in view of the inflation and declining value of the dollar seen across the period.[94] Writing in the mid-1970s, Lucian Pye, the noted MIT theorist of political development and a frequent adviser to the State Department, observed how "the congeries of sentiments and rationales which sustained and gave respectability to foreign aid during the 1960s have been shattered; and few seem to have the spirit to try to pick up the pieces or to reason through again the problem of finding political support for transferring resources and knowledge to less developed lands." In Pye's opinion, it had never been resolved "whether we were giving aid primarily because it was in our immediate national interest or whether we were practicing indiscriminate worldwide generosity.... Out of the confusion of reasons we were never able to untangle a clear sense of purpose either for foreign aid in general or even in particular cases."[95]

International development projects attracted the ire of conservatives distrustful of government-based solutions to social and economic problems, whether on a global or local basis. During the early 1980s, the World Bank and the International Monetary Fund—those two repositories of global Keynesian thinking—were refashioned under the influence of the Reagan administration so that they became evangelists for a monetarist economic agenda that sacrificed social provision for controls on inflation and a stress on opening up markets.[96] Buoyed by a wave of new "neoliberal" thinking, the free market became venerated for the growth it was expected to deliver.[97] Other critics pointed to the incidence of corruption, where aid was siphoned into the private bank accounts of Third World politicians or used to shore up authoritarian regimes that abused the human rights of their citizens. By the 1990s, and contrary to its self-image as a generous nation, the United States gave a smaller proportion of its gross national income as foreign aid—less than 1 percent—than any other country in the developed world (despite the fact that opinion polls showed that a majority of Americans supported foreign aid in principle).[98]

The emergence within the United States of a vigorous critique of foreign aid was accompanied by developments that suggested that freedom from want at home might be an ideal that was becoming attainable. Between the mid-1960s and early 1970s, the number of Americans classed as "poor" began to fall quite rapidly, while at the same time social welfare programs expanded. Numbers of those classified as poor fell from 39 million (or 22 percent of the population) in 1959, to 32 million (17 percent) in 1965, to 25 million (13 percent) in 1968, to 23 million (11 percent) in 1973.[99] In October 1968, as his presidency drew to an ignominious close, President Johnson was keen to stress the point that over the previous six years federal spending on the poor had gone up from $12 billion to over $27 billion, while twelve million people had moved out of the official classification of poverty. But ascribing such major and long-term movements in the incidence of poverty to the effects of federal measures that had only been in operation for a short time stretched credulity. In fact, the War on Poverty, and particularly the Community Action Program, had been marked by bureaucratic infighting, inadequate funding, patchy results, and disinterest from a White House soon consumed by another war overseas.[100] One important long-term source of change was the lifting out of poverty of many older people as social security payments began to be received, but of even greater significance was the steady growth of the economy in the 1960s. Definitions of poverty also tended to shift over the period; in 1977, the poverty line for a family of four was now set at an annual income of $6,600, a figure that allowed for more actual spending power than was accorded a previous generation, reflecting the fact that a wealthier society expected its poorest members, buoyed also by various forms of in-kind benefits such as food stamps and public housing, to enjoy more than simply subsistence living.[101]

By the 1970s, and to some extent mirroring the debates over foreign aid, liberal solutions to the problems of poverty and inequality in US society were in wholesale retreat (the Office of Economic Opportunity, for example, was finally wound up by Congress in 1974), and conservative commentators, finding a voice in journals such as *Public Interest*, were eager to assail examples of government intervention that were seen as worsening social conditions rather than alleviating them. At a local and state level, the decade saw the rise of tax revolts, where popular attempts were made to curtail the tax-and-spending powers of government and protect private wealth from public officials who might squander resources on costly and ineffective welfare programs. The ascendancy of a long-heralded new Republican majority at a national level, buoyed by the antigovernment and antiregulation mood, was marked by the election of Ronald Reagan in 1980; efforts to reduce federal spending were thereafter reflected in cutbacks to discretionary federal programs of public assistance. Hostility to "handouts" and attacks on welfare dependency were given prominence in works such as Charles Murray's 1984 book *Losing Ground*.[102]

The conservative resurgence coincided with far more challenging conditions for the US economy—triggered by the oil price shocks of 1973–74 and increased international economic competition—that helped reverse the encouraging trends of the previous decade when it came to levels of poverty. The stagflation of the period was followed from 1979–80 by another wave of deindustrialization as some of the traditional US manufacturing and mining industries went into steep decline (just to take one example, plant closures reduced US steel-making capacity by 10 percent between 1977 and 1981), unemployment rose (particularly in the older cities of the North and East), and the percentage of people living at or below the poverty line returned to the levels of the mid-1960s. As the economy expanded with the end of recession in 1982, the labor market picked up, and some real incomes showed signs of improvement (though jobs were increasingly in the low-paid service sector, with few benefits), but when recession returned between 1989 and 1992 the proportion of the population classed as poor rose again to 14.5 percent, amounting to 36.9 million people. One-third of this total were African American, and a steadily increasing number of the poor were children, many being raised in single-parent households (almost one-half of all black children under eighteen were by then living in poverty).[103]

At the moment when the Cold War came to an end, therefore, the United States was still far from surmounting some of its major social and economic problems, and a considerable proportion of its population—many of who were from nonwhite minorities—were a long way from enjoying the benefits that Roosevelt had wanted to confer through his January 1944 economic bill of rights. Despite the strong, steady growth in the economy that was such a feature of the decade that followed the end of the Cold War, one of the key characteristics of those years was widening inequalities. Low levels of unemployment certainly alleviated the conditions of those who found themselves squeezed by cuts to social welfare spending in the 1990s, but the stratification of divisions within society was accentuated by the extreme concentrations of wealth that could be found in its upper reaches. Indebtedness among middle-income earners was a growing phenomenon: an increasing number of American households had "negative wealth," where debts exceeded worth and assets (18.5 percent by 1995). If inflation was taken into consideration, average wages in 1999 had still not recovered to the same level as in 1973, when the long postwar boom came to an end, while Americans were tending to work longer hours (between 1981 and 1993, in an important side-effect of de-unionization of the workplace, the income of median wage earners fell by 5 percent in real terms; across the same period, the income of the top 5 percent of tax-payers increased by 30 percent). Health insurance coverage was a perennial concern of many social commentators. In 1998, less than two-thirds of those employed by private companies benefitted from employer-provided schemes, and there was a less than 30 percent chance that those in the bottom fifth of the wage-earning bracket would have health insurance. Although on a pure measure of per capita income per employee the United States in 1996 had the edge over the average for the other eighteen developed economies in the world (though not by much), this comparison discounted the value of the social and health services that were available in many of America's advanced competitors via public sector provision.[104]

By the 1980s, it is apparent, the liberal notion of freedom from want as a serious goal of national policy had been comprehensively overtaken by the idea that free enterprise and the unbridled market were instead the keys to unlocking future prosperity for all who were prepared to seize the chance. Freedom for American capitalism, with a minimal role for the state, was the lodestar of a conservative backlash against liberal reform that had been gathering pace since the mid-1960s. But its deeper origins can actually be discerned in the years between 1943 and 1945, when the OWI's attempts to popularize the third of Roosevelt's four freedoms, for example, had been checked by corporate promotion of a fifth freedom of free enterprise as embodying the true ethos of the American creed. As Ira Katznelson in his assessment of the Great Society reforms of the 1960s once observed, the "political space" for the left in American politics had already been decisively contracted in the 1940s by the redefining of the "social forces undergirding social democratic possibilities in the Democratic party" which "changed the locus of

political debate from questions of social organization and class relations to issues of technical economics and interest group politics."
American politics during the era of the Great Society had featured
similar trends: "The reduction of labor to an interest group; the cen-
trality of race; and an economist's definition of public policy and
political choice.... The subsequent turn to the Right that culminated in the election of President Reagan on an explicit pro-market,
anti-state platform with significant working class support thus was
facilitated by the way the Great Society embedded the trajectory of
the 1940s."[105] With supreme irony, the conservative heir to the "common man" populism of Henry Wallace would prove to be a politician who had begun his political affiliation as a New Deal Democrat
and had swung decisively against big government during the early
postwar period.[106] Ostensibly a means to bring Americans together
during wartime, in the post-1945 era the idea of freedom from want
had conversely polarized many views about the proper role of the
state in the economy and how best to provide economic security for
America's citizens. By the 1990s, it was apparent, the argument had
been settled as the Democratic Party under President Bill Clinton
moved to embrace free market and pragmatic-liberal ideology, where
corporate power could flourish, while a New Deal–era conception of
economic democracy, enshrined in the vision of an economic bill of
rights, was discarded.[107]

Notes

1. See James MacGregor Burns, *Roosevelt: The Soldier of Freedom, 1940–1945*
   (London: Weidenfeld & Nicolson, 1970), 53–54.
2. See Paul Addison, *The Road to 1945: British Politics and the Second World War*
   (London: Cape, 1975), 125, 168.
3. See Samuel I. Rosenman, *Working with Roosevelt* (London: Rupert Hart-Davis,
   1952), 247–48.
4. For the text see the Franklin Delano Roosevelt Presidential Library website: http://docs.fdrlibrary.marist.edu/od4freed.html. A good summary of the
   background to the speech can be found in Elizabeth Borgwardt, *A New Deal for
   the World: America's Vision for Human Rights* (Cambridge, MA: Belknap Pres of
   Harvard University Press, 2005), 48–53.
5. See Eric Foner, *The Story of American Freedom* (New York: W. W. Norton,
   1998), 223.
6. See Borgwardt, *New Deal for the World*, 22–26; for the Charter generally see
   Douglas Brinkley and David R. Facey-Crowther, eds., *The Atlantic Charter*
   (London, 1994).
7. See Burns, *Soldier of Freedom*, 387.
8. "The Price of Free World Victory," 8 May 1942, in Henry A. Wallace, *The Price
   of Vision: The Diary of Henry A. Wallace, 1942–1946*, ed. John M. Blum

(Boston: Houghton Mifflin, 1973), 635–40. See also Norman D. Markowitz, *The Rise and Fall of the People's Century: Henry A. Wallace and American Liberalism, 1941–1948* (New York: Free Press, 1973), 48–54; Edward L. Schapsmeier and Frederick H. Schapsmeier, *Prophet in Politics: Henry A. Wallace and the War Years, 1940–1945* (Ames: Iowa State University Press, 1970); Graham White and John Maze, *Henry A. Wallace: His Search for a New World Order* (Chapel Hill: University of North Carolina Press, 1995), 162–64.

9. See Wallace, *Price of Vision*, 29, 34.

10. John M. Blum, *V Was for Victory: Politics and American Culture during World War Two* (New York: Harcourt Brace Jovanovich, 1976), 29.

11. See Elizabeth B. Crist, *Music for the Common Man: Aaron Copland during the Depression and War* (New York: Oxford University Press, 2005), 180–3.

12. Stuart Murray and James McCabe, *Norman Rockwell's Four Freedoms* (New York: Grammercy, 1998).

13. See Allan M. Winkler, *The Politics of Propaganda: The Office of War Information, 1942–1945* (New Haven, CT: Yale University Press, 1978), 5–7, 38–45. For a recent examination of the OWI, see Justin Hart, *Empire of Ideas: The Origins of Public Diplomacy and the Transformation of US Foreign Policy* (New York: Oxford University Press, 2013), 95–106.

14. Quoted in John C. Culver and John Hyde, *American Dreamer: The Life and Times of Henry A. Wallace* (New York: W. W. Norton, 2000), 278.

15. For the idea of 1942 as representing the end point of such transatlantic cross-fertilization of ideas, see Daniel T. Rodgers, *Atlantic Crossings: Social Politics in a Progressive Age* (Cambridge, MA: Harvard University Press, 2000), 485–508.

16. Full background to the report's compilation can be found in José Harris, *William Beveridge: A Biography*, 2nd ed., (Oxford: Clarendon, 1997), 365–404.

17. See Addison, *Road to 1945*, 169–71, 211–28.

18. Janet Beveridge, *Beveridge and His Plan* (London: Hodder & Stoughton, 1954), 122.

19. See Daniel T. Rodgers, "An Age of Social Politics," in *Rethinking American History in a Global Age*, ed. Thomas Bender (Berkeley: University of California Press, 2002), 269.

20. Borgwardt, *New Deal for the World*, 49. See also Charles E. Merriam, "The National Resources Planning Board: A Chapter in American Planning Experience," *American Political Science Review* 38, no. 6 (December 1944): 1075–88.

21. Entry for December 11, 1942, Wallace, *Price of Vision*, 143.

22. Beveridge, *Beveridge and His Plan*, 173–74.

23. See Warren F. Kimball, "The Atlantic Charter: 'With All Deliberate Speed'," in Brinkley and Facey-Crowther, *Atlantic Charter*, 90.

24. William E. Leuchtenburg, *Franklin D. Roosevelt and the New Deal, 1932–1940* (New York: Harper & Row, 1963), 272–73.

25. See Barry D. Karl, *The Uneasy State: The United States from 1915 to 1945* (Chicago: University of Chicago Press, 1983), 210.

26. Statement on Lend Lease, February 26, 1941, in Robert A. Taft, *The Papers of Robert A. Taft*, ed. Clarence E. Wunderlin, Jr., vol. 2, *1939–1944* (Kent, OH: Kent State University Press, 2001), 230–31; hereafter *Taft Papers, 1939–1944*.

27. Address, January 27, 1943, *Taft Papers, 1939–1944*, 407.

28. Commencement address at Grove City College, May 22, 1943, *Taft Papers*, *1939–144*, 443, 447. See also James T. Patterson, *Mr. Republican: A Biography of Robert A. Taft* (Boston: Houghton Mifflin, 1972).

29. See James T. Patterson, *Congressional Conservatism and the New Deal: The Growth of the Conservative Coalition in Congress, 1933–1939* (Lexington: University of Kentucky Press, 1967), and David L. Porter, *Congress and the Waning of the New Deal* (Port Washington, NY: Kennikat, 1980).

30. Blum, *V Was for Victory*, 230–33; Ira Katznelson, *Fear Itself: The New Deal and the Origins of Our Time* (New York: Liveright, 2013), 378.

31. For coverage of the soldiers for ballots issue, see Katznelson, *Fear Itself*, 195–222, and also Burns, *Soldier of Freedom*, 429–32.

32. Katznelson, *Fear Itself*, 182–94; see also Karl, *Uneasy State*, 217.

33. Alan Brinkley, *The End of Reform: New Deal Liberalism in Recession and War* (New York: Alfred A. Knopf, 1995), 164–71; Foner, *Story of American Freedom*, 242–47.

34. See Karl, *Uneasy State*, 217–18.

35. See Winkler, *Politics of Propaganda*, 54–56, 63–72.

36. Brinkley, *End of Reform*, 137–45; Karl, *Uneasy State*, 217.

37. See Richard Polenberg, *War and Society: The United States, 1941–1945* (Philadelphia: Lippincott, 1972), 81; Karl, *Uneasy State*, 221.

38. For Hull's rebuttal of Wallace, see Robert A. Divine, *Second Chance: The Triumph of Internationalism in America during World War II* (New York: Atheneum, 1967), 66–68; entry for February 16, 1943, Wallace, *Price of Vision*, 191.

39. White and Maze, *Wallace*, 174–79.

40. Quoted in Polenberg, *War and Society*, 73.

41. On this important point see Rodgers, *Atlantic Crossings*, 496–500.

42. See Brinkley, *End of Reform*, 246–55 (with *The Nation* quotation on 254); Markowitz, *People's Century*, 59–62; Karl, *Uneasy State*, 214.

43. See Burns, *Soldier of Freedom*, 422–24.

44. See Foner, *Story of American Freedom*, 233–34.

45. Rosenman, *Working with Roosevelt*, 383–84, 391.

46. See Chester Bowles, *Promises to Keep: My Years in Public Life, 1941–1969* (New York: Harper & Row, 1971), 117–20; Rosenman, *Working with Roosevelt*, 417–27; Markowitz, *People's Century*, 83–86; Burns, *Soldier of Freedom*, 424–26.

47. Entry for March 10, 1944, Wallace, *Price of Vision*, 313. See also Karl's comment: "By 1944 Roosevelt's leadership in domestic policy had become pure form; his authority was reduced to management of the war. There was little suggestion of direction for the future." *Uneasy State*, 222.

48. See Wallace, *Price of Vision*, 367–72; Blum, *V Was for Victory*, 289–91.

49. Quoted in White and Maze, *Wallace*, 204.

50. See Brinkley, *End of Reform*, 154–60; Foner, *Story of American Freedom*, 235–6.

51. Brinkley, *End of Reform*, 160–64, with Niebuhr quotation on 161.

52. Katznelson, *Fear Itself*, 375–80.

53. Entry for August 3, 1944, Wallace, *Price of Vision*, 374. On this revealing theme, see William E. Leuchtenburg, *In the Shadow of FDR: From Harry Truman to Ronald Reagan*, rev. ed. (Ithaca, NY: Cornell University Press, 1983), 18–25.

54. See Blum, *V Was for Victory*, 329–32.

55. Entry for November 6, 1946, Adolf A. Berle, *Navigating the Rapids, 1918–1971: From the Papers of Adolf A. Berle*, ed. Beatrice Bishop Berle and Travis Beal Jacobs (New York: Harcourt Brace Jovanovich, 1973), 574–75.

56. For UNRRA see William I. Hitchcock, *The Bitter Road to Freedom: A New History of the Liberation of Europe* (New York: Free Press, 2008), 211–48, with the Lehman quotation on 218.

57. On this point see David Ekbladh, *The Great American Mission: Modernization and the Construction of an American World Order* (Princeton, NJ: Princeton University Press, 2010), 87, 116–17.

58. See ibid., 80–86. For Ekbladh's original formulation, see his sweeping and suggestive article " 'Mr. TVA': Grass-Roots Development, David Lilienthal, and the Rise and Fall of the Tennessee Valley Authority as a Symbol of US Overseas Development, 1933–1973,' *Diplomatic History*, 26, no. 3 (2002): 335–74, with Wallace's advocacy noted at 347.

59. Bowles, *Promises to Keep*, 245–46; and see in general Howard B. Schaffer, *Chester Bowles: New Dealer in the Cold War* (Cambridge, MA: Harvard University Press, 1993).

60. Inaugural address, 20 January 1949, as quoted in Ekbladh, *Great American Mission*, 77–78.

61. See Ekbladh, "Mr. TVA," 349.

62. Quoted in Nick Cullather, *The Hungry World: America's Cold War Battle Against Poverty in Asia* (Cambridge, MA: Harvard University Press, 2010), 109.

63. On the background to Point Four see Clark Clifford with Richard Holbrooke, *Counsel to the President: A Memoir* (New York: Random House, 1991), 248–52.

64. See Thomas G. Paterson, "Beginning to Meet the Threat in the Third World: The Point Four Program," in *Meeting the Communist Threat: Truman to Reagan* (New York: Oxford University Press, 1988), 147–58.

65. See Cullather, *Hungry World*, 72–77.

66. Chester Bowles, *Ambassador's Report* (New York: Harper, 1954), 323–24.

67. See Ekbladh, *Great American Mission*, 91–102.

68. See William Conrad Gibbons, *The US Government and the Vietnam War: Executive and Legislative Roles and Relationships*, vol. 1, *1945–1960* (Princeton, NJ: Princeton University Press, 1986), 68–70.

69. See Burton I. Kaufman, *Trade and Aid: Eisenhower's Foreign Economic Policy, 1953–1961* (Baltimore: Johns Hopkins University Press, 1982).

70. See Ekbladh, *Great American Mission*, 153–57.

71. Odd Arne Westad, *The Global Cold War: Third World Interventions and the Making of Our Times* (Cambridge, UK: Cambridge University Press, 2005), 30–32.

72. See Westad, *Global Cold War*, 66–68.

73. Bowles, *Ambassador's Report*, 401–2.

74. See Cullather, *Hungry World*, 77–91.

75. See Nils Gilman, *Mandarins of the Future: Modernization Theory in Cold War America* (Baltimore: Johns Hopkins University Press, 2003), 190–98.

76. See Laura Belmonte, "Selling Capitalism: Modernization and U.S. Overseas Propaganda, 1945–1959," in *Staging Growth: Modernization, Development, and the Global Cold War*, ed. David C. Engerman, Nils Gilman, Mark H. Haefele, and Michael E. Latham (Amherst: University of Massachusetts Press, 2003), 107–28.

77. See William Taubman, *Khrushchev: The Man and His Era* (London: W. W. Norton, 2003), 417–18.

78. See Maurice Isserman, *The Other American: The Life of Michael Harrington* (New York: PublicAffairs, 2000), 177–81.

79. Theodore White, *The Making of the President, 1960* (New York: Atheneum, 1961), 106.
80. Isserman, *Other American*, 191; see also Petra Dolata-Kreutzkamp, "Kennedy and Central Appalachia: Fighting Unemployment and Poverty," in *John F. Kennedy and the "Thousand Days": New Perspectives on the Foreign and Domestic Policies of the Kennedy Administration*, ed. Manfred Berg and Andreas Etges (Heidelberg: Winter, 2007), 242–60.
81. Isserman, *Other American*, 195–98; see also Allen J. Matusow, *The Unraveling of America: A History of Liberalism in the 1960s* (New York: Harper & Row, 1984), 218–21.
82. See William Issel, *Social Change in the United States, 1945–1983* (Basingstoke: Macmillan, 1985), 140.
83. See James L. Sundquist, *Politics and Policy: The Eisenhower, Kennedy, and Johnson Years* (Washington, DC: Brooking Institution, 1968), 112–14; Arthur Schlesinger, Jr., *A Thousand Days: John F. Kennedy in the White House* (Boston: Houghton Mifflin, 1965), 1009; Dolata-Kreutzkamp, "Kennedy and Central Appalachia," 256–57.
84. Lyndon B. Johnson, *The Vantage Point: Perspectives of the Presidency, 1963–1969* (New York: Holt, Rinehart, & Winston, 1971), 104.
85. See Sundquist, *Politics and Policy*, 134–54.
86. See, for example, Ekbladh, *Great American Mission*, 228–29.
87. Special Message to Congress on Foreign Aid, March 22, 1961, *Public Papers of the Presidents, John F. Kennedy*, vol. 1, *1961* (Washington, DC: US Government Printing Office, 1962), 204–6.
88. See Michael E. Latham, *Modernization as Ideology: American Social Science and "Nation Building" in the Kennedy Era* (Chapel Hill: University of North Carolina Press, 2000), 122–33; Cullather, *Hungry World*, 91–92.
89. As quoted in Walter S. McDougall, *Promised Land, Crusader State: The American Encounter with the World Since 1776* (Boston: Houghton Mifflin, 1997), 172.
90. On the fascinating story of IR-8 in Asia and its connections to American ideas of modernization, see Cullather, *Hungry World*, 159–79.
91. Cullather, *Hungry World*, 239–52.
92. See Schlesinger, *Thousand Days*, 596–99.
93. Patrick Dean to Michael Stewart, September 30, 1965, CAB 21/5552, National Archives, Kew, London.
94. Cullather, *Hungry World*, 255.
95. Lucian W. Pye, "Foreign Aid and America's Involvement in the Developing World," in *The Vietnam Legacy: The War, American Society and the Future of American Foreign Policy*, ed. Anthony Lake (New York, 1976), 374–75. On the decline of modernization theory in the late 1960s and early 1970s, see Gilman, *Mandarins of the Future*, 242–55.
96. See Westad, *Global Cold War*, 358–60.
97. See Ekbladh, *Great American Mission*, 234–38.
98. Godfrey Hodgson, *More Equal than Others: America from Nixon to the New Century* (Princeton, NJ: Princeton University Press, 2004), 273, 282.
99. James T. Patterson, *America's Struggle against Poverty, 1900–1994* (Cambridge, MA: Harvard University Press, 1994), 157.
100. See the strong critique in Matusow, *Unraveling of America*, 240–71.
101. Patteson, *America's Struggle*, 161.

102. See Patterson, *America's Struggle*, 212.

103. Patterson, *America's Struggle*, 225–26.

104. Data from this paragraph is drawn from Hodgson, *More Equal than Others*, 90–94, 99, 291.

105. Ira Katznelson, "Was the Great Society a Lost Opportunity?" in *The Rise and Fall of the New Deal Order, 1930–1980*, ed. , Steve Fraser and Gary Gerstle (Princeton, NJ: Princeton University Press, 1989), 187.

106. See Foner, *Story of American Freedom*, 320–23; Sean Wilentz, *The Age of Reagan: A History, 1974–2008* (New York: Harper, 2009), 127–28, 283–84.

107. See Hodgson, *More Equal Than Others*, 22–30.

Freedom from Fear. Franklin D. Roosevelt Presidential Library and Museum, 1930. Hyde Park, New York.

CHAPTER 5

Freedom from Fear

FRANK COSTIGLIOLA

WHAT COULD FRANKLIN D. ROOSEVELT as a person know about freedom of speech and religion or about freedom from want? Although his political ideas generated some vehement opposition, he was never blocked from saying what he wanted. Nor did this vestryman in the Episcopal Church, the closest thing twentieth-century America had to an established religion, ever fear repression of his faith. Born into an old money Hudson River Valley family, he never experienced material want. Roosevelt did, however, suffer fear, indeed terror, in an intensely personal way.[1] For two years after he contracted polio and suffered paralysis of his legs at age thirty-nine, he despaired that he would never again lead an active life. There were days when it took him till noon to master his feelings enough that he could paste on a smile and leave his room. Terrified that he might remain helpless, Roosevelt responded with a vigorous, at times brutal, regimen of physical therapy to mobilize the potential in his remaining muscles. He endured painful falls as he hobbled on crutches back and forth along the long driveway at his Hyde Park estate. His paralysis aggravated a phobia, stemming from his childhood witnessing of a cousin burning to death, of being trapped in a fire. He responded to that fear by practicing, again and again, the drill of dropping from his chair or bed onto the floor, crawling backwards across the room and then down the stairs. After his triumphant return to politics, as governor of New York State in 1928–32

165

and then as president in 1933, Roosevelt choreographed his public appearances so as to downplay the paralysis of his legs while displaying his muscular upper torso.

Roosevelt's personal ordeal sharpened his appreciation of the political utility of fear. While shapeless fear was paralyzing, he knew that focused fear, the kind he experienced in spades after contracting polio, could mobilize action. He put this knowledge to good use. Roosevelt as president underscored dangers, indeed at times exaggerated them, in order to energize and discipline Americans into combating the Depression and the dictators. Subsequent presidents would similarly mobilize and at times instigate fear in order to get Americans to accept their foreign policy agendas. Freedom from fear, then, was more than merely one of Roosevelt's four aims outlined in January of 1941. Freedom from fear instead underlay his entire call to arms in response to the growing Nazi threat, a tactic employed, repeatedly, by American presidents ever since.

Although FDR in his Four Freedoms speech pledged to free Americans from fear, neither he nor his successors have made good on that promise. What America does abroad influences the level of fear at home. At play is a basic dilemma. Since 1941, US leaders have engaged with the messy affairs of the world to pursue American military, political, and economic interests. They have tried, not always consistently, to promote freedom of speech and religion and freedom from want and fear in other countries. The United States has accordingly taken on difficult responsibilities, gotten entangled in intractable regional disputes, and succumbed in many instances to the temptations of power and empire. This entanglement in hot, cold, and covert wars has yielded a mixed record of successes and failures. What this involvement in world affairs has undoubtedly failed to produce for Americans, however, is true freedom from fear. Despite the trillions of dollars spent and the hundreds of thousands of lives lost in the pursuit of national security, America's global role has not eliminated, but rather has multiplied, the fears of the American people regarding dangers at home and abroad. Most of the presidents who came after Roosevelt followed his precedent of enlisting and even promoting public fears to mobilize support for their agendas. The Cold War and the post-9/11 "War on Terror" nurtured the symbiotic relationship between public anxiety and presidential power that is part of the mixed legacy of Franklin D. Roosevelt.

Ironically, Roosevelt personified the basic dilemma. In his Four Freedoms speech, he interpreted "freedom from fear" to mean "a world-wide reduction of armaments to such a point ... that no nation will be in a position to commit an act of physical aggression ... anywhere in the world."[2] Yet he made that pitch for eventual disarmament in the context of urging a ramping up of US weapons production for national rearmament and for supplying Britain and China. Resolving that contradiction was a challenge that even a political wizard like FDR might not have been able to accomplish. The stratagem was to arm sufficiently so as to beat the Axis, secure a peace conducive to the big powers limiting their weapons, and then, finally and with the most difficulty, muster the wisdom and will to step back from military predominance. Making that trick even tougher was the widespread belief, which Roosevelt shared, in American exceptionalism.

America's broad freedoms stand out as a marker of that supposedly exceptional status. Roosevelt appreciated freedom of speech and religion and freedom from want and fear as core American values and as key elements of US ideology. He understood that "freedom" ranked as the most powerful word in the American political lexicon.[3] FDR crafted his January 6, 1941, Four Freedoms speech as an ideological rebuttal to Nazi Germany and Fascist Italy, which stood astride most of Western Europe by this point in the war, and Japan, which had conquered most of China and was menacing Southeast Asia. The Axis powers were boasting that their New Order promised greater political and economic vitality than the supposedly worn out ideology of democratic capitalism. Also asserting they had a better system were the Communists, who were in charge in Moscow, claimed loyal party members throughout much of the world, and were loosely aligned with Germany following a Soviet-German accord in 1939. Giving credence to these claims was the failure of Roosevelt's New Deal to restore the US economy to full employment. During the Great Depression, democracy and capitalism themselves appeared at risk; indeed, they were viewed by many as systems whose best days were in the past. Fascism and communism, with their command control by the state, appeared ascendant as economic strife persisted through Roosevelt's first two terms. Glowing prosperity returned only in 1940–41 as weapons production soared. Defying the ideological and military challenge of the Axis, Roosevelt's rubric of the Four Freedoms insisted on the continuing vibrancy of American ideals and institutions and their relevance as a model for the world.

In reaffirming an American ideology of freedom in his January 1941 State of the Union address, FDR sketched an outline that was filled in only weeks later by publisher Henry Luce in his influential "American Century" essay in *Life* magazine. Luce insisted that although Americans opposed entering the conflict, "We are, for a fact," he wrote, "*in* the war."[4] He ascribed the aversion to war as stemming not only from a reluctance to kill and be killed, but also from "the fear that if we get into this war, it will be the end of our constitutional democracy."[5] Americans might nevertheless preserve their freedoms if they transformed the war into a crusade for spreading the tenets of their way of life: free elections, "free economic enterprise," and free choice by consumers. In grandiloquent terms, Luce urged Americans, as citizens of the world's foremost military, political, economic, and cultural power, to "share with all peoples our Bill of Rights, our Declaration of Independence, our Constitution, our magnificent industrial products, our technical skills."[6] Revitalizing the crusade of Woodrow Wilson a generation earlier, Luce prodded Americans to "create the first great American Century."[7] Despite the pledge by Roosevelt and by Luce that an American century would secure freedom of speech and religion and freedom from want and fear for the nation and for much of the world, that aim was only partly realized in subsequent decades. The greatest failure was in securing freedom from fear.

And yet it is freedom from fear for which FDR is best remembered, at least in the popular imagination. The coffee mug featured at the Franklin D. Roosevelt Presidential Library in Hyde Park, New York, is inscribed with the peroration from FDR's first inaugural address on March 4, 1933: "The only thing we have to fear is fear itself." A 2014 Google search yielded forty-six million references to this famous phrase, versus six million for "a day which will live in infamy" and two million for "rendezvous with destiny." In that iconic 1933 speech, Roosevelt did not target all fear—rather only "nameless, unreasoning, unjustified terror which paralyzes needed efforts to turn retreat into advance." After stressing the seriousness of the economic crisis, the new president employed military metaphors to underscore his approach: The nation had "to turn retreat into advance.... We must move forward as a trained and loyal army willing to sacrifice." He warned in 1933, as unemployment soared and the American economy sank into its fourth year of depression, that, if need be, he would ask Congress for "broad Executive power to wage a war against the [economic] emergency."[8] Drawing an analogy between the economic crisis and war allowed him to justify extraordinary executive power while also legitimizing the federal government's intervention in an arena that many Americans thought should remain the private domain of businesses and individuals. Given America's limited tradition of reform and the nervousness that many citizens felt about a leviathan state, depicting the Depression as a war seemed the only way to forge the consensus needed for aggressive federal action.[9]

In insisting that Americans confront the looming crisis in Europe and Asia in the late 1930s and early 1940s, Roosevelt returned to the strategy he had pursued in 1933. Once again he stoked and mobilized fear to advance a vigorous plan of action. For example, in his annual message to Congress on January 4, 1939—months before Hitler violated the Munich agreement by taking over the remainder of Czechoslovakia or began threatening Poland—FDR used repetition and vivid language to accentuate fears of the threat from abroad. He warned Americans: "All about us rage undeclared wars— military and economic. All about us grow more deadly armaments— military and economic. All about us are threats of new aggression—military and economic." Enemy control of vital markets and sources of raw materials could strangle America's economy. Moreover, the nation's ocean moats no longer sufficed as protection. "The world has grown so small and weapons of attack so swift that no nation can be safe." In August 1940, by which time Hitler had conquered most of Western Europe and the Japanese were menacing Southeast Asia, Roosevelt told Americans that whereas in 1917 we "were completely safe from any attack, that will never happen again in the history of the United States." He added, "If the United States is to have any defense, it must have total defense."[10]

As he had in fighting the Great Depression, Roosevelt enlisted the fears of Americans. The president had in mind more than merely justifying increased spending for warships, airplanes, and the expanding army. He aimed also to link the domestic achievements of the New Deal with his foreign and military goals. He told Americans that New Deal reforms had fostered "internal preparedness" to meet foreign challenges. He also sought to expand traditional notions of territorial and economic defense into a new focus on "national security." National security was a far broader concept that justified both the integration of domestic and foreign policy aims and the pursuit of a vigorous role in regions far beyond the United States and its territories. Finally, Roosevelt stressed the importance of technology as simultaneously a problem and a solution. While advanced weaponry imperiled the United States, Americans had a natural predilection for developing even more advanced weapons with which to protect the homeland and, if necessary, fight the enemy. Although advances in aviation meant that foreign bombers might reach America, the United States, Roosevelt insisted, could produce more and better airplanes than the dictatorships.[11] With regard to technology as in other arenas, practices and ideas that developed in 1940–41 would prove a precedent for the Cold War. Roosevelt tried to manage Americans' fears of ever more deadly weapons by assuring them that they could maintain the lead in a technological arms race.

Despite FDR's efforts to mobilize fears of an Axis victory, most Americans feared going to war even more. The prospect of a totalitarian-dominated world seemed real but still theoretical; war meant that many American boys were sure to die in far-off lands. Sentiment for keeping the United States out of the conflict therefore remained stubbornly strong throughout the country and in Congress. Mindful of these political winds, the president was careful to justify the sending of weapons and other materiel to the Allies (under the Lend-Lease program) by arguing that if the United States served as the "arsenal of democracy," Britons, Chinese, and Russians would do the actual fighting and dying. As France tried to resist the invading Germans in June 1940, Americans by a striking 77–17 percent margin opposed entering the fray.[12] The spectacle of Nazi troops goose-stepping through the Arc de Triumph after France surrendered on June 22, 1940, only hardened Americans' reluctance to fight. The proportion favoring entry into the war slumped to 11 percent, with an overwhelming 79 percent opposed.[13] Hitler seemed invincible, and the costs of defeating him too high to contemplate. Even in December 1945, with the carnage now over and the United States triumphant in Europe and in the Pacific, Americans by a ten-to-one margin still believed that Roosevelt in 1940–41 "should have been trying to keep us out of the war" rather than "trying to get us in."[14]

Despite their not wanting to fight, Americans largely dreaded a Nazi victory. In December 1940, only weeks before FDR's Four Freedoms speech, polls showed that Americans by a 60–32 percent margin worried that if Germany and Italy defeated Britain, the aggressors would provoke a war with the United States.[15] Nearly three-quarters feared that even if the United States stayed at peace, a German triumph would affect them personally.[16] Defeating Germany seemed yet more crucial than staying out of the war, Americans by a 55–41 percent margin agreed.[17] Nevertheless, Americans by a decisive 85–12 percent split still feared entering the war.[18] Of those opposed to fighting, 69 percent remained against even if a US victory were assured.[19]

How could this be? How could the people of the United States both believe that Germany had to be defeated and yet resist participation in the war? The answer is twofold. First, memories of World War I lingered, especially in the broad sense of disappointment that the American war effort and losses, endured in hope of a better world safe for democracy, had seemed for naught. Second, and more important, Americans in 1939–41 told themselves that their suffering and dying to defeat Hitler were not necessary because Britain, armed with US weapons and supplies, could win the war on its own. This was optimism bordering on fantasy. As England stood virtually alone against the Nazi armies that had swept across most of Western Europe, Americans by an astonishing 70–9 percent margin professed confidence that Britain would defeat Germany without the United States entering the war. This rose-colored view stemmed in part from Roosevelt's assuring Americans that their material aid would enable a British win. FDR stressed that argument to stifle charges that he was sending scarce war materiel to a lost cause. This assumption, that the United States could secure the defeat of the enemy without suffering either destruction of the homeland or horrific casualties, would in ensuing decades shape how Americans balanced their fears and ambitions regarding US actions on the world stage. Roosevelt, a superb politician who won six straight electoral victories from 1928 to 1944, understood that while he could not directly challenge Americans' opposition to entering the war, he had to mobilize their fears of the Axis in order to step up aid to Britain and other opponents of the Axis. He could not allow the fear of war to lead to isolationism or to attempts to settle with Nazi Germany. Roosevelt warned that appeasing the dictators would yield neither peace nor security.

Regarding the Four Freedoms address, Roosevelt's main speechwriter later recalled that the president "worked on it very hard" through all seven drafts.[20] FDR wanted to get across three lessons while reaffirming American ideals. His first lesson emphasized the extraordinary extent of the danger: "At no previous time has American security been as seriously threatened from without as it is today," he wrote. Each time the speech was redrafted, the language was strengthened by accentuating the urgency of the peril.[21] His second lesson was that Americans should act on their concerns by engaging in concrete activities, specifically accelerating armaments production, delivering weapons to the British and Chinese on the basis of what Congress would pass in March 1941 as the Lend-Lease Act, and having all major interest groups—business, labor, and agriculture—set aside their differences for the duration of the war. In an implicit nod to the opposition of a vast majority of Americans to entering the war, FDR emphasized that while the Allies needed "billions of dollars' worth of the weapons of defense," they did "not need manpower." He reinforced the comforting notion that Americans could help defeat the Axis without having to fight. Roosevelt's third lesson addressed what he called "the social and economic problems which are the root cause of the social revolution which is today a supreme factor in the world." He urged an expansion of the New Deal in order to make medical care available to all, bring more people into the social security system, secure full employment, and enhance equal opportunity. Americans could improve the world, he promised, even as they formed a more perfect union at home.

In this context of envisioning a better world for all, Roosevelt concluded the speech with his peroration pledging freedom of speech and religion and freedom from want and fear—"everywhere in the world." Underscoring his ideological challenge to the Axis, FDR pitted the "good society" of the four freedoms against "the so-called new order of tyranny" of the dictators. He saw the battle over ideals as a global one: "Freedom means the supremacy of human rights everywhere."[22]

For millions of Americans, these ideas came alive through Norman Rockwell's paintings of the Four Freedoms. Rockwell's images were first published in the *Saturday Evening Post* in 1943 and then printed on millions of war bond posters. They have circulated ever since as icons of an idealized America. Struggling for a way to bring the abstractions down to earth, Rockwell suddenly had an inspiration at three in the morning: "I'll illustrate the Four Freedoms using my Vermont neighbors as models. I'll express the ideas in simple, everyday scenes."[23] "Freedom from Fear," an unused *Post* cover painted in 1940 during the German bombing of London, depicts a middle class couple checking on their two sleeping children before they turn in for the night. The mother adjusts the bed sheet covering the children while the father in shirt sleeves and suspenders looks on. He is holding a folded *Bennington Banner* with the partially visible headline "Bombing Ki . . . Horror Hit." The irony here is that what succeeded as a war poster originated as an illustration of pre–Pearl Harbor sentiment that America could and should stay out of the war. Rockwell later recalled that " 'Freedom from Fear' was based on a rather smug idea." The message was: "Thank God we can put our children to bed with a feeling of security, knowing that they will not be killed in the night." He later admitted, "I never liked 'Freedom from Fear.' "[24] Despite Rockwell's misgiving about the painting, millions of Americans took this and the other three illustrations to heart. Thousands of praise-filled letters poured into the *Post*, including one from the president of the Pioneer Suspender Company, who wrote of the father standing by the children's bedside: "Of course he has freedom from fear. His trousers are held up by a pair of our suspenders."[25]

In contrast to Rockwell's depiction of freedom from fear as an essentially domestic matter of safeguarding homes and families, Roosevelt's Four Freedoms speech sketched a context of high politics and international relations. In ensuing decades, the failure of US leaders to secure freedom from fear in the domain of world politics would aggravate dangers that instilled fear in the homes of Americans. FDR in effect foreshadowed that failure when he called in his address for both an increase in weapons production and an eventual reduction of such arms.[26] Did Roosevelt really intend that the United States would also drastically disarm? While he might have believed that such universal disarmament was possible in the long run—and though he had argued for arms reductions in the 1920s and early 1930s—by the 1940s he expected that for at least the immediate postwar period the United States would retain significant military forces, especially in air and naval power.

Moreover, by mid-1942 FDR was moving away from Luce's American Century vision of US unilateral predominance. Reflecting the military reality that Russia was emerging as a major European power, Roosevelt increasingly envisioned a postwar peace in which the Four Policemen—the United States, Russia, Britain, and perhaps China—would collaborate after the war. The four would keep their arms to enforce the peace (and, if necessary, discipline smaller nations) following the defeat of Germany and Japan.[27] And indeed, although the United States after World War II demobilized much of its army, it still maintained the greatest navy and air force in the world and a global system of naval and air bases. It also possessed a terrifying new weapon, the atomic bomb.[28]

Fear of the unleashed power of this deadly device dulled Americans' joy at the surrender of Japan in August 1945. In reporting that an atomic bomb had destroyed Hiroshima, H. V. Kaltenborn, the dean of radio news commentators exclaimed: "We have created a Frankenstein!" He was afraid that the weapon would "be turned against us."[29] Edward R. Murrow, made famous by his broadcasts from London under the Blitz, observed that Americans, despite their overwhelming victory, displayed "uncertainty and fear" about their very survival.[30] Still another arbiter of informed opinion, *Time* magazine, asserted that the titanic world war had suddenly shrunk to "minor significance." The hard-fought triumph now seemed the "most Pyrrhic of victories."[31] In its "Man of the Year" cover, *Time* depicted Harry S. Truman dwarfed by a mushroom cloud, explaining that in the "giant shadow" of the bomb "even Presidents, even Men of the Year" ranked as "pygmies."[32] Atomic warfare threatened the most painful encounter imaginable between technology and corporality. The theologian Reinhold Niebuhr believed that the "strange disquiet" and "very great apprehension" ignited by the bomb seemed most intense among "the more sober and thoughtful sections of our nation."[33] Niebuhr no doubt had observed how American business was responding to the shock of the bomb. Within days of the Hiroshima attack stores were running "atomic sales," while radio stations were broadcasting "Atomic Polka." The General Mills Corporation offered kids an "atomic bomb ring" for fifteen cents and a cereal box top. Three-quarters of a million American children ordered a toy that promised to display "genuine atoms SPLIT to smithereens."[34]

Amidst the hoopla and the warnings at war's end, many ordinary Americans remained uncertain whether to dread or welcome the future. They understood that the development of planes like the B-17 Flying Fortress, B-24 Liberator, and the B-29 Superfortress, each long-range bombers that US forces had used to pulverize Germany and Japan, could in enemy hands cross America's ocean moats. The Germans' development of the V-2 rocket made inevitable the deadly marriage of the ballistic missile and the atomic bomb. Polls taken in late 1945 found that the overall mood of Americans was one of "awe, fear, cynicism, confusion, hope—but mostly fear and hopeful confusion." Over half the public expressed confidence that America's scientists, "these great master-minds," would soon develop an effective defense against the atomic bomb.[35] A majority were also open to international control of the bomb. In October 1945, Americans by a nearly three to one margin favored having the major world nations ban using the bomb in war.[36] Even as the Cold War was breaking out in 1946, three-quarters of Americans approved allowing international atomic inspectors to "search any property in any country," including the United States.[37] Although the Cold War soon dashed hopes for such international control, Americans remained generally receptive to atomic agreements with Moscow if they could be made enforceable.

Americans also remained susceptible to manipulation by political leaders who appreciated that fear could mobilize action. Strategists perceived a growing communist threat in the aftermath of war, yet the Republican-controlled Congress was in no mood to fund expensive international aid programs so soon after voting unprecedented sums for World War II. Eager to aid anticommunist forces in Europe, President Truman followed the advice of Senator Arthur Vandenberg, Republican of Michigan, who told him in 1947 that if he wanted to get Congress to approve funding for aid to Greece and Turkey, the president had to "scare hell out of the American people." Truman used that tactic successfully. Congress voted for the Truman Doctrine. Truman again stoked fear to push congressional approval of the stalled Marshall Plan bill, which provided billions of dollars for Western Europe to rebuild its economy and resist communism. The resulting anxiety in the country, aggravated by the Russians' explosion of an atomic bomb in 1949 and the victory of Mao Zedong in China that same year, established an emotional context in which Senator Joseph McCarthy, Republican of Wisconsin, could plausibly claim that the State Department was riddled with twin security risks, "political perverts" and "sexual perverts." Fear had become the emotion through which elites managed public life and adherents of traditional values policed perceived transgressors.[38]

In February 1950, the month that Senator McCarthy made national headlines with his claim (false, as it would turn out) to have a list of 205 card-carrying Communists employed by the State Department, an official of that agency boasted of having fired ninety-one homosexuals because they were, by definition, security risks. The ensuing witch hunt would drive thousands of loyal Americans from their jobs. Like the better known Red Scare, the parallel Lavender Scare additionally fed on older prejudices and fears. "Can [you] think of a person who could be more dangerous to the United States of America than a pervert?" a Senator challenged his colleagues.[39] Truman's advisers warned that "the country is more concerned about the charges of homosexuals in the Government than about Communists."[40] Queried about the most salient reason why a government employee might be labeled a security risk, Americans chose, first, "belief in communism" and, second, "questionable moral character," which was code for homosexuality. Farther down the list and apparently less dangerous were those "suspected of sabotage or espionage."[41] Public obsession with rooting homosexuals and a handful of communists or former communists out of government, the universities, Hollywood, and elsewhere was probably, at least in part, a displacement of anxiety about nuclear attack from Communist Russia. This latter threat was neither imaginary nor susceptible to management by scapegoating hapless Americans.

Even if Americans dismissed the supposed threat of "security risks" and the actual threat of atomic war, they could not escape the hazards created by the US government in the name of national security. Between 1951 and 1963, when nuclear tests were moved underground, some one hundred atomic weapons were exploded in the Nevada desert. Despite the hush-hush secrecy, the tests became public spectacles. In one eleven-day period, the military set off five bombs, the largest of which was felt 250 miles away in Los Angeles and seen in Boise, which was five hundred miles distant. Local television stations broadcast the flash, while the shock wave shattered windows in Las Vegas. The *New York Times* quoted an airline pilot who reported from his "balcony seat" that "it was just like the sun exploding. All of Nevada looked like it was on fire." He concluded, "It was a frightening thing, really terrifying, far worse looking than anything I had imagined."[42]

Radioactive fallout brought home the deadly dangers of the atomic age. People were being exposed to rays that could sicken, kill, and spur mutations. In 1954, a US hydrogen-bomb test poisoned a seven-thousand-square-mile swath of the Pacific Ocean with radioactive fallout. Changes in wind direction exposed more than twenty Americans working at a weather station and hundreds of Marshall Islanders to dangerous levels of radiation. The disaster blew up into an international incident when the captain of the *Lucky Dragon*, a Japanese tuna trawler fishing twenty miles outside the US-designated danger zone, reported that "about 90 minutes after the blast snow-white ashes began falling all around [his] ship."[43] The showering continued for two hours, resulting in the death of one crewman and sickness in the others. The uproar grew louder once the Japanese realized that the highly radioactive tuna aboard the trawler had been allowed to enter their food supply. The tuna catch of other trawlers in the test area also set Geiger counters clicking. Fish, a major component of the Japanese diet, rotted in the stores as panicked consumers refused to buy it. Coming only nine years after the Hiroshima and Nagasaki bombings, the fallout incident sparked anti-American street demonstrations. In his report to Washington, the US ambassador underscored that holding fast in the Cold War meant accepting such atomic perils, but the Japanese "government and the people cracked," he complained.[44] The Japanese were mollified neither by President Eisenhower's offer of a $2 million indemnity nor by the US Atomic Energy Commission blithe assertion that the fish were safe to eat. That assurance lost all credibility when tuna canners in California refused to buy Japanese-caught fish registering even the slightest level of radioactivity.[45]

Popular culture reflected and reinforced anxiety about atomic radiation. Media companies became adept at playing on such fears to generate excitement and profits. Japanese moviemakers introduced Godzilla, a prehistoric monster supposedly brought to life by radioactivity stemming from Hiroshima and Nagasaki. The story struck a chord. An American version soon appeared and then a series of sixteen Godzilla films. A top-grossing movie of 1954 was *Them*, which depicts a rapidly breeding colony of eight-foot-long human-eating ants burrowed near the site of the first atomic bomb test. As the breathless drama of the film's trailer indicated, the perils of the atomic age could thrill as well as frighten: "Born in that swirling inferno of radioactive dust were things so horrible, so terrifying, so hideous there is no word to describe THEM."[46] Just as mated pairs of the giant ants are about to fly off to start new colonies, the US military finally manages to incinerate them. The Oscar-nominated film ends on an ominous note:

GRAHAM: If these monsters got started as a result of the *first* atom bomb in 1945, what about all the other ones that have been exploded since then?

MEDFORD: When man entered the atomic age he opened a door to a new world. What we'll eventually find in that new world nobody can predict.[47]

The surge in claimed sightings of UFOs, notably the uproar over the supposed crash landing of an alien space ship in Roswell, New Mexico, probably reflected similar anxieties about technology's evil spawn. Despite repeated denials by the US government, conspiracy buffs and others continued to believe that military authorities were not only covering up the crash but had killed or were holding captive the aliens from outer space.[48]

Cold War America seemed to accept fearfulness as an inescapable state of mind. Even taking into account such indisputably frightening elements as the atomic bomb, Americans seemed impelled to embrace fear. Fear seeped into diverse aspects of American life. Many men and some women fretted about women moving beyond the domestic sphere and into public life.[49] Much of the population worried about the supposed security threat posed by a handful of communist or gay Americans, by far-off Vietnamese guerrillas, and even by rock 'n' roll–loving "juvenile delinquents."[50]

Washington incorporated fear into its principal strategy for deterring a possible Soviet nuclear attack. The US military establishment amassed an arsenal of thousands of atomic weapons that could be launched against the Soviet Union with long-range bombers, undetectable submarines, or land-based missiles. The strategic reasoning was that no matter how badly the United States was hurt by a Soviet first strike, this triad of nuclear forces would retain the capability to launch a retaliatory strike obliterating the Soviet Union. With this doctrine of mutual assured destruction (MAD), US leaders and defense strategists enshrined fear at the core of national security policy.[51]

The American people responded to the threat of all-out nuclear war in often contradictory ways. Albert Einstein observed that "most people go on living their everyday life: half frightened, half indifferent."[52] Many Americans remained confident that their leaders would protect them and the nation's best interests. Such faith would be weakened by the anti–Vietnam War protests of the 1960s, the Watergate scandal of the 1970s, and President Ronald Reagan's saber-rattling in the 1980s. Americans also implicitly trusted in the old saw that God took special care of children, drunks, and the United States. Surely this exceptionalist nation would be spared the suffering that might befall less chosen nations. Still another source of comfort was the belief that the very destructiveness of nuclear weaponry militated against a third world war.[53] A mixture of confidence and wishful thinking encouraged Americans to accept the risks arising from Washington's policy of playing the world policeman and protecting the "free world." Nonetheless, anxiety spiked during times of crisis. In January 1951, after the American (and United Nations) forces suffered a humiliating defeat when "Red China" intervened in the Korean War, Americans by an astounding two-thirds margin feared that the United States was "in more danger now than it was in December 1941, when Pearl Harbor was attacked."[54] The near-panic level of fear stemmed from perceptions that not only were the communists a global threat, but these enemy forces had defeated—not just attacked, as at Pearl Harbor—Americans in battle. By 1951, moreover, Americans were burdened with far wider global commitments than at the time of the Japanese attack a decade earlier.

For most of the Cold War, Americans contained such fears by trusting in the technological and numerical superiority of US weaponry, the capability of the Navy and the Air Force to pummel the enemy far from US shores, and the willingness of allies to share in the fighting. Acutely aware of US might, the Kremlin backed down in crisis after crisis, from Iran in 1946, to Berlin in 1948–49, to Berlin again in 1958–1961, and most dramatically in the Cuban missile crisis in 1962. Observing this pattern of the Russians retreating, many Americans were emboldened to take an uncompromising stance in Cold War crises. During the Berlin crisis in 1959, for instance, Americans by a more than seven-to-one margin favored resisting Soviet pressures and remaining in West Berlin, even if that course ignited an armed conflict. This toughness was bolstered by the simultaneous belief that the crisis would end without war and without losing Berlin.[55]

Nevertheless, fear of dying in a nuclear World War III persisted. In 1956, 51 percent of Americans believed another world war would likely break out in their lifetime, while 27 percent did not expect such a war. Among Americans under age fifty, the proportion fearing such a war rose to 59 percent.[56] Asked in 1961 whether they "worried about atomic war," 59 percent answered they were very or fairly worried, while 38 percent were not at all worried. Atomic dread was to some extent gendered. While 51 percent of men acknowledged anxiety about a possible war, 65 percent of women did so.[57] As for surviving an atomic holocaust, only 5 percent of Americans rated their chances "very good." Thirty-seven percent chose "just 50–50," and a majority, fifty-two percent, "poor."[58] Four-fifths of Americans said they would be willing to donate their labor and or money to building community atomic fallout shelters, and two-thirds acknowledged that they had thought about what it would be like living in such a shelter.[59] The readiness to spend time and money building fallout shelters evidenced not only fear of nuclear war but also the partial success of an extensive US government program to manage the emotions of frightened Americans. In the late 1950s, Senator John F. Kennedy of Massachusetts stoked such fears as he ran for the Democratic nomination for president in 1960. Kennedy charged, falsely, that the Eisenhower administration had allowed the Soviet Union to surge ahead in the development of nuclear-weapon-carrying intercontinental ballistic missiles (ICBMs), and that Americans should fear the resulting "missile gap." Although it was the United States, in fact, that had more accurate and more numerous ICBMs, the Russians' success in launching

Sputnik, the first artificial satellite, enabled Kennedy to succeed with this scare campaign.

Meanwhile, Washington officials worried that efforts by the Federation of Atomic Scientists (mocked as the League of Frightened Men) and other peace groups to warn Americans about the horror of nuclear war might undercut the public's willingness to run the risk of nuclear war. In order to make the strategy of deterrence credible, the United States had to be willing to launch a nuclear war, or at least appear willing to do so. In January 1946, *Collier's* published an open letter to the American people written by the prominent physicist Harold Urey. Graphically describing the damage wreaked by the atomic bomb, Urey declared: "I'm a frightened man myself. All the scientists I know are frightened—frightened for their lives—and frightened for **your** life."[60] The US government pushed back with a strategy to transform supposedly irrational nuclear terror into the more rational and hence mobilizable nuclear fear. In 1953, the director of the newly created Federal Civil Defense Administration warned in a popular magazine article that it was not the atomic bomb but rather the nuclear terror induced by enemy attack that was "the ultimate weapon" that could defeat the United States. In communities across the nation, survivors of an atomic attack could descend into "a hungry pillaging mob—disrupting disaster relief, overwhelming local police and spreading panic in a widening arc."[61]

Governmental agencies contracted with social scientists on Project East River, a program to manage emotions so as to head off such panic. The voluminous report recommended blurring the line between conventional and nuclear weapons to make the latter appear less terrifying, encouraging such self-help-oriented civil defense activities as drills and the construction of family fallout shelters, and educating citizens about the bomb so that it would seem like a survivable danger. The government circulated twenty million copies of *Survival under Atomic Attack*, which explained that an atomic bomb was "just another way of causing an explosion." The booklet promised: "You can live through an atomic bomb raid and you won't have to have a Geiger counter, protective clothing, or special training in order to do it."[62] Basements provided protection from the blast, while those caught outside during an attack, the booklet advised, should "jump in any handy ditch or gutter." Most of those exposed to radiation would suffer little more than the equivalent of a bad sunburn. If sprayed with radioactive debris, take a good shower: "You can get rid of all the radioactive dirt you've picked up if you keep scrubbing."[63]

Among the contradictions in this effort to reduce terror through education was the fact, as an internal government report acknowledged, that "the greater the knowledge of nuclear fission phenomena, the greater the fear it engenders."[64] Project East River was yet another attempt by government officials and their allies in the private sector to manage and channel fear. In carrying out a policy of nuclear deterrence, Washington leaders and nuclear strategists aimed at stoking the Russians' fear of a US nuclear attack while not panicking the American public. Though FDR in January 1941 was no doubt sincere when he had promised Americans freedom from fear, the activist world policies he and his successors had pursued made fulfilling that pledge nearly impossible.

To mitigate panic, civil defense planners urged schools and other institutions to institute drills so that Americans would respond in an organized and disciplined way when under attack. As the East River report put it, "It is not whether you feel afraid, but what you do when you are afraid that counts. The fear you experience will make you more alert, stronger, and more tireless."[65] Fear could and should be mobilized. Typical was a drill at PS 75 in Manhattan, where Mrs. Bertha Smith suddenly gave her sixth grade class the "take cover" signal and students dove under their desks and curled into a ball with their backs to the window. "It's good to know that we are ready for anything," the principal explained. "It's like having money in the bank."[66] Merely doing something was more important than doing something actually effective. Another principal sent a note to parents: "In order to save your child from burns in the case of direct exposure to an A-Bomb," have "him or her bring to school a piece of sheet large enough for him to curl under."[67] While some children took all this in their stride, others were terrified. One asked, "Please, Mother, can't we go some place where there isn't any sky?"[68]

The administration of John F. Kennedy redoubled efforts to convince the Kremlin of America's willingness to run the risk of nuclear war, mobilize public anxieties for civil defense activities, and blunt dissent from nascent antinuclear groups, such as the National Committee for a Sane Nuclear Policy. During the height of the Berlin crisis in September 1961, a *Life* magazine cover ran the banner "A LETTER TO YOU FROM PRESIDENT KENNEDY. HOW YOU CAN SURVIVE FALLOUT. 97 OUT OF 100 PEOPLE CAN BE SAVED." Although Kennedy realized the claim about survival was wildly exaggerated, he refused to correct the record. One of Kennedy's more liberal advisers, the former Harvard historian Arthur M. Schlesinger, Jr., explained how civil defense was useful in channeling otherwise disruptive emotions: "Civil defense has become the focus for all anxieties over foreign policy. When people read about American and Russian [confrontation] they feel they can do something about it themselves—they can decide whether or not to build a fallout shelter."[69] The *Life* pictorial essay on shelters depicted a white, suburban, and patriarchal family, with Father bravely scanning the sky for danger while Mother busied herself with household chores and Sis sipped Coke and chatted on the phone.[70] The overarching message here was that while the Russians had to take care lest they provoke a US attack, and the American people had to take precautions while remaining calm, the traditional values and consumerist culture of the United States were adaptable to this more fearful age.

Kennedy's focus on fallout shelters fit his strategy of enlisting both excitement and fear in his effort to build up military forces and "get the country moving again." In January 1961, he went so far as to assert that the United States faced peril comparable to that of early 1942, a time when the Japanese had just sunk the US fleet at Pearl Harbor and Hitler stood astride most of Europe.[71] Although the president was exaggerating the actual danger faced in 1961, his effectiveness in evoking fear was enhanced by his reputation as an authority on such threats. In 1940, while still in his early twenties, he had published a bestseller, *Why England Slept*, about Britain's failure to meet the Nazi challenge in the late 1930s.

The escalation of the Cold War by Kennedy and by Soviet premier Nikita S. Khrushchev culminated in the October 1962 Cuban missile crisis. As the two superpowers grappled for advantage, millions of Americans feared a nuclear holocaust. The scare seared the memories of many children. A boy would remember years later that on the Sunday at the peak of the crisis, "Our church was packed," with nearly triple the usual number of worshippers. "Most were sad, many were crying, the fear could almost be felt."[72] A nine-year-old girl would "recall going down to our basement, curling up on an old red couch, and waiting in terror for the bomb to drop and end the world."[73] Children's imaginations could magnify the dangers. A girl was horrified when her mother set "a bottle of Wishbone brand Russian salad dressing on the supper table." She thought: "Why is my mother doing this? Why would she want to eat this?! The Russians have probably put poison in it!!"[74] Yet not all children were terrified. Some later boasted, "No one was scared"; "We would be fine: we were Texans!"[75]

Although in the aftermath of the crisis Kennedy put relations with the Kremlin on a safer and more stable basis, he also stepped up the US commitment to the unpopular government of South Vietnam, which was under attack from a largely indigenous revolt aided by communist North Vietnam. Escalated further by Kennedy's successor, Lyndon B. Johnson, America's war in Vietnam did much to undermine the certainty of the American people that their government was truthful, competent, and waged only necessary wars. The Watergate scandal of the 1970s further undermined trust in the presidency.

By the early 1980s, growing numbers of Americans were challenging Cold War verities that had gone unquestioned for decades. By increasing military spending and reviling the "evil empire," President Ronald Reagan raised fear levels to heights not seen since the early 1950s. By now, however, the willingness of the American people to risk nuclear war was on the decline. Even though a majority of voters chose Reagan as president in 1980, one-third of those polled feared "he would get us into a war."[76] By October 1983, 53 percent of Americans agreed that "the way Reagan is handling relations with the Russians is increasing the chances for war." Only 32 percent disagreed.[77] A month later, *The Day After*, a frightening television movie depicting the destruction of Lawrence, Kansas, in a nuclear war, was watched in its initial broadcast by some one hundred million Americans. After previewing the film, Reagan confided in his diary: "It's very effective & left me profoundly depressed."[78] The president was also disturbed upon learning that Kremlin leaders mistakenly believed that an elaborate NATO war game was actually a rehearsal for an all-out nuclear attack on the Soviet Union. The Soviets raised their military alert level in response, and nearly precipitated an unprovoked preemptive strike. Concerned that he might stumble into a nuclear war or lose the 1984 election, Reagan moderated his anti-Soviet rhetoric. He began moving slowly toward the stance that would enable him in 1985–88 to accept overtures made by a new kind of Soviet leader, Mikhail Gorbachev.

The end of the Cold War reduced but did not remove fears of attack. As the United States assumed a more activist role in Middle Eastern quarrels in the 1990s, it amassed enemies among various jihadist groups. In 1993, Islamic terrorists set off a truck bomb in a garage under the World Trade Center in New York City, killing six people and injuring over a thousand. A year later, when pollsters asked Americans whether the United States stood "vulnerable to a surprise attack similar to that of Pearl Harbor," 40 percent answered yes, and 56 percent no.

The 1941 attack on Pearl Harbor was much on the minds of Americans following the terrorist attacks of September 11, 2001. In that assault nineteen Arab Islamic terrorists hijacked four airliners bound for the West Coast and laden with jet fuel. The terrorists crashed two planes into the World Trade Center towers, which subsequently collapsed; plowed one into the Pentagon, damaging that building; and crashed the fourth plane in Pennsylvania during a fight with passengers for control of the aircraft. Americans reacted to the attacks with a variety of feelings related to fear. They told pollsters they felt "shocked," "bad," "devastated," "horrified," or "violated."[79] Three-quarters believed the attacks would "fundamentally change things forever."[80]

Reflecting that shock as well as their sketchy knowledge of history, two-thirds of Americans ranked 9/11 as "more serious than Pearl Harbor," while an additional one-quarter equated the terrorist attack with the 1941 assault.[81] In other words, nine out of ten Americans judged the attack by a group of stateless enemies as equal in gravity to, if not worse than, the hostilities forced upon the United States by Japan and Germany, military juggernauts that then controlled much of Asia and Europe. Even five years after 9/11, Americans by a six-to-one margin appraised the 2001 attacks as equal to, if not worse than, Pearl Harbor.[82] Much of Americans' vulnerability stemmed from suspicion that their government had failed to protect the nation, something similarly raised during World War II by the investigation into the Roosevelt administration's possible knowledge of the impending Japanese attack. No proof for such claims ever arose after 1941, though conspiracy theorists persist to this day in arguing that FDR knew of it in advance, and moreover that he in fact embraced the opportunity afforded by Pearl Harbor to pursue the foreign policy he desired. Since fear had not sufficiently motivated the American people to go to war, he had supposedly reasoned in the darkest Machiavellian vein, he would have to sacrifice thousands of casualties and the Pacific fleet based at Pearl Harbor in order to get the war he wanted. In a similar vein, after 9/11 more than half of those polled believed that intelligence agencies should have been able to discover and prevent the attacks.[83] Two-thirds, moreover, feared further attacks by the same terrorists, a fear exacerbated by nearly simultaneous, though by all accounts unrelated, deadly anthrax attacks on public officials in Washington through the mail.[84] This widespread fear slowly dissipated. By 2011, nearly two-thirds of Americans judged the country safer from terrorism than it had been before September 2001.[85] This meant that the proportion of Americans fearing an assault had declined to roughly the pre-9/11 level.

In looking back at the post-9/11 decade with its frustrating wars in Afghanistan and in Iraq and its "enhanced" interrogation and surveillance abuses, 43 percent of Americans believed that the United States had overreacted to the terrorist attacks, while 27 percent believed that it had underreacted, and 36 percent appraised the reaction as just right.[86] This divided judgment reflected the persistence of sharp differences over the performance of the George W. Bush administration. What Americans agreed on, however, was that the world remained a fearsome place; indeed, the very name assigned to the enemy, "terrorists," underscored the pervasiveness of fear.

The Bush administration played on that apprehension to mobilize support for its war of choice in Iraq. While Vice President Dick Cheney beat the drums for a war to remove Saddam Hussein from power, National Security Adviser Condoleezza Rice warned that skeptics waiting for smoking-gun evidence of an Iraqi atomic bomb project might be confronted with an actual mushroom cloud. While exploiting public fears, administration leaders were themselves deeply shaken by the terrorist attacks. President Bush later recounted, "Six mornings a week, [CIA director] George Tenet briefed me on what they called the Threat Matrix, a summary of potential attacks on the homeland. Between 9/11 and mid-2003, the CIA reported to me an average of 400 specific threats each month. . . . For months after 9/11, I would wake up in the middle of the night worried about what I had read."[87] Tenet remembered that you could not "be anything other than scared to death about what [the Threat Matrix] portended. . . . You could drive yourself crazy believing all or even half of what was in" it.[88] Rice admitted that she had slipped into a state of "rational paranoia."[89] Such fears are not what FDR had promised to eliminate in his January 1941 speech.

FDR understood that fear is most fearsome when it is diffuse, free floating, and apparently impervious to action.[90] Just as he himself had embarked on vigorous physical therapy to recover mobility, Roosevelt urged the American people to energetically confront the Depression and the dictators. Despite his wise leadership during times of crisis, Roosevelt also led the United States in a dangerous direction. By urging Americans to pursue their ideals and interests around the globe, FDR helped push the United States further along the path of informal empire. While America's strategic commitments before World War II were limited Hawaii, Alaska, Puerto Rico, the Caribbean, the

Panama Canal Zone, the Philippines, and a few other islands in the Pacific, by war's end the United States had strung together a network of air and naval bases on every continent except Antarctica. The Cold War then provided the justification and opportunity to build the "free world," that is, a US-led alliance spanning most of the globe. After the Cold War, US influence extended still further into central Asia, the Baltics, and other areas formerly under Soviet control. Meanwhile, Washington used covert operations to make or break governments to suit perceived US interests. A widespread belief in American exceptionalism blinded most Americans to the envy and resentment that arises from such an empire. Although the Four Freedoms embody values that are shared widely around the world, they are not universal values. Nor has the United States always honored its best values when dealing with the intractable dilemmas of global politics. It is not surprising, then, that US engagement in the world has sparked among some people a hatred intense enough to motivate terrorist attacks on the United States. There is, then, an intrinsic contradiction between America's pursuing the global responsibilities that FDR helped initiate, in part to spread the Four Freedoms, and actually safeguarding the United States from fear.

Some Americans pointed to this contradiction soon after Roosevelt pledged to promote the Four Freedoms across the globe. Edwin M. Borchard, a renowned international law expert, remarked caustically that even the "crusades of a thousand years ago had a more limited objective." Another skeptic, University of Chicago president Robert Hutchins, warned that implementing the Four Freedoms entailed "a program of perpetual war in Latin America, war in the Far East, war in the South Seas." Mindful of the still unfinished work of the New Deal, Senator Robert La Follette, Jr., of Wisconsin urged that "we make the 'four freedoms' prevail in America before we try to ram them down the throats of people everywhere in the world."[91] Implementing the American Century meant building an informal empire on which the sun would never set and in which American leaders could never sleep.

The development of this empire since 1941 is part of Roosevelt's legacy. Although FDR could not have foreseen, and probably would not have approved of, the literally worldwide, military-oriented nature of US involvement abroad in the twenty-first century, he did appreciate that channeling fear was effective in prodding the American people to accept such entanglement. He played up the real dangers of an Axis victory to spur a reluctant nation to prepare for and finally enter World War II. Although effort by millions of Americans contributed to a smashing victory over the Axis, the war also produced the atomic bomb and the expansion of dangerous responsibilities abroad. Cold War presidents often exaggerated those perils in order to frighten the American people into voting funds for rebuilding war-torn Europe and other foreign aid, fighting the Korean and Vietnam Wars, and assembling a fearsome nuclear arsenal. In the post–Cold War era, the George W. Bush administration exploited fears of another terrorist attack to get Americans to accept a war of choice against the Iraqi leader, Saddam Hussein, who had had nothing to do with 9/11. Even after a nearly decade-long war in Iraq had squandered enormous amounts of blood and treasure, former vice president Dick Cheney, a principal architect of the conflict persisted in exploiting, a critic charged, "the politics of fear in order to carry out state purposes."[92]

Despite the key role of Roosevelt in utilizing fear in developing the nation's global reach, he did see limits to the American Century. FDR envisioned Four Policemen managing world affairs, not a sole "hyper-power" intervening with military force wherever it pleased. Indeed, the fight against Hitler's Germany was waged to avoid unilateral world domination by a nation dangerously convinced of its own exceptionalism and superiority.

Does the troubling record of US foreign policy since FDR's pledge of the Four Freedoms in January 1941 mean there is no alternative to policies that perpetuate war without securing freedom from fear? The United States might become much more selective about which global problems it chooses to engage. Rather than promoting the Four Freedoms everywhere, America might set an example by focusing instead on fulfilling those ideals at home. This was the advice urged by the famed foreign policy strategist George F. Kennan when he quoted John Quincy Adams's 1821 peroration opposing intervention in the Greek struggle for independence:

> Wherever the standard of freedom and independence has been or shall be unfurled there will [America's] heart, her benedictions and her prayers be. But she goes not abroad, in search of monsters to destroy. [If America did try to bring freedom to others], the fundamental maxims of her policy would insensibly change from *liberty* to *force*. She might become the dictatress of the world. She would be no longer the ruler of her own spirit.[93]

In order to secure for themselves a greater measure of freedom from fear, Americans need to limit their campaign to bring this and other freedoms to nations with far different cultures and histories from our own.

Notes

1. Although historians commonly refer to the fear, anger, or other emotions of historical actors, it is difficult to know what they "really felt." Indeed, it can be problematic figuring out what the people around us feel, or even what we ourselves are feeling. Most of the recent work on emotions in history proceeds from the findings of cognitive scientists and others that emotions are an integral aspect of thought. All thought is a mix of the emotional and the rational. Although scholars cannot determine precisely what people in the past actually felt, they can analyze the culturally inflected language and other symbols that bear evidence of what people felt. Emotions are expressed through words, gestures, actions, or other signs—all of which reflect an individual's or a group's interpretation of prevailing cultural practices. As the anthropologist Clifford Geertz put it, "Not only ideas, but emotions too, are cultural artefacts." Clifford Geertz, *The Interpretation of Cultures: Selected Essays* (New York: Basic Books, 1973), 80–81. Because the objects of fear and the ways that fear is expressed or mobilized can change over time and across cultures, fear, despite its elusiveness, remains a useful topic for historical investigation.

   In this essay I use the word "fear" to refer to a variety of feelings that are dominated by sensations of apprehension, fright, horror, or dread. Fears can seize our being by displacing all other thoughts and sensations; they can manifest themselves as a dull ache of chronic worry; or they can be felt somewhere along the spectrum between those extremes.

   As Joanna Bourke has put it, "The emotion of fear is fundamentally about the body.... Fear is *felt*, and although the emotion of fear cannot be *reduced to* the sensation of fear, it is not present *without* sensation. The body is not simply the shell through which emotions are expressed. Discourses shape bodies. However, bodies also shape discourse: people are 'weak or pale with fright,' 'paralyzed by fear' and 'chilled by terror.'" Joanna Bourke, *Fear: A Cultural History* (Emeryville, CA: Shoemaker & Hoard, 2005), 8. For scholarship on fear, see Michael Laffan and Max Weiss, eds., *Facing Fear: The History of an Emotion in Global Perspective* (Princeton, NJ: Princeton University Press, 2012); Jan Plamper and Benjamin Lazier, *Fear across the Disciplines* (Pittsburgh: University of Pittsburgh Press, 2012); and Corey Robin, *Fear: The History of a Political Idea* (New York: Oxford University Press, 2004). See also William Ian Miller, *The Mystery of Courage* (Cambridge, MA: Harvard University Press, 2000).

2. http://www.fdrlibrary.marist.edu/pdfs/fftext.pdf.

3. The word "freedom" packs such punch because it links nearly universal values, such as freedom of speech and religion, with more controversial principles, such as freedom of enterprise, meaning the right to hire, fire, and do business as one pleases, or freedom from want, meaning the right to a job and a minimum standard of living.

4. Henry R. Luce, *The American Century* (New York: Farrar & Rinehart, 1941), 8. The article was soon published in book form.

5. Ibid., 13.

6. Ibid., 33.

7. Ibid., 40.

8. PPP, "Inaugural Address," March 4, 1933, http://www.presidency.ucsb.edu/ws/?pid=14473.

9. Michael S. Sherry, *In the Shadow of War* (New Haven, CT: Yale University Press, 1995), 15–24.
10. PPP, "Annual Message to Congress," January 4, 1939, http://www.presidency.ucsb.edu/ws/?pid=15684.
11. Ibid.
12. Gallup Poll (AIPO), June 1940, retrieved January 14, 2014, from the iPOLL Databank, Roper Center for Public Opinion Research, University of Connecticut, http://www.ropercenter.uconn.edu/data_access/ipoll/ipoll.html (hereafter iPOLL).
13. Gallup Poll, June 1940, retrieved January 14, 2014, from iPOLL. The poll was taken June 27–July 2, 1941.
14. Foreign Affairs Survey, December 1945, retrieved January 14, 2014, from iPOLL.
15. Office of Public Opinion Research War Survey, December 1940, retrieved January 15, 2014, from iPOLL.
16. Office of Public Opinion Research War Survey, December 1940, retrieved January 15, 2014, from iPOLL.
17. Office of Public Opinion Research War Survey, December 1940, retrieved January 15, 2014, from iPOLL.
18. Gallup Poll, December 1940, retrieved January 15, 2014, from iPOLL.
19. Gallup Poll (AIPO), November 1940, retrieved January 15, 2014, from iPOLL.
20. Samuel I. Rosenman, *Working with Roosevelt* (New York: Harper & Brothers, 1952), 262.
21. Laura Crowell, "The Building of the 'Four Freedoms' Speech," *Speech Monographs* 22 (November 1955): 266–83.
22. FDR, Four Freedoms Address.
23. Norman Rockwell, *Norman Rockwell: My Adventures as an Illustrator*, as told to Tom Rockwell (New York: Harry N. Abrams, 1988), 313.
24. Ibid., 315. See also Deborah Solomon, *American Mirror: The Life and Art of Norman Rockwell* (New York: Farrar, Straus & Giroux, 2013), 204–13.
25. Solomon, *American Mirror*, 213.
26. FDR, Four Freedoms Address.
27. Frank Costigliola, *Roosevelt's Lost Alliances: How Personal Politics Helped Start the Cold War* (Princeton, NJ: Princeton University Press, 2012).
28. Ira Katznelson, *Fear Itself: The New Deal and the Origins of Our Time* (New York: Liveright, 2013).
29. Paul Boyer, *By the Bomb's Early Light* (New York: Pantheon, 1985), 5.
30. Ibid., 7.
31. Ibid.
32. Ibid., 21.
33. Ibid., 15.
34. Ibid., 11.
35. Ibid., 23–24.
36. Gallup Poll (AIPO), October 1945, retrieved January 17, 2014, from iPOLL.
37. Costigliola, *Roosevelt's Lost Alliances*, 375–76.
38. For the Truman administration and Congress, see Melvyn P. Leffler, *A Preponderance of Power* (Stanford, CA: Stanford University Press, 1992); Campbell Craig and Fredrik Logevall, *America's Cold War* (Cambridge, MA: Harvard University Press, 2009); Laura McEnaney, "Cold War Mobilization and Domestic Politics: The United States," in *The Cambridge History of the Cold*

War, ed. Melvyn P. Leffler and Odd Arne Westad (Cambridge, UK: Cambridge University Press, 2010), 1:420–441; Jeffrey A. Engel, " 'Every Cent from America's Working Man': Fiscal Conservatism and the Politics of International Aid after World War II," *New England Journal of History* 58 (2000): 20–60. On McCarthyism see Ellen Schrecker, *Many Are the Crimes: McCarthyism in America* (Boston: Little, Brown, 1998). For the cultural aspect, see Alan Nadel, *Containment Culture: American Narratives, Postmodernism, and the Atomic Age* (Durham, NC: Duke University Press, 1995).

39. David K. Johnson, *The Lavender Scare* (Chicago: University of Chicago Press, 2004), 2.
40. Ibid.
41. ORC Public Opinion Index, January 1954, retrieved January 18, 2014, from iPOLL.
42. "Great Blast Ends Atom Test Series," *New York Times*, February 7, 1951, p. 16.
43. Walter LaFeber, *The Clash* (New York: W. W. Norton, 1997), 311.
44. LaFeber, *The Clash*, 311.
45. "Lucky Dragon Incident," Trade and Environment Database, http://www1. american.edu/ted/lucky.htm.
46. "1954 Them!—Trailer," YouTube video, posted by "ennemme," December 29, 2007, http://www.youtube.com/watch?v=f8xSo2MEPzQ.
47. *THEM!*, dir. Gordon Douglas (Warner Brothers, 1954).
48. For an introduction to the controversy, see Thomas J. Carey and Donald R. Schmitt, *Witness to Roswell: Unmasking the Government's Biggest Cover-Up* (Pompton Plains, NJ: Career, 2009), and Karl T. Pflock and Jerry Pournell, *Roswell: Inconvenient Facts and the Will to Believe* (Amherst, NY: Prometheus, 2001).
49. See, for example, Elaine Tyler May, *Homeward Bound American Families in the Cold War Era* (New York: Basic Books, 1988).
50. James Gilbert, *A Cycle of Outrage: America's Reaction to the Juvenile Delinquent* (New York: Oxford University Press, 1986).
51. For a classic expression of this doctrine, see Herman Kahn, *On Thermonuclear War* (Piscataway, NJ: Transaction, 2006).
52. Joanna Bourke, *Fear: A Cultural History* (London: Virago Press, 2005), 261.
53. In 1954, Americans by a 54–20 percent margin believed that the fearsomeness of the hydrogen bomb made another world war less likely. George H. Gallup, *The Gallup Poll: Public Opinion, 1935–1971* (New York: Random House, 1972), 1230.
54. Gallup Poll (AIPO), January 1951, retrieved January 19, 2014, from iPOLL.
55. Gallup, *Gallup Poll*, 1600.
56. Ibid., 1435.
57. Ibid., 1726.
58. Ibid., 1808.
59. Ibid., 1745.
60. Guy Oakes, *The Imaginary War Civil Defense and American Cold War Culture* (New York: Oxford University Press, 1994), 44.
61. Val Peterson, "Panic: The Ultimate Weapon?" *Collier's*, August 21, 1952, 99–101.
62. Oakes, *Imaginary War*, 52.
63. Ibid., 53–54.
64. Ibid., 147.
65. Ibid., 64.

66. Ernest Sisto, "Training School Children in the Event of a 'Sneak' Air Attack on the City," *New York Times*, February 8, 1951, 35.

67. Alfred E. Kahn, *The Game of Death: Effects of the Cold War on Our Children* (New York: Cameron & Kahn, 1953), 14.

68. Ibid., 23.

69. Richard Reeves, *President Kennedy: Profile of Power* (New York: Simon & Schuster, 1993), 234.

70. See also Laura McEnaney, *Civil Defense Begins at Home* (Princeton, NJ: Princeton University Press, 2000).

71. Frank Costigliola, "US Foreign Policy from Kennedy to Johnson," in Leffler and Westad, *Cambridge History of the Cold War*, 2:116.

72. Chris O'Brien, "Mama, Are We Going to Die? America's Children Confront the Cuban Missile Crisis," in *Children and War*, ed. James Marten (New York: New York University Press, 2002), 79.

73. Ibid., 80.

74. Ibid., 81.

75. Ibid., 82.

76. CBS News/New York Times Poll, September 1980, retrieved January 19, 2014, from iPOLL.

77. ABC News/Washington Post Poll, October 1983, retrieved January 19, 2014, from iPOLL.

78. Douglas Brinkley, ed., *The Reagan Diaries* (New York: Harper, 2007), 186.

79. CBS News Poll, September 2001, retrieved January 20, 2014, from iPOLL.

80. IPSOS-Reid Poll, September 2001, retrieved January 20, 2014, from iPOLL.

81. NBC News Poll, September 2001, retrieved January 20, 2014, from iPOLL.

82. Pew News Interest Index Poll, August 2006, retrieved January 20, 2014, from iPOLL.

83. CBS News Poll, September 2001, retrieved January 20, 2014, from iPOLL.

84. NBC News Poll, September 2001, retrieved January 20, 2014, from iPOLL.

85. ABC News/Washington Post Poll, August 2011, retrieved January 20, 2014, from iPOLL.

86. PIPA/Knowledge Networks Poll, August 2011, retrieved January 20, 2014, from iPOLL.

87. George W. Bush, *Decision Points* (New York: Crown, 2010), 153.

88. Jack L. Goldsmith, *The Terror Presidency: Law and Judgment Inside the Bush Administration* (New York: W. W. Norton, 2009), 22.

89. Elizabeth Bumiller, *Condoleezza Rice: An American Life* (New York: Random House, 2007), 168.

90. The sociologist Zygmunt Bauman makes a similar point. See his *Liquid Fear* (Malden, MA: Polity, 2006), 2.

91. Justus D. Doenecke, *Storm on the Horizon: The Challenge to American Intervention, 1939–1941* (Lanham, MD: Rowman & Littlefield, 2000), 43.

92. The comment was made by Lawrence Wilkerson, a former aide to Colin Powell, who had served as secretary of state in the George W. Bush administration. "Retired Army Colonel Lawrence Wilkerson Rips Dick Cheney: He Isn't Immoral, He's Amoral," *Huffington Post*, July 1, 2014, http://www.huffington-post.com/2014/07/01/lawrence-wilkerson-dick-cheney_n_5548352.html?utm_hp_ref=politics.

93. J. William Fulbright, ed., *The Vietnam Hearings* (New York: Vintage, 1966), 115.

World War II Victory Medal, given to every member of the American Armed Forces who contributed to World War II. Credit: Ronna Spitz, Center for Presidential History.

CHAPTER 6

"Everywhere in the World"

The Strange Career of the Four Freedoms since 1945

WILLIAM HITCHCOCK

THIS CHAPTER SETS OUT TO explain what happened to the core ideas about freedom that were inherent in Franklin Roosevelt's great 1941 speech. How did FDR's ideas shape the postwar world, if at all? Were his ambitions for a new "moral order" realized? In order to track Roosevelt's ideas in the postwar world, it is important to know just what those ideas really were. The first part of this chapter shows that the Four Freedoms address was a bold restatement of the basic ideas that lay at the heart of the New Deal. Roosevelt believed that if the world was ever to know real peace and stability, then governments would have to address the basic needs of their peoples. Not only would they have to provide for the protection of basic rights like speech and religion, but they would also have to provide for basic needs like employment, social security, and the public welfare.

The Four Freedoms speech proposed nothing less than the globalization of the New Deal. The Western industrialized world initially responded very favorably to this vision, and for twenty years made considerable strides toward building a fairer world. However, this chapter will argue that the vision of "freedom" in FDR's great speech has fundamentally failed to take root "everywhere in the world," and is in fact nowhere near being realized anywhere in the world. This failure is not the fault of FDR or his ideas. Rather, it is the result of many global forces that have conspired since the 1970s to weaken and fatally undermine the essential features of the "Four Freedoms." The Four Freedoms continued to inspire people in the United States and around the world, but at the start of the twenty-first century, they are only a distant dream indeed.

One of the most shopworn criticisms of Franklin Roosevelt's leadership, rehearsed by contemporaneous rivals as well as some later historians, was that the president had no consistent political philosophy or strategy: that he was an opportunist, a man forever reacting to events, leaving contradictory and confused policies and commitments in his wake. As his secretary of war, Henry Stimson, put it, "his mind does not follow easily a consecutive chain of thought;" trying to pin him down on any subject was like "chasing a vagrant beam of sunshine around a vacant room." FDR encouraged this perception as a way to cast him as pragmatic and broad-minded. "I am a Christian and a Democrat," he replied to a reporter who asked him for a summary of his political philosophy. "That's all." This view of Roosevelt as a man who "had no broad policies and simply reacted to the situations that confronted him" was effectively demolished by one of the keenest students of Roosevelt's wartime leadership, historian Warren F. Kimball. For Kimball, FDR was no philosopher or theorist; he frequently "reacted, shifted, rethought and recalculated." Yet he was always guided by a core set of assumptions and beliefs. "Franklin Roosevelt was no ideologue," Kimball argued, "but he had an ideology."[1]

Kimball summed up that ideology in one word: Americanism. On the eve of the Second World War, Franklin Roosevelt had concluded that the American political system, by withstanding and mitigating the severe economic and social crises of the 1930s, had proved itself resilient, adaptable, flexible, and enduring. The New Deal had restored the basic compact between the state and the citizen. It had vindicated the liberal argument that it was possible to pursue individual liberty and social justice at the same time. By contrast, Roosevelt perceived, European liberalism and parliamentarianism was collapsing in the face of a desperate onslaught from fascism, Nazism, and communism. Europeans had allowed social instability and economic crisis to push their continent into war. The European political order had been destroyed by the crises of the 1930s; the American political order had overcome them. It was natural to conclude that the United States could teach the world something about how to build a stable political system for the modern age.[2]

By the fall of 1940, it seemed increasingly likely that the United States would have an opportunity, however unwelcome, to impart the lesson of American exceptionalism to the Old World. The scene had darkened considerably in that awful year. In June, France had fallen to the German blitzkrieg; Britain, licking its wounds from the humiliation at Dunkirk, braced for an invasion of its home island, and in late summer fought a desperate aerial battle to keep the Germans from seizing control of the skies over the Channel. In September, Nazi Germany, Fascist Italy, and Imperial Japan signed the Tripartite Pact, an explicitly anti-American alliance that marked the division of the world into hostile camps. When Hitler launched a massive and unrestrained campaign of nighttime bombing of British cities in the fall of 1940, it was unclear just how long Britain might endure. The president, unlike most of his people and their congressional representatives, believed that America had a moral and a strategic reason to assist Britain in facing the German onslaught. He engineered a deal that sent fifty mothballed destroyers to Britain, and soon after his re-election in November, in response to a desperate appeal from Prime Minister Winston Churchill, he conceived of the Lend-Lease program to assist that endangered island nation. Such a step required an explanation to a skeptical nation, which came on December 29 in a fireside chat.

> Some of our people like to believe that wars in Europe and in Asia are of no concern to us. But it is a matter of most vital concern to us that European and Asiatic war-makers should not gain control of the oceans which lead to this hemisphere.... If Great Britain goes down, the Axis powers will control the continents of Europe, Asia, Africa, Australasia, and the high seas—and they will be in a position to bring enormous military and naval resources against this hemisphere. It is no exaggeration to say that all of us in the Americas would be living at the point of a gun.

Unwilling to accept this doom-laden scenario, Roosevelt announced that the United States would assist those nations under German threat by serving as "the great arsenal of democracy."[3]

Just one week later, the president used the annual State of the Union message on January 6, 1941, to restate his thesis: Britain's survival was crucial to America's well-being. "The safety of our country and of our democracy are overwhelmingly involved in events far beyond our borders," he told the Congress.[4] He cautioned his listeners against succumbing to the blandishments of appeasers and isolationists, and declared that America must arm itself and arm others who were resisting German aggression. But what made this speech so memorable was that Roosevelt made the case for aid to Britain by appealing to more than just national security. He nested the argument for military assistance in a broader vision of the kind of world Americans wished to see emerge from the coming conflict. Herein lies the true meaning of the Four Freedoms speech.

Roosevelt understood that many of his listeners would only agree to make these immense additional exertions on behalf of rearmament if they had "an unshakeable belief in the manner of life which they are defending." The way of life now under threat was, quite simply, democracy—the sort of democracy practiced and perfected in America. What made America strong was its ability to craft a political system that placed at its core a binding and mutually beneficial agreement between the government and the governed. For, FDR declared, "there is nothing mysterious about the foundations of a healthy and strong democracy."

> The basic things expected by our people of their political and economic systems are simple. They are: Equality of opportunity for youth and for others; Jobs for those who can work; Security for those who need it; the ending of special privilege for the few; the preservation of civil liberties for all; the enjoyment of the fruits of scientific progress in a wider and constantly rising standard of living.

Roosevelt called these "the simple, basic things" that all free people want and that modern states must provide if they wished to remain stable and peaceful. For, he went on, "the inner and abiding strength of our economic and political systems is dependent upon the degree to which they fulfill these expectations." This was a lesson in political science worthy of his illustrious predecessor Woodrow Wilson, who taught that subject at Princeton for many years. Democracies are stable and prosperous when they can provide their people not only with personal liberty but also with "basic things" that will protect them from hunger, joblessness, and the harsh winds of the free market. Democracies that fail to provide stability, fail to honor the social compact, and fail to provide jobs and economic security will court political and social crisis. Roosevelt was couching a plea for aid to Europe in the language of global social and economic transformation. In the same way that the New Deal had rescued the American system from collapse, so too could the New Deal be put to use in guiding the postwar nations toward a new social compact with their citizens.

To make the connection between the American experience and the global transformation he envisioned, Roosevelt wrote into the speech its memorable appeal for a world based on "four essential human freedoms." The language came directly from FDR himself, as speechwriter Samuel Rosenman recalled. "The president announced as he came near the end of the draft that he had an idea for a peroration. We waited as he leaned far back in his swivel chair with his gaze on the ceiling. It was a long pause—so long that it began to become uncomfortable." And then he dictated the closing and most memorable passage of the speech. "The words seemed to roll off his tongue as though he had rehearsed them many times to himself." And indeed, in a way, he had, for these words came close to summarizing his core political philosophy. His "Four Freedoms"—the freedom of speech and religion, the freedom from want and fear—constituted for him a "moral order" that was distinct from the order of violence and tyranny that the fascists offered. And this "moral order" was, in essence, the New Deal: an expression of mutual solidarity between the state and the citizen. Rosenman instantly saw the Four Freedoms speech quite simply as "a summation of the New Deal." Historian David Kennedy agreed: "At this basic level of principle, there was unmistakable continuity between Roosevelt's domestic policies during the Great Depression and his foreign policies in the world war."[5]

The genius of the Four Freedoms speech lies in FDR's ability to make the abstract concept of freedom concrete. Freedom of speech and religion and freedom from want and fear are specific aspirations "that make people conscious of their individual stake in the preservation of democratic life in America," Roosevelt declared. Yet hidden inside FDR's State of the Union address sit not one but two core ideas about what freedom really means. These two ideas of freedom are complementary but also in tension with one another.[6]

The first idea of freedom in FDR's speech concerns what political theorists call "negative rights": those rights that inhere in the human person and which no state or government may abridge. Negative rights are those things that a government may *not* do to individuals. In a free society, government may not imprison citizens without due process nor torture people in its custody; the government may not limit the right to free speech nor deny the practice of any religion. When FDR identified freedom of speech and religion as essential to any free society, he was speaking about the central importance of negative rights: the rights of individuals not to be harmed or abused by the tyrannical power of government. This must have resonated with his listeners, for such rights form the core of the Bill of Rights, the first ten amendments to the US Constitution, where the limits of the powers of the federal government are clearly adumbrated. And such rights clearly distinguished the American ideas of freedom from the tyrannical fascist ideologies on display in Europe and Asia.

FDR's second concept of the rights that free people enjoy is rather more political, and more controversial. These are "positive rights." Positive rights are those things that citizens in a civilized state can expect their government to do *for* them. These are the obligations that states have toward their citizens. Governments, Roosevelt asserted, have an obligation to provide "freedom from want" and "freedom from fear" to their people, meaning peace, prosperity, and an environment in which every person can achieve his full potential. A society is free and stable when it provides "the basic things expected by our people." Equality of opportunity for all, jobs, the ending of the special privileges for the few, civil liberties for all, old-age pensions, unemployment insurance, and adequate medical care. These are what citizens in a peaceful and prosperous society expect from their government. Without them the loyalty of citizens to their government weakens, and the prospects for a strong democracy are dimmed.

One of the twentieth century's most insightful political philosophers, the Russian-born Oxford professor Isaiah Berlin, perceived that it was Roosevelt's great contribution to intertwine these two threads of freedom and so create a powerful means to bind together the centrifugal forces of modern society. Writing on the tenth anniversary of FDR's death, Berlin tried to explain how important Roosevelt's example was to Europeans during the 1930s and early 1940s. "The most insistent propaganda in those days declared that humanitarianism and liberalism and democratic forces were played out, and that the choice now lay between two bleak extremes, Communism and Fascism." Roosevelt rejected this assertion and instead sought to "establish new rules of social justice ... without forcing his country into some doctrinaire strait-jacket." FDR's New Deal, Berlin perceived, aimed to build a system that would "provide for greater economic equality and social justice—ideals which were the best part of the tradition of American life—without altering the basis of freedom and democracy in his country."

And Roosevelt succeeded. He showed that the propaganda of the 1930s was wrong: it was possible "to be politically effective and yet benevolent and human." At a time when the fascists offered efficiency, unity and order, at the expense of individuality and dissent, Roosevelt showed the world that "it is possible to reconcile individual

liberty—a loose texture of society—with the indispensable minimum of organizing and authority." It is not surprising that soon after
writing this appreciation of Roosevelt, Berlin published his seminal
essay "Two Concepts of Liberty," in which he explored precisely the
tension between individual freedom and social responsibility. "The
extent of a man's, or a people's, liberty to choose to live as he or they
desire," Berlin argued in that essay, "must be weighed against claims
of many other values, of which equality, or justice, or happiness, or
security, or public order are perhaps the most obvious examples."
Here was a clear restatement of liberalism, one with which Franklin
Roosevelt could happily have agreed.[7]

And this is just what animates the Four Freedoms speech, this
powerful double-barreled message. Democracy at its best secures
both negative and positive rights. It must protect individuals *from*
abuse of power, tyranny, and oppression. But democracy must also
provide *for* the citizens, and build a foundation of equality, fairness,
and social security to insure that all citizens are treated with respect
and dignity. This, for FDR, is the "moral order" that America had created at home and would seek to export globally in the coming years.
Indeed, in issuing the Atlantic Charter in August 1941—a broad
statement of Anglo-American values—Roosevelt stressed themes
drawn from the Four Freedoms address: the free world was committed to achieving freedom from want and fear, as well as peaceful
trade, national self-determination, and "improved labor standards,
economic advancement and social security." Roosevelt and his fol-
lowers would insist that these same principles be written into the
preamble of the United Nations, founded in 1945. Member states
would "reaffirm faith in fundamental human rights, in the dignity
and worth of the human person, [and] in the equal rights of men
and women," and they would "promote social progress and better
standards of life." The Four Freedoms and the subsequent founding
documents of the postwar order represented for FDR a new moral
order that was, he said, "the antithesis of tyranny." For such a world of
individual liberties entwined with social and civic justice Americans
would fight, and so would millions of people around the world.[8]

* * *

For all the enthusiasm that greeted FDR's vision of a world based
on the Four Freedoms, it is a fact that since he made his celebrated
speech, the world has not marched toward freedom along a straight
and direct path. The struggle to realize both the negative and

positive rights inherent in FDR's great address has been a long, arduous, and ultimately incomplete one. During the thirty-year period after World War II, important political and economic institutions came into place that advanced some of the kinds of rights that FDR cherished. In the United States, Western Europe, and even the Communist bloc, certain aspects of the Four Freedoms took hold. Yet nowhere was the fulfilment of FDR's vision complete, and nowhere were these advances made easily.

The first major problem that beset FDR's vision of a world based on Four Freedoms was that in 1941 the United States was entering into a period of costly, global war—a poor time to start to build major social programs. As historian Alan Brinkley has shown, FDR "deflected ambitious and even modest liberal proposals by insisting that 'we must start winning the war . . . before we do much general planning for the future.'"[9] Leading New Dealers left the administration, while figures from business and corporations took on conspicuous roles leading the economic mobilization for war. One prominent liberal to be abandoned by FDR was his vice president, Henry Wallace, who was replaced on the 1944 ticket by Missouri senator Harry Truman. FDR explained this shift away from domestic reform in his usual disarming manner. The New Deal, he said, had come into being because of the economic crisis of the 1930s. The nation was ill and needed a doctor, he mused in a December 1943 press conference. So "Dr. New Deal" was called in to help the patient. But on December 7, 1941, America was in a "bad smash-up" and a new physician had to be called for: that was "Dr. Win-the-War." The country was being treated with a new kind of medicine, namely the rapid mobilization of the nation's industry to wage war. For now, the New Deal had to be suspended. Programs such as the Works Progress Administration, the Civilian Conservation Corps, the National Youth Administration, and the National Resources Planning Board were all disbanded in 1943. Moreover, the great nations that made up the alliance against Nazi Germany and Imperial Japan found that the only way to win war on such a massive scale was to abridge freedoms: whether through conscription, seizure of private property, incarceration of suspected subversives and aliens, forced relocation of peoples, or the massive expansion of governmental power, all the nations fighting on behalf of liberty and equality found it necessary to abridge those freedoms in wartime. This shearing away of the social justice dimension of the New Deal was a crucial result of the war, and it lingered even into the postwar years. New Dealers in Congress, for example, could remain in favor of policies that stressed economic fairness while halting policies to encourage racial and social justice.[10]

Harry Truman, who became president upon Roosevelt's death in April 1945, was a staunch advocate of Roosevelt's progressive legacy, but the country was in a different mood than it had been in the crisis-ridden 1930s, or even in 1941 when FDR outlined the Four Freedoms. With the war over and the economy humming along, there seemed little justification for continuing the grand experiment of the New Deal. It was possible to imagine a return to a free economy and a smaller national government. Truman attempted to extend the New Deal and even initiated his own Fair Deal, but he was swimming against the tide. When Truman vetoed the Taft-Hartley Act of 1947, a bill that weakened many rights of labor unions, the Congress swiftly and easily voted to override the veto. This was a crucial harbinger of a broad national reaction against the New Deal and the ideals of shared sacrifice, common struggle, and social progress that had animated it.

But there was more going on in postwar America than a reduction of government programs. There was also a surge of anxiety in certain political circles that the New Deal had violated a foundational principle of American public life: the need to protect individual liberties from a powerful government. As the Cold War began, and Americans sharpened their own ideological arguments for why they hated communism, they found themselves articulating a broad indictment of all utopian schemes of human improvement that in the name of perfecting mankind only sought to enslave it. Fascism, Nazism, communism—and even the left-wing schemes of the New Deal—all could be tarnished by association with their common belief that government always had the answer to the problems of modernity. Down this path lay nothing more than "the road to serfdom," to use the title of Friedrich Hayek's hugely popular tract decrying the expansion of state power and social welfare programs. Even with the best of intentions, the welfare state opened the door to an expansion of state power that could snuff out individual liberty.[11]

And the reaction against the New Deal did not come only from obscure theorists or marginal intellectuals like Ayn Rand, Russell Kirk, or William F. Buckley; nor from life-long conservatives like Robert A. Taft of Ohio, who had opposed the New Deal from the start; nor from conspiracy-minded demagogues like Senators Joe McCarthy of Wisconsin and William Jenner of Indiana. No; even a moderate and apolitical public figure like Dwight D. Eisenhower chimed in about the lurking threat to liberty. Taking the oath of office as Columbia University's president in October 1948, he declared that "human freedom is today threatened by regimented statism.... In today's struggle, no free man, no free institution, can be neutral." This barb was aimed not only at the Soviets but also at the New Deal. Eisenhower confided in his diary at the start of 1949 that "in the name of 'social security' we are placing more and more responsibility upon the central government—and this means that an ever growing bureaucracy is taking an ever greater power over our daily lives." To an audience of two thousand graduates of the Seven Sisters colleges, gathered at a banquet at the Waldorf-Astoria in New York, he proclaimed: "We are drifting toward something we hate with all our hearts ... centralized government." If Americans did not strive to combat this "constant trend," they could expect "a kind of dictatorship" to emerge. Eisenhower would carry this argument into the White House in 1953.[12]

Of course, the main legacies of the New Deal endured, even if the political rhetoric of the 1950s claimed to find in them the taint of "socialism." Eisenhower himself, despite his campaign speeches, actually extended Social Security to millions of Americans and made important legislative proposals to provide affordable, federally backed health insurance to those unable to provide for themselves. Eisenhower also invested large sums in major public works projects like the construction of the Saint Lawrence Seaway and Interstate Highway system. In addition, Eisenhower presided over a massive expansion of the national security state, spending on average $45 billion each year on defense, including a vast program of nuclear weapons research and construction. Massive government spending contributed to rapid postwar economic growth, full employment, and widespread prosperity. In a curious political development, then, Americans embraced an antigovernment philosophy even while benefitting substantially from a still-expanding government. This was contrary to FDR's vision, in which citizens could expect their government to aid them in return for their duty, sacrifice, and taxes. In popular parlance, Americans in the 1950s and early 1960s spoke of their freedoms by stressing their individual rights and their desire to be free of government coercion. This, after all, is what made American government different from the "statist" regimes of the Eastern Bloc. In actual practice, however, Americans lived in a society in which government played an ever larger role in stimulating the free market, promoting employment, providing services, and enhancing positive rights.[13]

Unprecedented prosperity and a culture of consumerism in postwar America tended to mask the fact that millions of US citizens continued to live unfree lives. In an America steeped in a Cold War culture of individualism, affluence, and consumption, it was embarrassing and even infuriating to be reminded that African Americans did not enjoy basic civil rights. During the peak of the civil rights movement from 1955 to 1965, black Americans had to fight bitterly to lay a claim to their positive rights—their rights, as FDR had put it, to "equality of opportunity for youth and for others; jobs for those who can work; security for those who need it; the ending of special privilege for the few; [and] the preservation of civil liberties for all." As it turned out, the Cold War—which had led Americans to proclaim on a global stage their commitment to individual rights and freedoms—created an opening for civil rights demands: a nation that was waging a war between "freedom" and "slavery"—the word often used to describe the Soviet system—could hardly keep millions of its own citizens out of schools, restaurants, and public parks, nor could it systematically disenfranchise them. The arguments in favor of redressing centuries of racism and Jim Crow segregation were overwhelming, yet even so it took a great social movement, combined with creative leadership, to secure even basic civil rights through the passage of the 1964 Civil Rights Act and the 1965 Voting Rights Act. These laws were part of a major legislative effort, including the creation of Medicare and Medicaid, that tried to make good on the progressive vision that Roosevelt held out during the New Deal and that other leaders from Truman to John Kennedy had attempted to develop. It had taken twenty years, but by the mid-1960s the United States had made important if halting strides toward a society based on "four essential human freedoms."[14]

In Europe, the road to the fairer society that Roosevelt had outlined was somewhat less twisted. Having learned the lesson that timid government intervention in the social and economic crises of the modern age could invite extremism and lead to war, millions of Europeans after 1945 demanded that their governments be bold in rebuilding a new political order—and no democratic nation went further or faster than America's stalwart·wartime ally, the United Kingdom. Unlike Americans, Europeans had few qualms about embracing socialism as the best means to mobilize national energies in wartime and to build the foundations for an equitable postwar order. At the outset of the war, George Orwell had boldly welcomed the political radicalization that the war would demand. "We cannot win the war without introducing Socialism," he believed. The war had been the result, in his view, of the failure of capitalist states and their anemic leaders to solve the economic and social crises of the

1930s; the only way to fix those problems was to introduce a planned economy and the national ownership of the means of production. What Orwell envisioned was "new blood, new men, new ideas—in the true sense of the word, a revolution."[15]

If there was any European document that rivalled FDR's Four Freedoms speech for influence, it was the 1942 Beveridge Report, written by a British technocrat named William Beveridge, which outlined a plan for the extension of social security and health insurance to all citizens. Beveridge laid out five "evils" that government must attack: want, disease, ignorance, squalor, and idleness. It would be the test of good government to see that such perennial social problems were attacked, and he sketched out the government programs—mainly unemployment and health insurance—that would provide a minimum level of social security to Britain's working people. Beveridge's ideas were wildly popular not just in wartime Britain but inside the European resistance movements on the Continent that were fighting Hitler. The war could open the path to the creation of a new, fairer society.

It is not surprising, then, that when Winston Churchill led his Conservative Party into postwar elections in mid-1945, he sought to link the Socialist ambitions of the Labour Party to the totalitarian ideology that the western allies had so recently defeated. Churchill, on the hustings in the summer of 1945, declared that socialism of the kind Labour was offering was "an attack . . . upon the right of the ordinary man or woman to breathe freely without having a harsh, tyrannical hand clapped across their mouths. . . . Socialism is inseparably interwoven with Totalitarianism and the abject worship of the State."[16] He went even further, declaring that Labour could not bring about the socialization of the British economy without resorting "to some kind of Gestapo." To this outrageous remark, Labour's leader, Clement Attlee, calmly replied that freedom had to be restrained by social responsibility. "People should have the greatest freedom compatible with the freedom of others. But there was a time when employers were free to work little children 16 hours a day. I remember when employers were free to employ sweated women on finishing trousers at a penny-halfpenny a pair. Here was a time when people were free to neglect sanitation so that thousands died from preventable diseases."[17]

And of course the British public agreed with Attlee. The old order, based upon freedom for capitalism and little else, was soundly rejected at the polls. In July 1945, the avowedly socialist Labour Party took the reins of power in Britain. Within six years, they had

shaped a welfare state based upon a massive degree of state intervention in all aspects of society. The first wave of legislation enacted
by the new Labour-dominated parliament placed one-fifth of the
country's productive capacities under the control of the state. With
amazing speed, the government proclaimed the nationalization of
the Bank of England, civil aviation, telecommunications, coal, rail-
ways, road haulage, and electricity, gas, iron, and steel. This was not
a full-fledged workers' democracy: many former owners of national-
ized industries went to work on national oversight boards, helping to
run their companies in the public interest. But, no doubt, this was
a new synthesis of capitalism and socialism: the "mixed economy."
Britain's experiment showed that even a once rigidly free-market
society could adopt new methods that stressed economic distribution and social equality.

Much of Western Europe followed the same path. In France,
West Germany, the Benelux countries, and Scandinavia, governments brought about the nationalization of key industries, instituted a wave of progressive social security legislation, and worked
out new economic arrangements designed to shield workers from
the harsh workings of unfettered capitalism. Such ambitious plans
for social reform were initiated because the war seemed to bear out
FDR's observation that stable societies are those that meet the expectations of their citizens. Looking at the war years, political leaders
concluded that governments must take an active role in enhancing
prosperity, stimulating job growth, and encouraging a renewed faith
in the viability of democratic institutions.[18]

Could Roosevelt's vision of a world based on four basic human
freedoms be constructed across the Iron Curtain, in the states of
the Eastern Bloc? Clearly not: the communist states had no interest in protecting individual freedoms such as freedom of speech or
religion. Nor did they want to protect workers from the harsh winds
of capitalism; they wanted to destroy capitalism itself and replace
it with an entirely new form of economic production that elevated
workers to the status of owners. In such a revolutionary and ideologi-
cally extreme environment, freedom could find no secure footing.

Yet even so, the communist states found it valuable to borrow
from the language of western liberalism from time to time to promote the belief that communism was in fact a kind of worker's utopia. The 1936 Constitution of the Soviet Union—issued at the very
moment that Stalin was waging a brutal war on the rural kulaks and
other unfortunate peoples across the Soviet Union—reads like a
blueprint for a Western European welfare state, filled as it is with

an itemized list of the many "rights" that Soviet citizens allegedly possessed: the right to work, to rest, to old age pensions, education, and health care, as well as freedom of speech, freedom of the press, and the right to form labor unions. However, there was a thorn in this bed of roses. Such benefits were granted only in exchange for fulfilling "duties and obligations" toward the state. The individual had no inherent rights, negative or positive. Those rights were only meaningful within a political system that could provide for them, in exchange for the loyalty of the citizen to the state. The 1977 Soviet Constitution was even more pointed: "Citizens' exercise of their rights and freedoms is inseparable from the performance of their duties and obligations" (article 59), which meant that if the state decided that a citizen had failed to fulfil his duty, his rights could be taken away. Rights were contingent, not universal, and they were awarded in return for loyalty.[19]

Obviously, the Soviet Union never intended to provide "freedom" of any kind. But what is notable is that the Soviets found it politically advantageous to present their system as part of a liberal project that was advancing certain "rights"—the right to work, to health care, to education, and so on. Crucially, the Soviet and Eastern Bloc states in the 1960s and 1970s were able to deliver sufficient "freedom from want" in the form of social goods and services to mask the total absence of negative rights—that is, personal freedoms and protections against coercion—that characterized life in the communist world. Growth rates in the Eastern Bloc states in the 1950s certainly looked impressive, and matched those in the west. Consumer goods, perhaps shoddier and less abundant, nonetheless began to appear in Eastern Bloc storefronts. Eastern Bloc citizens accepted cradle-to-grave insurance, medical care, schooling, and employment in return for surrendering their claims to individual rights and liberties. For a region coming out of the turmoil of World War II, this was not an intolerable bargain, even if it was to be a temporary one.[20]

* * *

In the thirty years after World War II, then, the industrialized states evolved a consensus in favor of a new economic and political order. It was based on substantial government intervention to provide basic services, education, health care, and insurance for citizens; it required a new kind of managerial, managed capitalism to stimulate employment, allocate resources, and direct government spending into key sectors of the economy; and it required a high degree of global cooperation from trading partners, built around a shared set of social and political goals. Strange as it may seem, these cooperative agreements were even able to breach the Iron Curtain, bringing the Eastern European states into some degree of integration into the world economy. This was no utopia: even as the postwar welfare state was being built, inequality, racism, sexism, poverty, and other problems persisted in western market democracies, while violation of individual liberties occurred in the Eastern Bloc states as a matter of daily life. But there can no doubt: the progress toward the "moral order" that FDR envisioned in 1941 had been real, even if halting.

Alas, expanding these postwar economic and social arrangements—making them available "everywhere in the world"—proved to be a major challenge, filled more with disappointment than with progress. This is for two reasons. First, the postwar decades in the non-Western world ushered in dramatic political turmoil, as the wars of decolonization postponed the fulfillment of the kind of rights and benefits FDR envisioned. And second, starting in the 1970s, the industrialized world itself began to face serious economic crises that halted and threatened to unwind much of the social progress made since 1945.

It is essential to recall that at the very moment that the United States and Western Europe were constructing the postwar welfare state, millions of people around the world still lived under colonial rule. While Europeans spoke of freedom of speech and religion and freedom from want and fear, much of the world remained locked into an exploitative colonial system that was premised upon the subservience of non-Western peoples to foreign overlords. In the turbulent decades of the 1950s and 1960s, in Africa, the Middle East, Latin America, and Asia, powerful mass movements began to fight against the colonial system, and as they articulated their political goals, they spoke not in the words of the Beveridge Report but in the language of revolution. The overwhelming priority of the anticolonial liberation movements that sprang up in these years was national self-determination. For what good was the right to free speech, the right to assembly, the right to join a labor union, or the right to social security if one's nation itself could not be free? To this goal of national self-determination and the expulsion of the colonial system all social goals would be subordinated.

There is a cruel and sadly predictable irony to the story of decolonization: the nations that were most eager to embrace and implement the vision of the Four Freedoms in their own national communities were also those that clung most tenaciously to the exploitative colonial order. For two decades after the war, British, French, Dutch, Belgian, and Portuguese soldiers fought nasty, often prolonged colonial conflicts aiming to arrest the momentum of decolonization. Even when anticolonial nationalist leaders tried to throw the Western language of "freedom" at colonial rulers, the arguments failed. Ho Chi Minh's clever 1945 declaration of Vietnamese independence pointed directly to Western hypocrisy. He began by quoting the words of Thomas Jefferson, as well as the French Declaration of the Rights of Man, and then followed with a grim catalogue of French abuses of these same rights:

> For more than eighty years, the French imperialists, abusing the standard of Liberty, Equality, and Fraternity, have violated our Fatherland and oppressed our fellow-citizens. They have acted contrary to the ideals of humanity and justice. In the field of politics, they have deprived our people of every democratic liberty.... They have built more prisons than schools. They have mercilessly slain our patriots—they have drowned our uprisings in rivers of blood.... They have fleeced us to the backbone, impoverished our people, and devastated our land.[21]

To be lectured on the meaning of freedom by a Vietnamese nationalist should have been a deep embarrassment for leading Frenchmen; that it was seen instead as impudence reveals the powerful hold of racist and colonial ideology among French elites. How else to explain the decade of bitter, savage war that followed Ho's declaration? How else to explain the tragedy of the Algerian struggle, where again the demands for self-determination were met with bullets, not ballots?

Tragically, during the wars of decolonization, the colonial powers and the anticolonial nationalists struggling against them turned their gaze away from the basic rights that FDR had outlined. The pure and simple call for universal respect of freedom of speech and religion and freedom from want and fear—these concepts found no hold across two decades of bloody colonial conflict. The colonists deployed atrocious violence in order to sustain their rule; in reply, nationalist guerrillas justified their own acts of terrorism and violence in the name of that one right they most desired, and which FDR had neglected: the right to national self-determination. That right—to define, create, and protect a sovereign state—trumped any claims among anticolonial movements to the protection of individual personal rights. The anticolonial leaders wanted sovereignty for their peoples; after that, their own governments could provide human rights. But national independence and freedom from the colonial yoke would have to come first, and this was going to come only through violent struggle.[22]

With profound sadness and anger, Frantz Fanon explained this logic of violence in his masterwork, *The Wretched of the Earth.* Fanon, born in colonial Martinique, served in the Free French army during the war and trained as a psychiatrist in the late 1940s. He practiced his trade in Algeria, and had ample opportunity to observe the ways that colonialism had deeply warped the minds of both colonizers and the colonized. Joining the movement for Algerian independence, he came to see that colonialism was a structure that had been premised on profound violence, and could only be destroyed through violent struggle. "The naked truth of decolonization," he wrote in a chilling passage, "evokes for us the searing bullets and bloodstained knives which emanate from it. For if the last shall be first, this will only come to pass after a murderous and decisive struggle between the two protagonists." What made Fanon's cry for upheaval so powerful was its determination to reject not only the West but the very ideals of freedom and rights that the West had so blatantly failed to respect. "Let us not pay tribute to Europe," he wrote, "by creating states, institutions, and societies which draw their inspiration from her. Humanity is waiting for something from us other than such an imitation, which would be almost an obscene caricature." No: the liberal ideals of the West had soured. Now it was time, Fanon declared, for "new concepts" and a "new man."[23]

For all its political significance in ending the colonial order, decolonization failed to advance the Four Freedoms. Born in violence, most of the Third World successor regimes that emerged from the independence struggle were controlled by tyrants, ideologues, and dictators. It is pointless to assign blame: if the anticolonial nationalists were not ready for pluralist democracy, it is because they had been deliberately denied opportunities to develop democratic political institutions by their colonial overlords. The Four Freedoms and their hopeful language of human freedom and social progress seemed almost to mock the tragedy and global catastrophe that now opened across most of the Third World in the post-independence years.

In searching for explanations for why the Four Freedoms have been so fragile and embattled in our times, we must look not just to the troubled history of decolonization but also to the troubled history of the capitalist world. For beginning in the early 1970s, something happened to the Western world that jolted its confidence in its ability to sustain the consensual politics of the welfare state. The crucial foundation for postwar prosperity among the industrialized states was laid in 1944–45, when international agreements governing the rules for global trade were created. The lessons of the 1930s seemed to point to the need for free trade and maximum expansion of employment. These goals could be achieved by creating a stable international trading environment through a system of stable exchange rates in which nations fixed their currencies to the value of the world's most important currency, the dollar. The dollar itself was pegged to the value of gold. These arrangements meant that the global trading order had a high degree of predictability, so that a truly global market for goods could be established. The results were impressive: high export-led growth spurts in most of the industrialized world. This growth in turn created the conditions for full employment and rising standards of living.[24]

However, by the late 1960s, the global engine keeping all this growth churning—the United States—began to falter. Its long-running war in Vietnam, which was a hugely expensive undertaking that put stress on the budget and pushed up inflation, weakened the US economy just at the same period that rapidly industrializing states like Germany and Japan became powerful new competitors on the global marketplace. In 1971, the United States sought to increase its global competitiveness by devaluing the dollar and taking it off the gold standard. This policy signaled the end to an era of stability in world trade, one largely driven by American leadership. When the oil shock hit in 1973—the result of an oil embargo imposed by OPEC due to Western support for Israel during the Yom Kippur War—the cheap fuel the industrialized world depended upon quadrupled in price. The global economy entered a tailspin, and growth rates sagged dramatically. Large deficits, a falloff of industrial activity, and inflation all hit the industrialized world hard. In the major industrial economies, the so-called misery index—the combined percentages of unemployment and inflation—soared from 5 in 1959 to 17.1 in 1974. Powerful Western states like the United States, Germany, and Britain sharply curtailed spending and tightened up monetary policies, contributing to a sharp contraction of global economic growth. Latin American and Eastern Bloc states, which had exposed themselves to loans through the IMF, now faced massive debt crises. Perhaps most important in all this, the authority of states to oversee the economic activity of their peoples, and to protect them against the harsh realities of capitalism, was irrevocably damaged. The glad era of managed capitalism, which had sustained broad social progress and buoyed the lives of working people in the decades after the war, had come to a sharp halt.[25] What impact was this global economic crisis going to have on the future of the Four Freedoms, whose progress had depended so heavily upon prosperity, growth, and heavy government support for social welfare?

* * *

The policy prescriptions that industrial states followed to address the collapse of the postwar economic order have been termed "neo-liberalism" by social scientists, which implies a return to classically "liberal" policies, namely, relying upon the natural dynamism of capitalism to spur growth while getting government out of the way. Neoliberal solutions to the global crisis were pursued in the United States and Britain by two leaders with great political gifts and strong economic views. Ronald Reagan and Margaret Thatcher viewed the economic crisis of the 1970s through the lens of their own ideological beliefs: each of them had long been antigovernment conservatives, certain that the New Deal and the European welfare state had promoted lethargy, sloth, indulgence, and a culture of dependence upon government handouts. The economic crisis had proven that the New Deal was a failure, they believed, and the best solution to the problem was to restore the values of hard work, industry, savings, productivity, and self-reliance.

From these conventional social ideas these two leaders extrapolated their overall economic policies. Margaret Thatcher declared the postwar welfare state to have been "a miserable failure in every respect." The vision of a new "moral order" announced by FDR in 1941 had devolved into a "centralizing, managerial, bureaucratic, interventionist style of government" that "jammed a finger in every pie" and hailed "the virtues of dependence."[26] Ronald Reagan took a page from Thatcher's book. In his 1981 inaugural address, he declared, "Government is not the solution to our problem; government is the problem." Unlike Roosevelt, Reagan's conception of freedom privileged only negative rights. In his view, the government should limit itself to protecting the right to individualism, the right to pursue personal enrichment and self-fulfillment. He believed that America had become a powerful nation because it had nurtured individual freedom. "If we look to the answer as to why, for so many years, we achieved so much, prospered as no other people on Earth, it was because here, in this land, we unleashed the energy and individual genius of man to a greater extent than has ever been done before. Freedom and the dignity of the individual have been more available and assured here than in any other place on Earth." He also believed that America's troubles began when government became intrusive. "It is no coincidence that our present troubles parallel and are proportionate to the intervention and intrusion in our lives that result from unnecessary and excessive growth of government."[27]

Far from offering a cushion against the harsh jolts of the free market, government had no place at all in the marketplace. Reagan's plan for restoring greatness, then, stressed cutting welfare benefits, tightening budgets, strictly controlling the money supply and sharply increasing interest rates, privatizing sectors of the economy that had been under public governance, and lowering labor costs and weakening labor unions, all of which he believed would serve the broad purpose of spurring individual initiative and economic growth and thus restoring confidence in the capitalist system. The crisis of capitalism of the 1970s had opened the way for a new economic order to be erected—and it would be sharply different from the ideals Franklin Roosevelt had outlined in 1941. The goal now was not to create a just and fair society but to create opportunities for global investors to make money in the expectation that a rising tide of global prosperity would eventually lift all ships. To trigger this economic renewal, though, it was essential to lower workers' wages, increase productivity while reducing costs, and squeeze more out of a smaller and cheaper labor force. Meanwhile, the United States deregulated many of its industries and its banking sector, thus drawing in global capital and spurring growth—but growth that would benefit multinational corporations rather than the workers who toiled in them. Neoliberalism triggered dramatic changes in economic patterns, the most baleful of which was the sharp increase in income inequality in the United States. Small numbers of wealthy investors and capitalists made fortunes, but wages stagnated in the post-1980 period for the vast majority of working people. The momentum toward building a fairer society that was gained in the era of managed capitalism had now been reversed.[28]

How was it possible that American voters supported policies that seemed to hurt the majority of wage-earning citizens? Part of the answer has to do with ideology: Ronald Reagan made a powerful and compelling political argument that welfare handouts were un-American, that self-reliance, industry, and wealth accumulation were by contrast the most proud characteristics of American civilization. The American public was drawn to these ideological principles, even as their pay dwindled and their labor unions crumbled. Yet another reason these ideas were so popular is that from 1986 until 1989, the western world watched as the Eastern Bloc imploded. The rapid collapse of the Soviet Union and its Eastern Bloc allies seemed to vindicate the argument that capitalism, once unleashed from the maze of regulations and restrictions that the welfare state had imposed on it, possessed revolutionary capabilities, and even the power to destroy communism. What could be a clearer example of the universal benefit of capitalism than its sweeping away of the failed communist experiment?

Yet it is still an open question as to why the collapse of communism in 1989 occurred. Certainly, there are powerful economic explanations. The economic crisis of the 1970s severely hampered the communist economies. In the 1970s, Eastern Bloc states had borrowed significant sums from western banks in order to try to jump-start their faltering industrial economies. They did so because they were aware of their failure to provide a decent quality of life in their countries. But the oil shock of the 1970s as well as the slow-down of the global economy meant that the Eastern European "jump-start" never happened. Instead, Poland, Hungary, and East Germany were stuck with large debts they could not pay off. Worse, the controlled economies had to trim their large subsidies for food and other services, with the consequence that prices on basic staples—meat, fish, sugar, butter—rose sharply in Eastern Europe in the 1970s. Shortages, long lines, and an absence of consumer goods triggered widespread anger. The Eastern Bloc states had once demanded obedience in exchange for social security and a worker's utopia. But by the late 1970s, the state could not meet its end of the bargain, and a surge in dissent and unrest resulted. It is no accident that the Polish underground workers' movement gained strength just as the Polish economy was collapsing in the late 1970s. When the KOR (Committee for the Defense of Workers) was formed in 1976, its principal demand to the Polish government was to address the rise in prices of basic foodstuffs, the decline in the quality of health care, and the endemic paucity of decent housing.[29]

And yet it would cheapen the extraordinary events of the late 1980s in Eastern Europe to suggest that dissidents risked their lives to stand against communism just because they wanted more sausage. There was something much deeper going on in the communist world than mere material demands. What was happening in the late 1970s was the growth of a global movement that sought to focus attention on the broad failure of modern states, whatever their ideological makeup, to attend to basic human rights: those inherent rights that all humans possess, above all the right to freedom of conscience, freedom of speech and assembly, and the freedom to maintain one's personal dignity in the face of oppression. Here we can see that the spirit of the Four Freedoms was in fact still alive, ready to be rekindled.

* * *

Historians have identified the stirrings around the world in the 1960s and 1970s of a new approach to the struggle for freedom. Inspired less by the language of social, economic, and political rights, numerous activist and dissident organizations around the world began in these decades to hone a new vocabulary of human rights. Grander and yet more narrowly focused than positive rights, the human rights campaigns of these years responded to the stark failure of governments everywhere to provide for even the most basic negative rights—the rights to freedom of speech and conscience. Historian Samuel Moyn, like a number of other scholars, takes the founding of Amnesty International in London in 1961 as a leading indicator: the British lawyer who started it focused its efforts narrowly on specific people who had been jailed simply for political speech. The contrast with the overarching ambitions of the Universal Declaration of 1948 was obvious. "Amnesty International invented grassroots human rights advocacy," Moyn argues, and many later groups learned from Amnesty how to push the agenda of human rights onto the world stage. Revolution was passé, tarnished by the grotesque violations of rights by revolutionary movements in the developing world. What mattered now was not the utopian scheme or the claim to some set of political rights, what mattered now was to secure universal recognition for the most basic right of all: the right to be treated as a human being.[30]

As it happened, Amnesty's efforts coincided with similar stirrings elsewhere. Inside the Soviet Union, dissidents had been developing a legalist strategy, calling on the socialist state to abide by its own constitutionally protected laws. Soviet scientists since the 1950s had been active in transnational networks organized especially around disarmament and arms control. The Group for the Defense of Human Rights, founded in 1969, and the Human Rights Committee, founded in 1970, revealed the emerging space inside the Soviet Union to talk about rights, even while the 1968 Soviet invasion of Czechoslovakia made it plain that states still retained the ultimate power to coerce and control. These efforts were met with repression inside the Soviet Union: nuclear scientist Andrei Sakharov, one of the founders of the Human Rights Committee, was subject to constant harassment and internal exile for most of the 1980s; Yuri Orlov, the physicist who founded Moscow Helsinki Watch, was tried and imprisoned in 1977 and spent almost a decade at forced labor; Anatoly Shcharansky, a young mathematician who had joined the Moscow Helsinki group, was imprisoned in 1977. These tribulations, however, were registered and elevated to international awareness by a thickening network of scientists in the United States and Europe who formed pressure groups that lobbied on behalf of their incarcerated colleagues. They did so not through a framework of Cold War rhetoric but by championing the ideal of international scientific cooperation. The new human rights activism was most successful when it left the politics out.[31]

The return to human rights activism was not limited to Europe. In South Africa, human rights had long been at the center of the antiapartheid movement. In the early 1940s, the African National Congress "explicitly embraced human rights as a fundamental goal of its struggle for racial justice." The Freedom Charter of 1955 laid out civil and political goals for all peoples in South Africa, and helped transfer the principles of human rights into local community struggles. By the time of the 1960 Sharpeville massacre, the violations of the South African regime against basic human rights were internationally known, and the foundations for a transnational network of antiapartheid activism could be created. In Argentina and Chile, meanwhile, groups of protestors, most notably the Mothers of the Plaza de Mayo in Buenos Aires, brought international attention to bear on the problem of the "disappeared": victims of the regimes who had been captured and murdered. A wide array of transnational NGO networks brought their plight to public awareness globally.[32]

The United States, too, had its human rights moment. In 1976, with the election of Jimmy Carter to office, a new American commitment to rights talk could be discerned in the public pronouncements emanating from the White House. "The world itself is now dominated by a new spirit," Carter declared in his inaugural address, accurately diagnosing the universal dissatisfaction with the politics of revolution that had so marred the 1960s. "Peoples more numerous and more politically aware are craving, and now demanding, their place in the sun—not just for the benefit of their own physical condition, but for basic human rights." Americans would rededicate themselves to this vision, Carter said. "Because we are free, we can never be indifferent to the fate of freedom elsewhere. Our moral sense dictates a clear-cut preference for those societies which share with us an abiding respect for individual human rights." Carter's rhetoric in favor of a foreign policy based on human rights was a dramatic departure for the country. Carter took human rights seriously because he believed a foreign policy guided by human rights advocacy would raise America's diminished moral standing around the world, and also because it would help in "achieving other broad or particular goals, such as greater credibility in the Third World," according to Carter's National Security Council. Yet in practice Carter's administration found it nearly impossible to use human rights advocacy as its sole guide. While human rights had its uses, for example in criticizing the Soviet Union, Carter chose not to stress human rights in the fragile and emerging relationship with China, while in the Third World the degree of human rights criticism often aligned with the friendliness of the regime toward the United States. Scholars have been quick to point to cases where Carter failed to pursue a vigorous human rights policy abroad, in Cambodia, Indonesia, Central America, and elsewhere. Very rarely did the Carter administration change its policy on loans or financial support as a result of human rights concerns. For Carter, human rights as a foreign policy was part of a change in tone and a question of emphasis; it did not lead to a dramatic change in the assessment of the national interest or in the deployment of power.[33]

If we look only to American presidents for evidence of human rights activism, we are bound to be disappointed. We must look instead to the streets. In the late 1970s, activism and dissidence bubbled away beneath the surface, most notably in communist Europe. Charter 77 in Czechoslovakia gave voice to a small but vibrant intellectual movement calling for the Czechoslovak state to respect human rights laws as contained in the Helsinki Accords, while the Polish Committee for the Defense of Workers demanded the right to strike. But Charter 77 was a tiny movement, and its leaders were harassed and arrested; it did not by itself threaten the Czechoslovak government. The Polish Solidarity movement of 1980 was far more political and powerful, and did pose a genuine threat to the regime. It was not merely a gang of café bohemians but an incipient revolution. And in December 1981 it was suppressed by force, as martial law was imposed in Poland.

The Solidarity experience suggested that communism in Europe was not going to be brought down by direct assault. But it could be eroded from within. And here the language of human rights proved enormously powerful. The activists who went out into the streets of East German cities in the fall of 1989 did not appear to be revolutionaries, nor did they claim to be antagonistic to the interests of the state. All they demanded was that their government respect their basic human rights to speak, assemble, and think without fear of retribution. The claims of the dissidents of the 1980s were expressed in the language of negative rights, not social justice or revolution. This made them subversive and dangerous: they appeared to ask only for the basic respect of the human person, yet this was an idea that mobilized millions of people, and even the communist regimes of Eastern Europe could not turn back its force.

There can be no doubt, then, that the desire for freedom—the right to speak freely, to worship freely, and to fend off the coercion of a tyrannical regime—that these basic human instincts played a major role in ending the Cold War. The basic human desire for "negative rights" had managed to survive, and even to help end, the Cold War. But in saying that, we must also recall that the world Franklin Roosevelt wished to build was going to be based not just on individual freedoms but also on collective shared responsibilities, on fairness and on social justice. In celebrating the unquenchable human desire for individual freedom, we too often forget its important corollary: that freedom thrives best in a society that is itself committed to equality.

If we want to honor Franklin Roosevelt's Four Freedoms, we must do so by recalling that they were the product of a remarkable time in American life—a time when the global economic crisis of the 1930s, combined with the rise of militant and aggressive fascist empires, truly threatened to snuff out the very life of democracy. At that dark hour, Roosevelt called on Americans and all the peoples of the world to join together in creating what he called a new "moral order," one based not only on individual liberties but also on collective responsibility for other human beings. This latter part of Roosevelt's message, which reflected the ethos of the New Deal, was absolutely central to the Four Freedoms speech and to his vision for the postwar world. And it is here where our postwar world has failed. The world of the early twenty-first century, with its shocking inequalities of wealth, its war-ravaged nations, its bulging refugee camps, its torture chambers and violations of human freedoms, its unceasing religious conflicts, its depleted natural resources, its long-term unemployed—is a far cry indeed from FDR's hopeful vision. It is safe to say that Franklin Roosevelt would tell us that there is still work to be done to bring about the triumph of the Four Freedoms— "everywhere in the world."

Notes

1. Warren F. Kimball, *The Juggler: Franklin Roosevelt as Wartime Statesman* (Princeton, NJ: Princeton University Press, 1991), 7–19, 185–200; Hull quoted on 14. For the "Christian and a Democrat" quotation, see Frances Perkins, *The Roosevelt I Knew* (New York: Viking, 1947), 330.

2. Kimball, 186–87. This connection between the New Deal and the postwar plans for global reconstruction is the central concern of an excellent study by Elizabeth Borgwardt, *A New Deal for the World: America's Vision for Human Rights* (Cambridge, MA: Harvard University Press, 2005); for a discussion of the Four Freedoms, see 46–53.

3. Radio Address Delivered by President Roosevelt, Washington, December 29, 1940, quoted from United States Department of State, *Peace and War: United States Foreign Policy, 1931–1941*, publication 1983 (Washington, DC: US Government Printing Office, 1943), 598–607, PPP, "Fireside Chat," December 29, 1940, http://www.presidency.ucsb.edu/ws/index.php?pid=15917. https://www.mtholyoke.edu/acad/intrel/WorldWar2/arsenal.htm.

4. These passages are quoted from the text of the speech available at the Miller Center, University of Virginia, http://millercenter.org/president/speeches/detail/3320.

5. Samuel I. Rosenman, *Working with Roosevelt* (New York: Harper Brothers, 1952), 263–65; David M. Kennedy, *The American People in World War II* (New York: Oxford University Press, 1999), 45.

6. A perceptive discussion of these themes is given by Eric Foner, "Freedom in a Global Age," *American Historical Review* 106, no. 1 (February 2001): 1–16.

7. Isaiah Berlin, "Roosevelt through European Eyes," *Atlantic*, July 1955, and "Two Concepts of Liberty," published in 1958, reprinted in *Four Essays on Liberty* (Oxford: Oxford University Press, 1969).

8. United Nations Charter, "Preamble," http://www.un.org/en/documents/charter/preamble.shtml.

9. Alan Brinkley, *The End of Reform: New Deal Liberalism in Recession and War* (New York: Knopf, 1995), 144–45.

10. PPP, "Excerpts from the Press Conference," December 28, 1943, http://www.presidency.ucsb.edu/ws/?pid=16358. For a powerful discussion of the way the war compelled the consolidation of power and the abridgement of freedom in the United States, see Ira Katznelson, *Fear Itself: The New Deal and the Origins of Our Time* (New York: Liveright, 2013), especially chapter 9. For the Congress and the New Deal during the war see Nancy Beck Young, *Why We Fight: Congress and the Politics of World War II* (Lawrence: University Press of Kansas, 2013).

11. Brinkley, *End of Reform*, 154–64; see also his *Liberalism and Its Discontents* (Cambridge, MA: Harvard University Press, 1998), 105–6.

12. "Text of Eisenhower's Speech Pledging His Regime's Support to Keep Our Basic Freedom," *New York Times*, October 13, 1948; diary entry, January 14, 1949, *Papers of Dwight D. Eisenhower*, vol. 10, *Columbia*, 430–32; "Eisenhower Warns on Centralization," *New York Times*, January 30, 1949.

13. For a sophisticated treatment of how such contradictory values were constructed, see Wendy Wall, *Inventing the 'American Way': The Politics of Consensus from the New Deal to the Civil Rights Movement* (New York: Oxford University Press, 2008).

14. The classic account of the way the Cold War helped open a path for the civil rights agenda is Mary Dudziak, *Cold War Civil Rights: Race and the Image of American Democracy* (Princeton, NJ: Princeton University Press, 2000).

15. George Orwell, "The Lion and the Unicorn" (1941), in *The Collected Essays, Journalism, and Letters of George Orwell*, ed. Sonia Orwell and Ian Angus (New York: Harcourt, Brace, 1968), 2:83, 94.

16. "Winston Churchill's defense of Conservative Party Rule," in Douglas Brinkely, ed., *The New York Times Living History: The Allied Counteroffensive, 1942-1945* (New York: Times Books, 2003), 359.

17. Richard Holmes, *In the Footsteps of Churchill* (New York: Basic Books, 2006), 279.

18. William I. Hitchcock, *The Struggle for Europe: The Turbulent History of a Divided Continent, 1945–2002* (New York: Doubleday, 2002), 46–47, 54.

19. Benjamin Nathans, "Soviet Rights-Talk in the Post-Stalin Era," in *Human Rights in the Twentieth Century*, ed. Stefan-Ludwig Hoffmann (Cambridge, UK: Cambridge University Press, 2011), 166–90.

20. Eric Hobsbawm, *The Age of Extremes: A History of the World, 1914–1991* (New York: Random House, 1994), 259; Richard N. Cooper, "Economic Aspects of the Cold War," in *The Cambridge History of the Cold War*, ed. Melvyn P. Leffler and Odd Arne Westad (Cambridge, UK: Cambridge University Press, 2010), 2:48.

21. "Vietnamese Declaration of Independence, 1945," Modern History Sourcebook, http://www.fordham.edu/halsall/mod/1945vietnam.html.

22. Samuel Moyn, "Imperialism, Self-Determination, and the Rise of Human Rights," in *The Human Rights Revolution: An International History*, ed. Akira Iriye, Petra Goedde, and William Hitchcock (New York: Oxford University Press, 2012), 159–78; Roland Burke, *Decolonization and the Evolution of Human Rights* (Philadelphia: University of Pennsylvania Press, 2010), 26. For a critical view of Burke that stresses the thin and brittle quality of the statements in support of human rights at Bandung, see Reza Afshari, "On Historiography of Human Rights," *Human Rights Quarterly* 29 (2007): 1–67.

23. Frantz Fanon, *The Wretched of the Earth*, trans. Constance Farrington (New York: Grove Weidenfeld, 1963), 37, 315–16.

24. For a brief outline of these developments, see Robert Skidelsky, "The Growth of a World Economy," in *The Oxford History of the Twentieth Century*, ed. Michael Howard and William Roger Louis (New York: Oxford University Press, 1998), 50–62.

25. Skidelsky, "Growth of a World Economy," 60. See also Charles Maier, "Malaise: The Crisis of Capitalism in the 1970s," in *The Shock of the Global: The 1970s in Perspective*, ed. Niall Ferguson, Charles S. Maier, Erez Manela, and Daniel J. Sargent (Cambridge, MA: Harvard University Press, 2010), 25–48.

26. Margaret Thatcher, *The Downing Street Years* (New York: HarperCollins, 1993), 6–7.

27. Ronald Reagan's First Inaugural, January 20, 1981, at http://www.heritage.org/initiatives/first-principles/primary-sources/reagans-first-inaugural-government-is-not-the-solution-to-our-problem-government-is-the-problem.

28. Giovanni Arrighi, "The World Economy and the Cold War, 1970–1990," in Leffler and Westad, *Cambridge History of the Cold War*, 3:23–44. For a detailed analysis of global income inequality, see OECD, "An Overview of Growing Income Inequalities in OECD Countries: Main Findings," 2011, at http://www.oecd.org/els/soc/49499779.pdf.

29. Stephen Kotkin, "The Kiss of Debt: The East Bloc Goes Borrowing," in
    Ferguson et al., *Shock of the Global*, 80–96; "KOR Appeal to Society," October
    10, 1978, in *From Stalinism to Pluralism: A Documentary History of Eastern Europe
    since 1945*, ed. Gale Stokes (New York: Oxford, 1996), 194–99.
30. Samuel Moyn, *The Last Utopia: Human Rights in History* (Cambridge,
    MA: Harvard University Press, 2010), 129.
31. Paul Rubinson, "'For Our Soviet Colleagues:' Scientific Internationalism,
    Human Rights, and the Cold War," in Iriye, Goedde and Hitchcock, *Human
    Rights Revolution*, 245–64. On scientists and disarmament, see Matthew
    Evangelista, *Unarmed Forces: The Transnational Movement to End the Cold War*
    (Ithaca, NY: Cornell University Press, 1999), and Aryeh Neier, *The International
    Human Rights Movement: A History* (Princeton, NJ: Princeton University Press,
    2012), 138–45.
32. Jean H. Quataert, *Advocating Dignity: Human Rights Mobilizations in Global
    Politics* (Philadelphia: University of Pennsylvania Press, 2009), chaps. 2 and
    3. This is the overall thesis of Margaret Keck and Kathryn Sikkink, *Activists
    beyond Borders: Advocacy Networks in International Politics* (Ithaca, NY: Cornell
    University Press, 1998).
33. A positive appraisal is in David F. Schmitz and Vanessa Walker, "Jimmy Carter
    and the Foreign Policy of Human Rights: The Development of a Post-Cold War
    Foreign Policy," *Diplomatic History* 28, no. 1 (January 2004): 113–43. For a much
    more critical take, see Bradley Simpson, "Denying the 'First Right': The United
    States, Indonesia, and the Ranking of Human Rights by the Carter
    Administration," *International History Review* 31, no. 4 (December
    2009): 798–826.

INDEX